After the new
social democracy

MANCHESTER
UNIVERSITY PRESS

For my parents

After the new social democracy

Social welfare for the twenty-first century

TONY FITZPATRICK

Manchester University Press
Manchester and New York

distributed exclusively in the USA by Palgrave

Published by Manchester University Press
Oxford Road, Manchester M13 9NR, UK
and Room 400, 175 Fifth Avenue, New York, NY 10010, USA
www.manchesteruniversitypress.co.uk

Distributed exclusively in the USA by
Palgrave, 175 Fifth Avenue, New York,
NY 10010, USA

Distributed exclusively in Canada by
UBC Press, University of British Columbia, 2029 West Mall,
Vancouver, BC, Canada V6T 1Z2

British Library Cataloguing-in-Publication Data
A catalogue record for this book is available from the British Library

Library of Congress Cataloging-in-Publication Data applied for

ISBN   0 7190 6476 7   *hardback*
         0 7190 6477 5   *paperback*

First published 2003

11 10 09 08 07 06 05 04 03   10 9 8 7 6 5 4 3 2 1

Typeset in Palatino with Frutiger
by SNP Best-set Typesetter Ltd., Hong Kong
Printed in Great Britain
by CPI, Bath

Contents

List of figures

Preface and acknowledgements

A couple of years ago I was feeling pretty pleased with myself (the word is 'smug') at having published quite a few pieces of work, in a range of subjects, while barely out of short trousers (believe me, in academic years I'm still being bottle-fed). 'Do you know what you ought to do', I mused on one particular ego-fuelled day, 'you ought to publish a compilation'. What a sad sight. A young, handsome, eligible lecturer swanning around, imagining that society is awaiting his Greatest Hits collection. Not even the fact that academic books barely register on publishers' sale charts could stop me (they are usually only read by friends and family, and even they moan when you don't give them a discount). The world urgently needed my help and my help was what it was going to bloody well get. Fortunately, time and sobriety intervened – as time and sobriety have an irritating habit of doing – and the plan changed, as people to whom I described the original version began to inch away from me with eyes averted, so most of what follows is new. Inevitably, parts of my ego creep back into the following pages, perhaps as compensation for the fact that writing is a lonely business, but mainly because when addressing the contemporary state of social democracy, and trying to point out where you think it's going wrong, some soapbox oratory is impossible to avoid.

But hopefully the egoism does not get in the way of the book's main purpose: to make connections. The world is a frightening place at the moment (though when was it not?) filled with people who seem to imagine that what it is really missing is another set of fundamentalist dogmas. Having won the war against communism, for instance, it turns out that many anti-communists have yet to win the war against themselves. Yet there are many out there who are working for something different, for something more humane, and although not everyone who belongs to this group can or should be placed under the heading of social democracy, this isn't a bad heading from which to start. So this isn't a manifesto either but it is, hopefully, an attempt at dialogue which discerns, amid the clamour of the asylums within which we insist on living, some voices of sanity.

Many thanks to the usual suspects, Chris Pierson and Hartley Dean, who gave valuable feedback on the draft manuscript.

Chapter 3 is a revision of two earlier pieces of work: 'New Agendas for Criminology and Social Policy', *Social Policy and Administration* 35(2) (2001) and 'Critical Theory, Information Society and Surveillance Technologies', *Information, Communication and Society* 5(3) (2002). I am grateful to Blackwell and Routledge, respectively, for permission to use these.

Chapter 7 is also a revision of two earlier pieces of work: 'Dis/Counting the Future', *Social Policy Review* 13 (2001), edited by Rob Sykes, Cath Bochel and Nick Ellison, and 'Making Welfare for Future Generations', *Social Policy and Administration* 35(5) (2001). I am grateful to Policy Press and Blackwell, respectively, for permission to use these.

Chapter 8 is a revised version of 'Before The Cradle: New Genetics, Biopolicy And Regulated Eugenics', *Journal of Social Policy* 30(4) (2001). Reprinted with permission of Cambridge University Press.

The rest of the book was written between February and May 2002 during a semester's study leave and my thanks go to the School of Sociology and Social Policy, University of Nottingham, for that opportunity.

Introduction

I cannot now remember what else I did that day. I must either have pressed on into town to my office or else bought something for lunch and returned home to work. I do recall how beautiful the day was that mid-morning. How the pavements yawned and stretched under a sun clambering eagerly towards its dive into the windless blue sea of a sky. As if the light that precedes it had been scattered across the visible world, making it brighter than ever before. I also remember that the walk to the school took less than 10 minutes, or almost 18 years, whichever you prefer. And then that night. With millions of others into the dizzy dark hours, stunned witnesses to our impact upon each other's lives.

And what of the journey away from that school, once the ballot boxes had been rewarehoused and the children's desks returned? For that day has certainly joined the backward procession of memories. Of other days, when dark cars rolled towards Buckingham Palace, when industrial communities were transformed into museums of themselves, when social ties faded behind the very individuals they bind together, when an elderly women stood in Downing Street and tears drained finally down a face that must have seen, but never acknowledged, the tears of others. But what else? We no longer have recourse to that old standby, 'the jury is still out'. In fact the jury returned long ago and its members have been beating each other up ever since. For the thing about New Labour is that it has both fulfilled expectations and betrayed them. It has fulfilled the expectations we had and betrayed the expectations we should have had. New Labour succeeded and failed because our expectations of it, and it of us, were always too low. And if you want to understand why New Labour became so popular *and* so disliked you have to understand the lack of trust in ourselves that those low expectations have engendered.

But this is not a book about New Labour. Blair and Co. have an important walk-on part, but are then killed off before the first act is over. It *is* a book about the new social democracy (NSD) of which New Labour has been perhaps the best but by no means the only representative. More specifically, it is a book about imagining a social democratic future that diverts from the NSD, about how we can raise our expectations once again and so learn to trust each other more.

Social democracy refers to the attempt to bring capitalist economies under some form of collective control using statist and gradualist reforms that work from within the framework of liberal democracy. Describing the aspirations of the Left it has united both socially-minded liberals and liberal-minded socialists, despite disagreements about the nature, speed and direction of reform that have often divided these groups. By the 1920s and 1930s social democracy had become the main alternative on the Left to Marxism and Communism (which is not to claim that it remained un-influenced by either), marginalising those who preferred anarchist, syn-dicalist and associative alternatives. Achieving its high-water mark in the quarter century following World War Two, social democracy had been placed on the defensive by the 1980s and 1990s, yet the exact nature of that crisis, and the solutions to it, differ depending upon the historical story that we tell ourselves.

Unfortunately, histories of social democracy are often simplified to reflect the prejudices of the present. The NSD's story goes something like this. Social democracy emerged in the late nineteenth century out of the international workers' movement as a reformist alternative to revolu-tionary socialism. Although initially dedicated to the replacement of socialism with capitalism, social democrats realised that for this to happen capitalism would first have to be saved from itself and made to work better. Hence the enthusiasm from the 1930s onwards for Keynesian eco-nomics which, in addition to nationalisation and state welfare, came to characterise the politics of social democratic governments after the war. During its heyday, most social democrats came to realise that the aspira-tion for a society substantially different from capitalism was an unrealis-tic dream and so social democrats dedicated themselves to maintaining a form of socialised capitalism. But with the eventual demise of social democratic governments, the resurgence of the Right and a series of eco-nomic and sociocultural changes, social democrats have had to rethink their commitment to Keynesianism, nationalisation and state welfare. Social democracy is therefore a history of decline. Revolutionary Marxism was replaced by a reformist socialism, which was replaced in turn by the desire for a socialised capitalism, and now the aim of socialising capital-ism has also died. Therefore, the only way to save what it left of social democratic aspirations is by abandoning Keynesianism, nationalisation and state welfare. Enter the NSD.

This is the story told by those such as Giddens (1998), Dell (2000), Plant (2002) and hints of it can even be heard in Sassoon (1996) and Moschonas (2002). The problem with it is that it tells only one part of the tale. For although the term itself was not conceptualised until the 1870s, significant elements of social democracy predate that period, whether within the trade unions and burgeoning workers' movement or on the Left of the bourgeois liberal movement. So, if social democracy is not a dilution of Marxist Communism, if they share a contemporaneous development, then the history of social democracy is not one of decline but, as with most ideologies, much more complex than this. And what the defenders of the NSD downplay, when they are not omitting it altogether, is the history of capitalism over the last century or more, for if we are to interpret history in terms of either ascent or decline, then it makes as much sense to talk about the decline of capitalism in the century following the last quarter of the nineteenth century. The so-called decline of social democracy might also be written as the decline of capitalism to a point where it would not have been recognisable to its eighteenth- and nineteenth-century forebears. More accurately, we should think of social democratic history as a complex evolution rather than as either an ascent or decline.

Ah, say new social democrats, but this only takes the story to the 1980s at best. The resurgence of market capitalism since then means that social democratic traditions have lost their former relevance. So whether the decline is measured in generations or decades *there has been a recent decline to which the NSD is the only viable response.*

Yet what this argument conveniently does is to resurrect the determinism which has usually been employed to caricature Marxism (and which Marxists have often used as caricatures of themselves). If the resurgence of market capitalism was and is inevitable, then what are the laws of history which will make the future an endless reflection of the present? New social democrats are understandably silent on this point. But what really gives the lie to their argument is that this insistence on inevitability ('There Is No Alternative') used to be deployed by conservatives – and often still is, of course – against *any* form of social democracy. So if the NSD really is a viable option then the resurgence of market capitalism must be political rather than deterministic, i.e. the result of social forces mobilising for ideological ends within particular, conjunctural circumstances, and if it is political, then although the NSD is *one* viable option it is not necessarily *the only one.*

However, the new social democrat has an additional argument. Even if the NSD is not the only option it is nonetheless the best given the immense problems that we face. Would today's socially excluded really thank us for spending time, energy and resources building radicalism for tomorrow? This question deserves an answer by presenting those to the Left of the NSD with a considerable challenge and it is this challenge with which the present book is concerned.

Although my conclusions will hopefully be based upon sturdier foundations, part of the answer lies in the current crisis of the NSD itself. In the 18 months following New Labour's 1997 victory, social democratic parties swept to power across Europe to an extent never seen before – by 1999, 12 out of 15 EU member states were governed either wholly or partially by social democrats. Given the tortuous slowness of academic publishing (apart from Manchester University Press, obviously), it is only fairly recently that I have finished reading books and articles celebrating this and heralding a brave new dawn for the Centre-Left. Unfortunately, by the time of writing (summer 2002), this situation had reversed with only New Labour looking particularly secure within Europe. Now because the electoral successes were not a victory for the NSD alone (see Chapter 4), despite some of the wilder claims made at the time, the electoral reverse undoubtedly holds lessons for all social democrats, old and new. Nevertheless, because the NSD was presented as the only possible future for the Centre-Left, and because its main strength was its apparent popularity, then recent events will hopefully produce some soul searching among new social democrats and raise questions not only about whether it is the *only* available option, but also about whether it really is the best.

But let me reiterate, the arguments of this book do not rise or fall depending upon political contingencies. For all I know, by the time you are reading this the electoral situation will have reversed again. It matters little since the long-term significance of the political fortunes of the NSD and any social democratic alternative can only be properly assessed once we understand the relative strengths and weaknesses of the relevant ideas. In short, we should not confuse psephology for philosophy.[1] Our objective is therefore to address the following two questions: 'does the intellectual case for the NSD bear scrutiny?' and 'what kind of alternative to the NSD can be imagined?'. The relevance of the second question obviously depends upon our answer to the first, but I have already indicated above why I think the second question deserves to be asked. To answer these questions we will be working from within the idiom of political philosophy and social theory as they relate to the subject of social policy. What we will *not* be doing is reviewing the full range of possible Centre-Left alternatives to the NSD (market socialism, stakeholding, etc.). Some of these make an appearance in the following pages, but what you are going to find is an attempt to summarise the key elements of an approach that I believe is essential to the future viability of social democracy. Nor will we be sketching a blueprint of an alternative welfare state. I will make occasional recommendations in this respect, but our principal concern is with the theoretical underpinnings of policy alternatives to the NSD.

Let me add that I consider the presenting of alternatives as essential to theoretical labour. Unfortunately, when considering philosophical problems and puzzles of one form or another, even most political philosophers are content to remain at an abstract level, reluctant to get their social hands dirty. It is as if debating institutional reform is either to sully the purity of philosophical endeavour or to invoke the kind of utopian, system-building that has now surely been discredited. To this extent I agree with David Miller (1999: x) when he complains that Rawlsian and post-Rawlsian ideas come across as detached from the social environments they are presumably meant to improve. Many social philosophers have come to resemble chefs who devise recipes, but are content to let others actually cook the food. Equally, I am also frustrated with non-philosophical polemics that consist of little more than menus for reform: lists of policies and prescriptions that often seem reasonable in themselves, but frequently adopt a take-it-or-leave-it approach. Here, the chef expects you to swallow the menu without sampling any of the meals for yourself. This book therefore steers a course somewhere between these two approaches.

One consequence is that although we cover lots of theoretical ground, we sometimes need to stray away from it. Chapter 4 is particularly guilty in this respect. But before crying 'where the hell is the theory?', as you will be tempted to do from time to time, please remember that in order to present a philosophical alternative to the NSD, but one which is still recognisably social democratic, we have to draw upon resources that are non-philosophical as well.

Finally, let me say something more about my basic ethical and social beliefs. In its synthesis of economic prosperity, political participation, social justice and cultural maturity, social democratic capitalism represents the best form of society that humans have yet managed to create for themselves. I make this claim with some feeling of ambivalence. I regret that we have not done better than social democracy and hope that we yet will.[2] But, despite its failings, social democracy offers the best opportunity for the progressive future for which many of us still yearn, especially in the face of a political Right that, across both Europe and America, appears to be more rabid than ever. A sense of ambiguity therefore pervades the book. We must both defend social democracy and criticise it, consolidate and improve it. This has been the professed aim of new social democrats also but, by accepting many of conservatism's assumptions (inclusion does not require equality, we possess what we deserve to possess, social problems are individualistic in origin and solution, the poor are morally and socially different from the norm, coercion is good), the NSD sends us in the wrong direction. We must therefore set our sights on the best examples that European social democracy has to offer, though here too we will see that the recent picture is ambiguous. European social democracy has made some concessions to the conservative hegemony that prevails at the global level (due largely to American influence), concessions that have driven some but by no means all into the arms of NSD. Therefore, reinvigorating social democracy means resisting the sirens of the NSD and finding ways in the face of conservatism to revive the 200-year old project of creating a better society for all rather than (as the current orthodoxy demands) a wealthier economy for the lucky. Our ultimate task then is to answer the following question: how can social democracy be rejuvenated?

Part I of the book deals primarily with the NSD. Chapter 1 offers a summary and critique of the NSD, treating New Labour as the best exemplar of these ideas. It argues that while it is simplistic to equate New Labour with conservatism, due to the continuing influence upon it of Left values and concepts, it fails to break away substantially from the conservative hegemony. The NSD therefore reinforces the grip of the mainstream upon the political imagination, a grip that excludes a much broader range of ideas, perspectives and values, with potentially dangerous repercussions for us all. However, the chapter spots a potential within the mainstream for genuinely radical alternatives if the simplistic narratives of the NSD can be successfully challenged.

In Chapters 2 and 3 we examine some of the main criticisms of New Labour in greater depth. Chapter 2 proposes that New Labour favours a combination of 'weak equality' and 'strong reciprocity' and I contrast this with an alternative vision of distributive justice and social citizenship. We then spend Chapter 3 exploring some of the implications of New Labour's preference, namely the extent to which it derives from and perpetuates what I call the 'security state'. The security state has not replaced the welfare state, but it has transformed the discourse of rights into duties, equality into inclusion and collective problems into individual pathologies. This transformation is illustrated through an analysis of New Labour's approach towards Information and Communication Technologies (ICTs).

Chapter 4 widens our focus beyond New Labour and the NSD and concludes that social democratic traditions across Europe are more robust than either has allowed for. The NSD represents an important strand in recent Centre-Left developments, but it is simplistic to imagine that the 'old' social democracy has been discredited. That said, social democracy undoubtedly faces some real challenges in adapting to a post-industrial and global economy. Yet it is premature to imagine that such adaptation requires social democrats to abandon egalitarianism and to prod as many people as possible into the service economy. This kind of productivist approach may create as many problems as it solves and Chapter 4 ends by proposing that social democrats should explore the prospects for post-productivism.

It is this conjunction of social democracy and post-productivism that is here termed 'ecowelfare' and Part II sets out to trace the main parameters of ecowelfare ideas. Chapter 5 contrasts productivism with post-productivism and shows that while the latter does not abandon the aims of increases in growth, productivity and well-being, it does recontextualise them in terms of what are called 'reproductive values', values that refer to the ecological and social conditions of a productive economy, conditions which that economy is increasingly unable to replenish. Economic practice therefore has to be assessed in terms of reproductivity and labour has to refer less to waged work and more to the kind of emotional and ecological labour that economic orthodoxies continue to neglect. Ecowelfare therefore guides social democracy in the direction of a post-employment society.

Chapter 6 provides a clearer overview of ecowelfare as referring us to three principles: first, the alternative version of distributive justice that was provided in Chapter 2; second, the principles of 'attention', by which I mean both recognition and care; finally, the principle of sustainability. The chapter defends a simple model of ecowelfare and suggests that the social theory of ecowelfare consists of an analysis of the links between these three principles.

These links are therefore examined over the next three chapters, not comprehensively but as a platform for further reflection. Chapter 7 investigates the principles of sustainability and distributive justice by outlining a theory of intergenerational justice and discussing some of the key issues to which this debate gives rise. It concludes that the ultimate conflict is less between present generations and future ones and more between those who would and those who would not favour a more equitable distribution of natural and social resources. Intergenerational justice therefore engenders a series of radical welfare reforms that have as many implications for ourselves as for the future.

In Chapter 8 we turn to the principles of sustainability and attention by studying the new genetics. Here I argue for a multidimensional conception of human nature where the maintenance of diversity through social solutions (rather than technological fixes) should be the priority. However, we are also obliged to prevent harm whenever it is possible and desirable to do so. This obligation, plus the fact that we cannot disinvent biotechnology, means that we have to make some difficult decisions regarding therapeutic and reproductive genetics. Such decisions have already begun to tax governments and Chapter 8 argues for a 'regulated eugenics' as an alternative to the '*laissez-faire* eugenics' of the free market and to a hands-off approach that tries to avoid these difficult decisions altogether.

Chapter 9 brings together the principles of attention and distributive justice and argues for a 'welfare democracy', i.e. a system of deliberative democracy within which discursive debate occupies a much greater role in the operation of welfare services. Welfare democracy represents an egalitarian alternative to conservatism (and the NSD) by empowering individuals as members of a political community rather than as members of consumer markets. It means that a more creative interface is required between parliamentary and non-parliamentary spheres of politics and between social movements and social democratic parties. The chapter ends by concluding that both associative and deliberative approaches are essential to a new politics of equality.

Notes

1 That said, the political *urgency* of our philosophising certainly changes with the electoral wind and, as I write, those winds have shifted considerably and alarmingly in recent months. The Centre-Left is in trouble not only in countries like France and Germany, but also in countries that are represented in Chapter 4 as archetypes of social democracy: Denmark, Netherlands and Norway. The analysis contained in this book is therefore set against the background that prevailed before this crisis, i.e. before the ascendancy of the far Right and the falling popularity of the Left in 2002. I will have more to say about the current situation in the concluding chapter and why I think that the ideas expressed in this book can assist the Left in fighting back.

2 I place to one side the question of whether the social democracy I will be arguing for is capable of eventually leading us beyond capitalism. As I argue elsewhere, it is less important to imagine a post-capitalist society than it is to think through the kind of radical reforms that might gradually take us away from where we are (Fitzpatrick with Caldwell, 2001).

PART I

1

The long march back

If Eric Hobsbawm (1994) is right and the twentieth century effectively ended in 1991, then the new millennium was considerably less new by the time we were popping the corks, the balloons and, most importantly, the aspirin. And if he is also correct to portray the last century as the 'age of extremes', then where does this leave us? Have we become wise enough to avoid the mistakes of the past or have we simply been experiencing the interregnum before the emergence of new forms of extremism? Tony Giddens (1994) had the foresight to recognise that these alternatives are not necessarily exclusive, that reflexivity and fundamentalism are both coherent responses to the risks of our 'second modernity' (Beck, 1992; Beck et al., 1994). This ambivalence has characterised the post-communist years, with the globalisation of deregulated markets, consumer values and western power being accompanied, first, by the mobilisation of social movements opposing corporate capitalism and then by the globalisation of insecurity, fear and revenge (Mouzelis, 2001).

Yet is Giddens (1998, 1999, 2000, 2001) also correct to suppose that the NSD is the best means of charting a way through this landscape of confusion and ambiguity? Possibly, *if* we accept the following reasoning. All attempts to construct ideal societies have failed. The state utopias of the Left have led either to totalitarianism or to a crippling backlash of taxpayers, consumers and capital markets; the market utopias of the Right have led to social exclusion and civic decline. Therefore, we should not only attach ourselves to the political Centre, but also seek to radicalise that Centre by evading the conceptual barriers between Left and Right, public and private, state and market, justice and efficiency, security and flexibility, equality and freedom. It is this radicalisation that Giddens refers to as the NSD.[1] By transcending these dichotomies – rather than simply trading off between them – we provide ourselves with an alternative not only to the 'Old Left' and 'New Right', but also to the siren calls of nationalist, ethnic and religious fundamentalists. For if we can find a way to negotiate the risks and hazards of this second modernity, through the emotional and cultural empowerment of reflexive citizens, then we can better resist the nihilistic certainties of the 'new extremisms'.

This is a powerful and compelling narrative but does it stand up to scrutiny? The purpose of this book is to engage with key features of the NSD in order to answer that question and to suggest why and how more radical alternatives *can* be developed. The aim of Part I is to criticise those key features in order to help us towards an outline of an alternative social philosophy in Part II, one that I shall term 'ecosocial welfare' or 'ecowelfare' for short. We begin in this first chapter by reviewing the main principles, justifications of and main objections to the NSD. Some of the following objections are then pursued at greater length in Chapters 2–4 as a means of setting us up for the arguments in Part II.

New Labour

A political ideology is a constellation of 'nodes' (ideas, principles and concepts) which establish a set of relations between one another that are constantly evolving, due to the theoretical developments of that ideology's supporters and its critics, and to changing circumstances both in society and in other ideological formations. The NSD undoubtedly constitutes such an ideology. It contains (a) a critique of existing society, (b) an impression of a better one and (c) an explanation of how to get from (a) to (b) (Ball and Dagger, 1991). Yet the core components of the NSD are by no means unique to itself. Instead, it borrows its primary values and principles from established ideologies but rearranges them in such a way that a distinctive ideological position emerges nevertheless. This not only makes the NSD what Freeden (1996) calls a 'thin' ideology, in that its nodes are not peculiar to itself, but means that the relational network linking its core components is in an accelerated state of flux, given the nature of the NSD's intervention into our social conjuncture. Indeed, some have argued that pragmatism and populism are *the* key features of the NSD (Powell, 2000) and that it is little more than a practice in search of a few philosophical trimmings that hardly constitute an ideology. While agreeing that the NSD lacks the focus and robustness of liberalism, socialism, feminism, etc., its possession of (a), (b) and (c) means that pragmatism is not its only feature.

And yet this pragmatism is perhaps the main problem with which we have to wrestle. How do we distil what new social democrats say and do into a coherent series of ideas? Do we treat the NSD merely as a political programme? Is the NSD merely a rhetorical device that governments have employed in trying to square various circles? How do we name something as NSD in the first place? All of these questions are relevant, but my solution is to take the line of least resistance and examine the NSD in what arguably remains its purest form, that of Tony Blair's post-1994 Labour Party and the ideas which have been deployed to both motivate and justify its approach. For whereas other ideologies cannot be reduced to the actions and pronouncements of political parties, it is the very thinness of the NSD which allows us to organise our analysis around the actions and discourse of political parties. And although there are certainly other recent governments which may qualify for the label – principally in the USA, Netherlands and Germany, as well as several countries in the Southern Hemisphere (Gledhill, 2001), especially New Zealand – it is in the UK that the NSD, and associated terms such as the 'Third Way', have been applied most often and most consistently.[2,3] Of course, this solution is not ideal, as it might be said that, as with any ideology, the NSD has no pure form, for even within New Labour the influence of old social democracy has still been visible.

So for our purposes the first question we need to ask, 'what is the NSD?', can be reformulated as 'what is new about "New Labour"?', a question that requires to plot the party on the political graph. Once we have addressed this question we should be in a position to outline the NSD's key principles and features (cf. Buckler, 2000).

First, let us dispense with two claims. The first claim is that there is no such thing as *New* Labour, i.e. that the party under Blair has been just as socialist/conservative (delete according to taste) as the Labour Parties of Attlee, Wilson, etc.; the second is that New Labour bears *absolutely no relation* to what preceded it. Both of these claims ignore the nature of ideology and the fact that the networks which relate nodes together are constantly evolving, as are the principles and concepts themselves. The first claim underestimates the scale of that evolution, whereas the second claim overestimates it by neglecting the continuities between present and past. Once we reject these claims we are left with the following six interpretations:

1   The party has frequently described itself as applying traditional values in a new context. What has changed are not the basic beliefs and ideals, but the social and economic environment within which they have to be realised, necessitating radically new policy instruments, practices and institutions. New Labour is new because the times are new and not the goals to be achieved (Mandelson and Liddle, 1996; Blair, 1998; cf. Blair and Schroder, 1999; Hombach, 2000).

2   Some academic commentators agree and go on to regard the continuities as outweighing the discontinuities (Rubinstein, 2000; Larkin,

2001; Allender, 2001). However, contrary to its self-image, the Labour Party has never been particularly radical (except when out of power) because it has always had to appeal to middle-class voters and ensure that international capital is not scared away by the prospects of a Labour Government. Social democracy has always been a politics of 'catch up', of adaptation to economic and social developments, and so New Labour is not really that new, despite the undoubted weaknesses of traditional social democracy.

3   However, these views have been disputed by those such as Driver and Martell (1998, 2000, 2001; cf. Coates, 2001) who insist that what has changed is not simply the *means* that the party employs, but the *ends* that it attempts to achieve. What is new about New Labour are underlying values and principles that are substantially different from those held prior to Blair's ascendancy. As such, New Labour is neither a social democratic party, as this has been traditionally conceived, but nor does it represent Thatcherism Mark II, since it retains an anti-Thatcherite emphasis. Instead, its politics are the politics of *post-Thatcherism*, i.e. an adaptation to the society and economy which Thatcherism engineered, and which involves a substantial leap to the Right, though with some tilting back towards the Left, albeit a Left that rejects socialism and embraces the market economy.

4   Others go further and insist that New Labour is effectively a kind of 'Left Thatcherism' in that it has accepted almost all of the radical Right agenda and has merely used the vocabulary of the Centre-Left to justify this surrender (*Marxism Today*, 1998; Mouffe, 2000; Heffernan, 2000; Callinicos, 2001).

5   Others have wondered whether New Labour is forming a Left version of Christian Democracy (Marquand, 1998). Having flourished across Europe, Christian Democracy is broadly on the Centre-Right, embodying the idea of a social market where everyone is able to participate in the market economy regardless of social background. Capitalism can be humanised through welfare institutions, strong families and strong communities without the need for large-scale upheaval. Although never really taking hold in Britain (though the paternalistic conservatism that Thatcher swept away might be construed in similar terms), New Labour could be thought of as a compromise between social and Christian Democracy (cf. Huntington and Bale, 2002).

6   Another interpretation suggests that New Labour is a reinvention of 'new liberalism' (Beer, 2001; cf. Freeden, 1999; Stears and White, 2001). New Liberalism flourished at the end of the nineteenth century and represented a shift away from classic liberalism in its recognition that individuals are socially interdependent. But because this interdepen-

dency is undermined by economic injustice, state action is required to rectify the flaws of capitalism, though a state which is still limited in scope and ambition lest the spaces of individual liberty be undermined. New liberalism had all but vanished by the First World War, after which British politics was dominated by a damaging stand-off between conservatism and socialism. But with the eventual discrediting of socialism, the way was open for a rejuvenation of new liberal ideas in the form of a social democratic politics that has divested itself of socialist myths. This is an interpretation which appeals to many within New Labour, convinced by David Marquand's (1991) contention that conservatism has dominated British politics because progressives of the Centre and the Left allowed themselves to be divided throughout the twentieth century, as the latter yearned for a post-capitalist society that the former always knew to be illusory.

Which of these interpretations should we prefer? In fact, I do not think we can identify any of them as exclusively right or wrong, as each helps to temper the potential excesses of the others. The attempt to weave the above interpretations together looks something like this. New Labour has reconfigured rather than abandoned many of its previous beliefs and values (1), i.e. it has altered the relational network *between* principles rather than jettisoning old principles for new ones. This means that we should not lose sight of the historical continuities (2) and acknowledge that the Labour Party has usually been forced to play catch-up. However, whereas from the 1950s to the 1980s the party was always readapting to a consensus that it had initially shaped between 1945 and 1950, by the 1990s the Keynesian agenda had been dispelled by the Right and so the politics of catch-up led to the most substantial Rightward revision in the party's history (Bara and Budge, 2001). Therefore, its reconfiguration *was* one of ends and not just means (3), so that its relational network came to resemble many aspects of Thatcherism (4) though this accommodation has been moderated by a paternalistic belief in the common good (5). So the party has abandoned all but the most harmless and general references to socialism, meaning that aspects of late nineteenth-century liberalism *have* been reinvented (6).

If this narrative is convincing then what does it tell us not just about New Labour, but about the NSD? First, it tells us that three conditions seem to be required for the NSD to have emerged:

- The Right must have adopted significant elements of both free market liberalism and social authoritarianism in its political programme (a combination which I will now refer to throughout this book as 'conservatism').[4]

- The Right must be in the ascendancy, constituting an actual or potential threat to the existing political settlement.
- The Centre-Left movement must lack confidence in itself, be divided and/or social democracy must lack any real social and institutional roots to the point where it is unable or unwilling to resist the hegemonic formation of a new settlement, a settlement to which it eventually adapts its traditions and values.

Obviously, this is no more than an hypothesis which extrapolates from the UK's experience and considerable research would be needed to assess the extent to which it applies to other examples of the NSD around the world. Nevertheless, the hypothesis suggests a second point. The ascendancy of a conservative agenda is only a necessary condition for a shift in the ideological spectrum. Even where this ascendancy is visible, it may nevertheless fail to alter the existing settlement *if* the Centre-Left holds firm and does not feel the need to dilute social democratic politics. I will return to this argument in Chapter 4, but the final point is this. The NSD is not merely an accommodation to conservatism, but a means by which the radical Right's agenda is socially and economically embedded to a degree that the Right could not manage on its own. As Heffernan (2000: 175) puts it, '... the conservative agenda underpinning the politics of Thatcherism may even be strengthened by Labour in office: a "Nixon goes to China" syndrome, one which marks the abnegation of the social democratic project'.

Therefore, the principles of New Labour and the NSD are not just a reconfiguration of the relational network of social democratic principles, but a means by which conservative concepts and values are embedded across the ideological spectrum, further colonising the repertoires and domains of the social field. What continue to be recognisable Centre-Left concepts are given a conservative content that inhabits and converts the space long populated by what, as a signature of this colonisation, comes to be designated as 'old social democracy' (and 'Old Labour'). The NSD is not equivalent *to* conservatism, but it is a conduit *for* conservatism: 'social democracy, even when it is neoliberalized, is *not neoliberal*' (Moschonas, 2002: 173). So, NSD principles are unremarkable in themselves. What is remarkable is the process to which they are being subject, due to the adaptive strategies of social democrats within a conservative context, a process which not only reconfigures those principles, but further embeds the radical Right hegemony that first impelled it. In short, what is new about the NSD is not so much the Rightward lurch of social democracy, but the 'social democratisation' of conservatism, i.e. the way in which, with the Centre ground having been dragged towards the Right, market liberalism and social authoritarianism have been given a Centre-Left voice. What we will need to decide by the end of this chapter is whether this social democratisation represents a new politics or whether it is little more than a sophisticated surrender to the Right's hegemony.

However, this account is to anticipate the critique that is pursued later on in this chapter and throughout Part I. Before examining it in more detail we obviously have to appreciate the NSD's basic principles, again using New Labour as our exemplar.

Principles and justifications

The NSD is based upon five key principles: community, meritocracy, reciprocity, inclusion, pragmatism. Note that this section and the next – which presents the main objections to the NSD – are only intended to outline the main arguments that have emerged from the debate. The aim is simply to establish a framework that will be elaborated upon over the course of the next three chapters.

Community

Many commentators have noted the attachment of New Labour to community (Lund, 1999; Heron, 2001). At its crudest New Labour represents community as a third way between the attachments of the Old Left to collectivism and of the New Right to individualism, with the former being criticised for ignoring civil society and the latter for reducing civil society to the blind interactions of economic exchange (Blair, 1998; Giddens, 1998: 78–89). Community is offered as a virtue in obvious opposition to Thatcher's proclamation that 'there is no such thing as society, only individuals and families', but avoids treating 'the social' as an abstract quality that abandons reference to the local and the private. Community therefore emphasises both the lived relations of family, neighbourhood and civic attachment, but also the broader social relations that make individuals interdependent and through which we express a need for ontological solidarity and belonging.

Because community is a notoriously vague, contested and all-purpose concept, there was an initial interest shown by New Labour in communitarianism, the political philosophy arguing that communal relations (*Gemeinschaft*) are constitutive of who we are and what we do, rather than being the contingent, ephemeral properties imagined by liberalism (Etzioni, 1994; Fitzpatrick, 2001a: 81–4). The attraction of communitarianism was that it enabled New Labour to define community as distinguishable from the state and the market, while allowing it to develop an economics that utilises both the public and private spheres. Subsequently, New Labour has made more reference to 'social capital' (Putnam, 2000) and 'stakeholding', each term signifying the interactive, associative networks through which we participate in society and contribute to the enhancement of 'human capital' (skills, qualifications, employability), trust and bonds of cooperation. The essential intention though is to reconcile social cohesion with individual effort, traditional values with modern circumstances, local needs with global imperatives.

Meritocracy

As a reaction against what it sees as state collectivism, New Labour has also rejected the egalitarianism of the Old Left, regarding this as an inhibition on economic prosperity and individual creativity that smothers social and cultural diversity (Commission on Social Justice, 1994; Gray, 1996). However, the solution is not to stumble towards either the market libertarianism of the 1980s or the moral libertarianism of the 1960's counter-culture. Instead, the emphasis should be on opportunity. This implies not only the removal of restrictions on aspiration and mobility, but also an attempt to embody the equal worth of individuals by providing everyone with an equal chance in life, i.e. *real* opportunities. This requires that everyone has an equal start regardless of social background, but not an equality of outcome since, by reducing the rewards for success and the penalties for failure, this would deter people from developing and applying their talents. Therefore, equal opportunities plus freedom of choice leads to a meritocratic system where inequalities are just, since they derive from individual efforts of will rather than brute luck or inheritance.

Equality therefore needs redefining in terms of life-chances and capabilities (or capacities) rather than simple redistribution from rich to poor. What matters is less what people possess than the use to which they can put their possessions. Because most deprivation is temporary (Leisering and Leibfried, 1999), what people need are non-material rather than simply material resources, such as income. Society consists of strata that are in a dynamic state of flux, with considerable individual mobility both up and down, rather than the rigid class hierarchies imagined by socialists and traditional social science. This necessitates an emphasis upon education, skills, training and retraining. The welfare state should be based upon 'active welfare', or provision that emphasises insertion into the labour market, rather than a 'passive welfare' that pays people to be idle.

Reciprocity

Similarly, whereas the Old Left based its ideas upon the social rights of citizenship and interpreted entitlements to welfare as unconditional (Plant, 1998), the NSD regards obligations as equally important. This does not mean abandoning the category of social rights, as the New Right advocated (Plant, 1993), but it does mean being clearer and firmer about attaching rights to responsibilities (Roche, 1992). This reciprocity mirrors the social interdependency that is expressed in the principle of community, since those who derive the benefits of belonging to a community have an obligation to contribute to the production of those benefits (White, 1999). Those who refuse to do so are 'free-riders', i.e. they accept the benefits but do not shoulder the corresponding burdens. Social membership therefore implies a combination of benefits and burdens and so a reciprocity of rights and responsibilities. It is a third way between a society consisting entirely of rights-holders or one consisting entirely of duty-holders, neither of which offers an adequate basis for social justice and progress.

This principle also provides support for active welfare. Benefits should be provided conditionally rather than unconditionally, based upon a willingness to work, train, job search, learn or perform some other valuable social contribution. Indeed, Tony Blair has referred to community as the product of opportunity in combination with responsibility (Levitas, 2000: 191). New Labour has gone as far as claiming that rights do not exist outside of the reciprocal relationships that are said to give them meaning: no rights without responsibilities (Giddens, 1998: 65). However, this reciprocity must consistently apply to *all* sectors of society, not only those at the bottom but those at the top. And responsible citizenship implies not only 'negative' actions (e.g. not dropping litter) and legalistic actions (e.g. paying your taxes), but also 'positive', civic actions (helpful interventions). Hence, New Labour's encouragement of civic virtues such as civility, neighbourliness, charity and volunteering.

Inclusion

The Left has tended to treat exclusion from the social mainstream as a threshold of income: those below a given income line being defined as excluded. This is taken to be too simplistic, as there may well be some above the line who are excluded (pensioners and disabled people) and some below it who are not (students and academics). In short, whereas 'poverty' refers to the static measurements of income distribution, exclusion is a far more qualitative term, capturing the dynamic, subjective and life-chances aspect of social membership (Oppenheim, 1998). It enables us to recognise the fracturing of public space and social norms due both to exclusion at the top, manifested most obviously in gated communities, and at the bottom as a result of welfare dependency. It follows that policies of social inclusion must involve much more than a redistribution of income, since this may only exacerbate the voluntary exclusion of both the affluent and the workshy. The objective should not be equality per se, but the inclusion of all in a new public space, through which common endeavours can be pursued and shared citizenship expressed (Dahrendorf, 1995; Giddens, 1998: 101–11).

To create this space we need to reconnect people to each other through a series of investment strategies (Mulgan, 1998). The labour market is of key importance and people must be equipped with the transferable skills and qualifications that are needed to thrive in the world of work. Through work people derive not only an income, but also self-esteem, social contacts, civic connectedness and ontological stability. However, free markets alone cannot achieve this. The state must ensure that work pays, by requiring employers to pay a minimum wage and by supplementing wages with in-work benefits or tax credits. Investment in potential rather than compensation for failure (passive welfare) should be the priority. Additionally, inclusion must not override the virtues of diversity and pluralism: communities should be empowered to take control of their fate based upon a knowledge of their local circumstances and needs.

Pragmatism

Pragmatism is not something that counter-balances the above principles, it is itself a principle which eschews dogma (of Left and Right) in favour of evidence, verification and realism (Taylor-Gooby, 2000). Pragmatism allows government to be flexible, testing what does and does not work and changing accordingly, to adapt to alterations in society and the economy (particularly important in a global environment) and to combine the best features from a range of political ideas. Pragmatism is suited to a post-ideological age where we recognise that there is no perfect social model. Yet pragmatism is not necessarily a form of conservatism, but that which can be made to serve an ambitious and radical agenda.

This means that once we have chosen our goals, e.g. reinvestment in the public sector, we should not be inflexible about the means of delivering them (IPPR, 2001). Public goals require more than public means of delivery and it may well be that private companies and voluntary organisations are equally capable. This kind of pluralism ensures that the dangers of vested interests monopolising the public sector are avoided and that public, private and voluntary agencies can learn from one another. Ultimately, political pragmatism simply reflects the pragmatism of ordinary people who are interested in 'outcomes' and do not much care about how the outcome is delivered. 'What works' must be the watchword and to automatically favour either the state over the market, or vice versa, is to prefer ideals to facts. But pragmatism is not only about the consumption of services, it is also that which favours a grassroots, bottom-up approach to social reform. Pragmatism allows people to make mistakes and learn from them. It is the learning which is important and not the imposition of a 'one size fits all' approach to social reorganisation.

In short, the NSD styles itself as a politics of the radical Centre that applies the principles of community, meritocracy, reciprocity, inclusion and pragmatism to a social environment shaped by conservative policies in an attempt to restructure society according to the social democratic belief in justice and opportunity for all within a humane form of capitalism. Is this the definition of the NSD with which we should be content or might the key objections to NSD arguments throw a different light on the matter?

Objections

What follows are the main criticisms of the NSD and New Labour, in response to the above principles and arguments, some of which we will return to over the course of the next few chapters. Note that these objections do not reject the above principles *per se*, merely what some see as their conservative content.

- Community only offers a middle way between collectivism/egalitarianism and individualism if these social philosophies are caricatured and simplified. Unless we recognise conflicts over its meaning and application, community is a vague concept that easily lends itself to romanticised visions of home, family and nation, perhaps explaining New Labour's uneasy relationship with feminism (McRobbie, 2000; Franklin, 2000) and environmentalism (see Chapter 6).
- Because it is ultimately intended to be compatible with global capitalism, New Labour's communitarianism tends to be authoritarian and moralistic rather than truly reflexive and heterogenous (Driver and Martell, 1997). Its commitment to pluralism is correspondingly shallow: excluding, *a priori*, calls for a more radical pluralism through the redistribution of wealth and ownership.
- Meritocracy is too weak a principle (Young, 1958). Genuine equality requires the removal of the structures that distribute power, wealth and capital unevenly. To graft a few 'meritocratic' policies onto a class

society means that (1) existing structural inequalities are justified, because inequalities are now wrongly held to result from individual efforts, and (2) those at the social bottom are held responsible for their disadvantages because they obviously did not make proper use of the opportunities provided for them.

- Equality of opportunity is meaningless without some equalisation of outcomes, otherwise the former ossifies into the very system of un-deserved advantage and disadvantage that it is meant to correct. 'Outcome equality' requires not just social protection (Giddens, 2002a: 39–40), but a substantial redistribution of material and cultural resources. Just distribution is not *only* a zero sum game, but it does depend upon some degree of redistribution from those with to those without.

- The distinction between active and passive welfare is spurious (Lister, 2001a). Welfare has always been 'active' in that there has always been some expectation that benefit claimants will work, hence the princi-ple of social insurance. The distinction has become popular to dis-guise the fact that what is now called active welfare is little more than a synonym for workfare policies that often coerce and punish the victim. Economic efficacy is now supposedly gained by reforming the worker rather than reforming the market.

- The idea that the Old Left ignored the importance of duties is another caricature (Deacon, 2000: 15). In fact, the NSD merely updates the principle of 'less eligibility' to which state welfare has always sub-scribed, both pre- and post-Beveridge. What *traditional* social democ-rats recognised, unlike New Labour, was the duty of the state to structure the job market. And at its worst what New Labour has done is to *decentralise responsibility* while *centralising power* upon those who already hold it.

- Responsibility is far more complex than new social democrats imagine. For instance, it might be said that duties correlate to powers rather than to rights *per se* (see Chapter 2), so that a real ethic of social responsibility necessitates a far greater redistribution of power than that envisaged by the NSD. By ignoring this point, New Labour might also be accused of decentralising responsibility but of centralising power even where they have attempted to be most radical, e.g. devo-lution. Therefore, this is yet another emphasis that attempts to legiti-mate existing inequalities.

- Reciprocity, too, is much more complex. There are general and par-ticular forms of reciprocity, as well as short-term and long-term ver-sions. There are rights that do not correspond to duties and duties that do not correspond to rights. We might claim that because rights are fundamental to human welfare, they *do* give rise to unconditional entitlements to those goods without which a minimal level of well-being cannot be maintained. Additionally, it could even be claimed that the NSD does not take responsibility seriously enough (Fitzpatrick, 2001b, 2001c) – see Chapters 2 and 7.

- New Labour has been extremely inconsistent in applying the principle of reciprocity. For instance, it has required claimants to jump through a number of hoops in order to qualify for state benefits, establishing continuity with the previous Conservative administrations, often justifying this as a means of empowerment ('by forcing people into employment they will benefit in the long run'). However, it has imposed few responsibilities upon affluent households or powerful corporations and individuals.

- Equality cannot be redefined as inclusion without betraying the essential aims of distributive justice (Levitas, 1998: Chs 7–8). Exclusion may imply more than the lack of an income, but possessing a decent income is the *sine qua non* of effective social participation. To ignore this is to substitute selectivist policies for redistributive ones. It condemns many on low incomes to a revolving door of retraining, low-waged work, retraining . . . *ad infinitum*. This misidentifies the source of social exclusion and the social problems that are thereby generated and, by imagining that large degrees of income inequality are compatible with social inclusion, favours only a weak form of inclusion.

- The NSD incorporates conservative conceptions of dependency in three senses. First, it fetishises market forms of independence. Second, it treats dependency upon the state as the main problem. This misses other forms of dependency that may be equally damaging, e.g. upon the labour market and upon the family. Third, it identifies the welfare state as the essential problem rather than the welfare state's market environment. The NSD's solution is then to make the benefit system more selectivist and conditional in order to adapt it to the very flexible and polarised labour market which is the real origin of most social problems.

- Social participation is equated with participation in employment, neglecting the informal sector and the unpaid forms of work that lie outside the wage contract and so marginalising the contribution that domestic labour (still predominantly performed by women) makes to national and global wealth.

- Without reference to robust principles and ideals, pragmatism is nothing more than a dissimulated form of conservatism. Pragmatism has an ideological force depending upon the political context within which it is applied and whether that context is being accepted or challenged. Pragmatism is the ideology that dare not speak its name. In New Labour's case, deciding 'what works' has involved introducing private sector ethics and practices into the public sector while there has been little hint of introducing the public into the private.

- The idea that what is important is output rather than the means of delivering the output rests upon a spurious distinction between ends and means: as if the nature of the latter does not affect that of the former. In reality, the means determine the ends (Leys, 2001: Ch. 4). Introducing private provision into public services subtly alters the nature of the latter by introducing commercial, competitive and profit-oriented values and standards into the public sphere. This may or may not be desirable, but the issue of whether it is cannot be side-stepped through a 'common sense' appeal to pragmatism.

If these objections are fair – and we will return to some of them throughout Part I – then we need to redefine the NSD. The NSD is indeed a politics of the radical Centre, but a Centre that has been hegemonised by the Right and from which the NSD is reluctant to escape. The essential criticism of the NSD is therefore this.

Post-war social democracy achieved an equilibrium of accumulation and legitimation: the capitalist market provided the finance for welfare services which, in turn, provided this form of 'welfare capitalism' with justification and validation (O'Connor, 1973; Habermas, 1975). By the 1970s this equilibrium had become increasingly unstable: it was claimed by both Left and Right that private markets had reached the limits of their social potential and that the state could no longer guarantee social and cultural stability. The proposed solutions were different, however. According to the Left, if private systems of accumulation were exhausted, then it would be necessary to find non-private forms, to socialise the means of accumulation by taking more of the economy into public ownership. According to the Right, if the state could not guarantee legitimacy, then it would be necessary to privatise the means of legitimation, of loyalty. With the inability of social democratic governments to reconcile this dis-equilibrium, the blame for economic turmoil was placed upon the Left and so the solutions of the political Right prevailed. The effect was the increasing use of markets, quasi-markets and private forms of investment, priority given to low inflation rather than full employment, privatisation and increased inequality.

But the conservative agenda dealt not only with economics, but also with morals and social expectations. People were taught to expect less from each other. Social relations were individualised and structured as forms of contractual exchange; social disadvantage was pathologised and treated as a source of menace and risk. Oppositional voices were defeated, silenced, harried and overworked. The public sector was infused with market-like reforms: league tables, centralisation, competition, standard-

Figure 1.1 Conservatism and social democracy

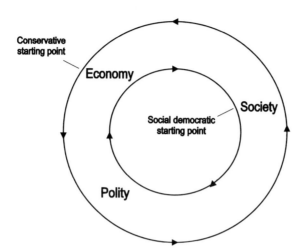

isation, auditing, bureaucratisation, remote control managerialism, perpetual reviews and reforms (Clarke *et al.*, 2000), as well as diversionary
criticism and demoralisation. The result has been a privatisation not
only of the economy, but of culture and discourse, the means of self-
description, the inner economies of the self.

It is this privatisation of legitimation, in both its economic and cultural
forms, that the NSD perpetuates. Whereas post-war social democracy
sought the social control of the economic, the NSD seeks the economic
control of society, helping the radical Right to reverse the political flow so
that the outer circuit of Figure 1.1 predominates over the inner. The NSD
'reverses the political circuit'. The defeat of 'old social democracy' and the
conservatisation of the Centre has now been promoted by the social
democratisation of the Right's hegemony. To put it simply, society is
reshaped by the above Centre-Left principles to fit the imperatives of the
free market. The NSD's emphasis is certainly different and more progressive, but the consequence is the same: the desocialisation of society.
To repeat: the NSD is not equivalent *to* conservatism, but is an effective
conduit *for* it, an unwitting accomplice or useful idiot.

The case against New Labour and the NSD has been stated bluntly and
so the task now is to justify it, not by substantiating each and every aspect
of the above objections, but by concentrating upon those that are most
useful to the book's aim and to the argument of Part II. In Chapter 2 we
examine the NSD in terms of justice and citizenship, Chapter 3 deals with
the state and the information society, while Chapter 4 furthers our under-

standing of the NSD by looking beyond New Labour to social democracy across Europe. But before we can initiate those discussions, we have to establish the basic case: that the NSD represents the conservatisation of the Centre and the social democratisation of conservatism, rather than anything more progressive.

The age of mainstreams

This basic case is established by looking at how and why the NSD conceives of politics and political struggle.

In the introductory chapter, I complained about those who simplified the history of social democracy. This simplification is performed by those who wish to distance themselves from the very tradition upon which they continue to draw and one consequence of this is that what they defend also ends up being simplified. Take the approach of Tony Giddens, for example. Giddens repeatedly succumbs to the temptation to homogenise his social democratic predecessors and peers. He ignores the extent to which the 'old' social democracy was already a complex negotiation between competing principles, though one that did not treat pragmatism as an end in itself (Callaghan, 2000; Pierson, 2001), and he overestimates the flexibility and reflexivity of the NSD. This overestimation is easily explained. New social democrats set out to collapse the conceptual and discursive distinctions between Left and Right, public and private, etc., but in so doing they have to elide the very real divisions, associations and identities which continue to exist and from which those distinctions derive their salience (Clift, 2001). Because new social democrats adopt the *vocabulary* of consensus they imagine that the *reality* of consensus must follow automatically (Fairclough, 1999). The NSD is therefore far more flexible and reflexive at the level of language than it has proved to be in practice. Indeed, it is far less flexible and reflexive than the old social democracy which, by recognising the structural depth of divisions such as class, is more able to effect a politics of reconciliation where consensus is (however imperfectly) built upon and through a recognition of enduring social conflict. By valuing the harmonies of big-tent politics, the NSD's version of consensus is quite shallow and, at worst, helps to mask the power of corporate capitalism (Callinicos, 2001). In fact, because social harmony has not followed the harmonies they construct within discourse, new social democrats frequently adopt a patronising attitude towards those who disagree with them, distinguishing sharply between allies, those whose 'therapy' is not yet complete and those who are allegedly 'incurable' (Giddens, 2001: Ch. 2; 2002a: 10–28).

This explains why the 'Third Way' debate was ultimately a non-starter. By setting up a crude contrast between the Centre and what they took to be either the far Left or Right, Third Wayers have neglected the simple fact that there are multiple Centres and many different forms of social democracy (see Chapter 4). Giddens (2000: 31; 2001: 3) briefly considers this possibility only to reject it – since accepting it might imply that the old social democracy is not so redundant after all – by ultimately appealing to a *deus ex machina* that supposedly reinforces the superiority of Third Way politics: the advent of globalisation and information society as that which allegedly renders all other strategies obsolete (Giddens and Hutton, 2000: 45–51). As noted in the introduction, the NSD therefore appeals to a TINA logic ('There Is No Alternative') which represents the intolerant closure of the social imagination, what I have elsewhere called the 'extremist Centre' (Fitzpatrick, 2002a), in stark contrast to the pioneering self-image that it likes to project.

If, then, the NSD simplifies both itself and its predecessors, and if it overlooks the extent to which there are multiple Centres and multiple forms of social democracy, why is this and what are the potential implications?

In essence, the NSD bases itself upon a limited theory of politics and political struggle, the strategy of which is to search for a unified coalition that will support a pragmatic instrumentalism where politics is about efficient management and 'what works'. Mouffe (2000: Ch. 5) characterises this approach as *politics without adversity*, the avoidance of enemy making in the belief that social partnership requires the absence of antagonism. In truth, new social democrats are perfectly willing to make enemies of those they consider to be ideologists, though because theirs has been a journey towards the political Right the ideologists have been identified more on the Left, i.e. in the gap left behind. Yet this kind of enemy making is inadequate because it ignores Mouffe's point that liberal democracy depends upon *creative* disagreement, not pluralism for its own sake, but one that drives a mutual learning process across the social and political fields. This notion of creative dissent is important not only for liberal democracy, which is otherwise emptied of the resources it needs to constantly renew itself, but for those who wish to bend liberal democracy in the direction of their favoured principles and values. Social democrats lost the initiative in the 1970s, not because they failed to adapt to the new realities of market capitalism, but because they treated those 'realities' as inevitable and failed to reconfigure social democracy across a broader spectrum of movements, organisations and alliances that pull away from the reductive logic of free market capitalism (see Chapter 9). So far from representing a break with the past, the NSD replicates the worst features of the old (Krieger, 1999: 170–1): a politics that yearns for the non-political.

So pluralism must not only be 'external' but 'internal', not only disagreement with political enemies, but also a constant search with friends for new forms of political friendship: a reflexive pluralism. What is objectionable about the NSD is not its alliance with Centrist politics – after the discrediting of centralised communism a retreat to the Centre was natural and inevitable – but its insistence that the meaning and implications of 'the Centre' are inevitably fixed around conservative configurations. Yet if politics must imply reflexive pluralism then there is no such thing as 'the Centre', since this is always subject to the flux of negotiation and contestation. This is not just the simple and obvious observation that 'the Centre' means different things in different countries, e.g. the Swedish Centre is still highly redistributive, whereas the American Centre eschews income equality; it is the point that even *within* particular political communities the Centre is a fractured alliance of forces that push and pull in opposing *ideological* directions. The Centre, then, is everywhere a multiplicity of 'Centres' and the agenda promoted by the NSD (where politics is reduced to managerial efficiency) is not determined for us, but is only one of many on offer. The NSD is the ideological attempt to colonise the space of social democracy once and for all and to banish those versions of Centre-Left politics that point us away from conservative capitalism.

Therefore, the definition of politics and struggle advanced by the NSD is very one-sided. Its vision of political struggle is the surmounting of dissensus so that we can all sit around a table and agree on how to run the trains: struggle is a journey towards a closure, a final consensus. By contrast, a politics of reflexive pluralism regards struggle as a paradoxical, never-ending loop of 'enclosure' and 'disclosure'. Enclosure implies the closing of social forms around one aspect of the social field; disclosure implies the breaking open of social enclosure by devising new descriptions, practices and alliances. Strategic disclosures then lead towards new forms of enclosure that, in turn, also require breaking open. So enclosure and disclosure are always interdependent and relative to one another: without disclosure, enclosure engenders social totalities (and eventually totalitarianism); without enclosure, disclosure is aimless, ineffective and chimerical. This distinction therefore cuts across the ideological spectrum: there are both Left and Right versions of enclosure *and* disclosure. But in our present conjuncture, after the reforms of the last quarter century, what we face is a Right-wing closure.

Therefore, the case against the NSD is that by either not recognising this at all or, at best, underestimating it the NSD not only fails to 'disclose' conservatism, but goes some way towards consolidating the conservative enclosure (Hutton, 2002). Through the conservatisation of the Centre and the social democratisation of the Right, the NSD conjures a totalitarian-ism of the mainstream.

We have received our first hint of why I refer to this as the age of main-streams. Mainstreaming signifies the contemporary closure of social cog-nition, value and action around conservatism. But because this process is less visible in some countries than in others, a politics of the mainstream may also offer the potential for reopening the social field. In order to un-pack this idea, and suggest what 'reopening' might imply, I have to say a bit more about political struggle.

I want to outline a theory of 'open hegemony', a notion of political struggle that derives from liberal, Marxist and post-structuralist perspec-tives on society, without being reducible to any one of them. The two key figures in this respect are Karl Popper and Antonio Gramsci.

Popper (1945) argued that only open societies could secure freedom and peace within the post-war world. For a society to be open, it must contain institutions and cultures that permit and encourage the scrutiny and criticism of leaders and the structures which lend them their author-ity. This requires an educated, liberal, free-thinking citizenry that does not allow closed hierarchies of power to be imposed upon the social order. Struggle is always the struggle of openness against closure.

Popper's argument is a simple yet ingenious redescription of liberal tenets. Its strength, though, is also a debilitating weakness, since even at a basic level there are many different versions of liberalism and, by impli-cation, different versions of the open society. By not following through this line of thought, and by rejecting Marxism upon spurious grounds (Hollis, 1994: 71–7), Popper invites the support of simplistic *apologias* and defenders. In particular, by regarding the state as the principal source of closure, Popper repeats the tendency of classic liberals to either overlook the dangers of market monopolies or even to prefer market domination as a barricade against statism (Hayek, 1982). Therefore, if the concept of openness is to be useful, then it must receive a treatment more sophisti-cated than that which Popper himself is willing to provide.

Gramsci's (1971) theory of hegemony is equally well known, denoting a form of domination effected either through the voluntary or forced consent of those dominated. This consent is secured because the dominant are able to project their particular interests, values and inter-pretations of the social world as common sense, as a neutral reflection of reality that is universally applicable. Such hegemony then allows the dominant to remake the world in their image, to confirm the universality of their worldview through a self-fulfilling reconstruction of society. To resist hegemonic dominance therefore requires counter-hegemonic strategies on the part of the dominated. Marxists should concern them-selves not only with revolutionising the economic base, but also with hegemonic struggle within civil society; indeed, the latter is a condition of the former.

Like Popper, Gramsci's vision of society lends itself to simplification. If the overwhelming organising principle of society is a conflict between capital/bourgeoisie and labour/proletariat, then Gramsci's interpretation of political struggle holds water. Yet if this conflict, however important, is just one of many, some of which intersect the capital/labour division and some of which do not, then hegemonic resistance becomes a much more complicated affair. This was the fundamental point made by Laclau and Mouffe (1985). If 'the social' is not reducible to an essential logic, then hegemony is no longer polarised along a class dimension, but is dispersed along manifold dimensions of identity and affiliation. Resisting oppression therefore requires a complex sociocultural critique that recognises the salience of non-class forms of domination. All struggle is profoundly political, since the political is not merely a set of representative mechanisms (liberalism) nor simply a reflection of economic dominance (Marxism).

Nevertheless, if this post-Marxist revision of Gramsci is persuasive, less persuasive is the post-structuralist alternative. As I will argue again in Chapter 9, by abandoning all reference to extra-contextual spaces, i.e. traditionless standards that enable us to judge traditions, post-structuralists leave themselves in something of a social vacuum. Take their response to those critical theorists such as Habermas who dare to imagine that they have theorised at least the outlines of the extra-contextual standards that post-structuralists deny exist. In rejecting such claims post-structuralists are neither able to deliver the knock-out blow that would dispel critical theory once and for all – since this strategy would undermine the agonistic pluralism that they support – but neither can they propose a *rapprochement* with critical theory, given the incommensurability of its premises.

We seem to be left in an impasse. A simple conception of the open society would be one populated only by free-market conservatives; and though a more complex reading of social openness might lead us towards the concept of hegemony this too is vulnerable to a simplistic appropriation. Yet how to devise more complex readings without falling into the traps that ensnared post-structuralists?

My solution is to propose a theory of open hegemony that captures the paradox of reflexive pluralism that has just been discussed. For political struggle redefined as an open hegemony, the ideal is neither openness nor utopia, but an oscillation that arcs elliptically between the two. The liberal ideal is admirable, but neglects the fact that attempts to curve the social grid around particular imperatives are inevitable and desirable: inevitable, because the grid's contours are already shaped by multiple gravities of power; desirable, because if an open society's only rationale was to maintain its openness then it would quickly lose legitimacy in the eyes of its citizens (something that has arguably been happening in our 'post-ideological age'). Therefore, openness is not the static property imagined by liberals, a redoubt against closure, but a perpetual fluctuation away from and towards itself.

Yet equally the horizon of openness must never be lost sight of. If the grid is allowed to curve totally around any one gravitational force, then it collapses in on itself, imploding into a totalitarian finality. Therefore hegemonisation must allows carry an alterior logic within itself, must never seek its own end. To repeat the point made in Fitzpatrick (2001a: 199), it is as dangerous to arrive at utopia as it is to avoid its call and utopianism must be a journey which avoids its own destination. Political struggle is therefore antimonious. It is the maintenance of a loop of enclosure/disclosure within which ideological principles and ideals, far from being abandoned, are activated. For as the loop circulates again and again, the aim is to approximate society more and more to one's vision of the good, to drag the Centre towards yourself. But this requires not a postmodernist celebration of difference-for-the-sake-of-difference, but the willingness to prioritise some struggles above others based upon a reading of the contemporary conjuncture (see Chapter 6).

Against this interpretation of society and political struggle the conceptions of the NSD appear naive, constantly invoking the tyranny of three: once we had the statist egalitarianism of the Old Left which, because it failed, gave way to the New Right's market libertarianism that wrecked society and so led electorates back towards social democracy, albeit one that must adapt to new social realities. On this reading, the 'reopening' of society is already underway due to the NSD's ability to synthesise what were traditionally considered to be opposites and apply this lesson to social and economic developments. However, on my reading, the NSD is wrong on two counts: wrong about counter-hegemonisation and wrong in its cartographic reading of where we are.

According to the NSD, it has successfully turned society away from conservatism by accepting the reality (and often the desirability) of its reforms, but redirecting the resulting environment towards the goals of social inclusion and communal responsibility. Counter-hegemonisation therefore implies that in order to defeat your opponents you have to wear some of their clothes. At the beginning of the new century we are now travelling from welfare to social investment states, having been briefly diverted towards the libertarian market. But according to the above theory of open hegemony, counter-hegemonisation requires a degree of reflexive pluralism that new social democrats, in their determination to crowd out alternative social democratic traditions and possibilities, have not come close to demonstrating. Counter-hegemonisation also needs a willingness to contrast what your opponents say with what they do. But by accepting much of what the radical Right has said and done, this contrast has been muted at best. New social democrats have played the game without trying to change many of the rules. For instance, it has appealed to a particular aspect of middle-class identity, the desire for security, but without a critique of privatisation and marketisation that would enable the goal of security to be redefined and allow other more progressive and cooperative aspects of middle-class identity to emerge and mobilise with other social groupings. Consequently, the NSD retains not only the economics of the Right, but also its moral authoritarianism and intolerance for dissent.

The NSD therefore confuses political struggle with electoral expediency: it assembles constituencies upon a middle ground that, having been shaped by the Right, is now held to be immutable. Its electoral successes have been impressive, but have not generated any long-term visions of social emancipation other than a process of permanent modernisation, or adaptation to social changes that are somehow held to evade political control. So the mainstream, the opposite of extremism that nevertheless replicates its exclusionary logic, its closure of social possibility, becomes the only acceptable reference point. The tyranny is internal, a dictatorship of the Centre reconfigured around the Right's conservatism.

Yet as we shall see throughout this book the social grid has not imploded entirely and oppositional voices have refused to be silenced. The mainstream can also become a site of renaissance and renewal since the values which are strong enough to keep us tethered to the authoritarian market must also be strong enough to loosen the grip. The freedom which mutilates itself in the desire for more security, more consumption, more competition, is also a freedom that can recognise alternative forms of social life, *can* recognise because such recognition has been clearer in the past, articulated by forms of social democracy that continue to survive (see Chapter 4). Therefore, although we are not locked within the existing mainstream we must think from within and through it if we are to spy the political spaces that lie beyond. This is why I base my philosophical alternative upon social democratic traditions, though not the NSD which seeks to enclose those traditions around conservative silences.

Conclusion

To summarise: the NSD represents the conservatisation of the political Centre and the social democratisation of conservatism. While not equating to conservatism, it does represent the hegemonisation *of* the Right rather than a counter-hegemonisation *to* the Right. However, the mainstream is not necessarily closed around a conservative agenda, as there are potentially multiple versions of the political Centre and social democracy on offer. And although NSD purists want us to believe that all nations will travel down the road pioneered by Britain and America, this is by no means inevitable.

As such, I contend that the NSD is *not* a new politics, but is at best the first steps on a long march back towards truly progressive ideals, one from which valuable lessons can be learned, if only about how *not* to proceed. My argument in Part I is that 'old' social democratic traditions are far from exhausted and that the kind of principles outlined earlier can be genuinely reconfigured away from conservatism. Therefore, the disclosure of the social field does not mean abandoning social democracy, but does mean radicalising it in ways that the NSD has not begun to imagine.

Notes

1 Though his initial enthusiasm was for the term 'Third Way', one that makes occasional appearances in this book, he subsequently tempered this enthusiasm.
2 I am not going to make much reference to the 'Third Way' for reasons that will become clear later.
3 In short, the UK will be our main point of reference, but note that Chapter 3 will make some reference to America.
4 This risks upsetting those social, one-nation conservatives and Christian Democrats for whom the term bears different implications. However, this is a tradition of thought that makes few appearances in this book and so I feel able to appropriate the term. I am not going to offer a critique of conservatism directly though it is possible to infer such a critique from my analysis of the NSD.

2

Justice and citizenship

Chapter 1 concluded by arguing that the NSD is not a counter-hegemonic strategy, because its notions of politics and political struggle are inadequate. Here we begin to examine some of the objections raised there in more depth. As noted already, our task is not to offer a comprehensive critique of the NSD, merely to investigate those features which most enable alternatives to the NSD to be imagined. In this chapter, we concentrate upon the principle of reciprocity, and associated terms such as rights and responsibilities. Effectively, my argument will be that if we are to be genuinely concerned with reciprocity and responsibility then we must attach them to a theory of egalitarian justice that I will term 'equality of powers'. What the NSD conveniently ignores is that if egalitarian justice really is defunct, then not only does this eliminate radical alternatives to conservatism, it also gives us very little reason to support reciprocity, responsibility, etc., thus undermining the NSD itself. The case is established by reviewing two concepts in turn: justice and citizenship.

Justice

As a working definition let us define justice as 'the fair distribution of benefits and burdens'. Let us also assume that the meaning of 'benefit' and 'burden' is relatively unproblematic. In making this assumption I certainly do not want to underplay the contestability of these terms. For if their meaning is determined by social norms, i.e. the shared understandings of social members, then it is not difficult to see why our ideas of what is and is not a benefit have developed with the development of social norms. Nevertheless, for the sake of space I want to concentrate upon the more controversial aspect of the above definition, that of fair distribution.

There are essentially seven theories of justice offering an answer to this question (cf. Barry, 1989, 1995): justice as equality, as reciprocity, as procedure, as virtue, as restoration, as retribution and as differential inclusion. Again, for reasons of space I am not going to deal with all of these but instead concentrate upon those that have dominated the debate during recent years: egalitarian justice, reciprocal justice and procedural justice.

Egalitarian justice

This theory states that justice requires an equality of either resources or welfare (Dworkin, 2000). Resources may be internal (talents, skills, abilities) or external (income, wealth, opportunities) and resource egalitarianism demands that because inequalities in endowments are undeserved, then some equalisation of external resources is called for. If a resource is a possession then 'welfare' in this context refers to that which our possessions allow us to achieve. Welfare egalitarianism has therefore received far less support than resource egalitarianism because an equalisation of achievement, and of the satisfaction that achievement brings, is widely held to be both impractical and undesirable. However, some have argued for an equal opportunities version of welfare egalitarianism (Cohen, 1989; Arneson, 2000; Roemer, 1998), as will I.

Reciprocal justice

Although any society depends upon forms of mutual cooperation what is to stop an individual from defecting from their side of the bargain (Barry, 1995: Ch. 2)? One solution is to instil moral standards so that agents regard reciprocity as the highest good and are not tempted to defect (Gibbard, 1991). This implies a strong emphasis upon desert (so that what you take from the social product is proportional to what you have contributed) and duty (so that your notion of advantage is other-regarding rather than self-regarding). Reciprocal justice is therefore attractive in an age where the ethic and practice of egalitarianism have waned. It preserves the 'socialism' of egalitarian justice and the ideal of communal belonging and identity (Selbourne, 1994), yet it also appeals to some notion of proceduralism (see below) where what is important is common adherence to just rules rather than the manipulation of outcomes, yet without the prominence that market libertarians give to entitlement, since reciprocity preserves the notion of moral desert (cf. Gauthier, 1986).

Procedural justice

Here, the most convincing account remains that of Nozick (1974) who contrasts procedural theory with 'end-state' theories of justice. Proceduralism is concerned with the means that generate a given pattern of distribution, rather than with the pattern itself. So if in a series of exchanges each individual transfer and transaction is just (including the initial acquisition of resources), i.e. does not violate anyone's rights, then the outcome of that series is also just, even if massive inequalities have been created. It is tempting to assess whether the outcome, the end-state, is or is not just, but doing so ignores the fact that justice consists in voluntary, harm-respecting exchanges between free agents where benefits and burdens are distributed according to entitlement. In short, procedural justice represents a challenge to all forms of egalitarian, socialist and welfarist ideas which aim at some ideal of social justice. For since redistribution requires the taxation of what people have legitimately earned, then taxation is theft and social justice a specious means of justifying theft.

New social democracy

Which of the above does the NSD come closest to embodying? We can eliminate procedural justice since the NSD is committed to some form of social justice that such theories do not permit. The problem with procedural justice is that entitlement cannot bear the weight it is expected to bear. The means can justify the end only if we ignore the moral arbitrariness (what I will call the 'undeservingness') of our endowments and say, as Nozick says, that although we may not deserve our talents we are nevertheless entitled to them (via the principle of self-ownership) and to the goods that they generate. Nozick therefore builds a theory of 'justice as voluntary transaction' upon involuntary grounds. Taking account of moral arbitrariness either means that we do not own ourselves in full or that full self-ownership does not necessarily translate into the full ownership of the goods that our endowments partially, but not wholly, create (Kymlicka, 2002: Ch. 3).

Yet nor does the NSD sit entirely within the egalitarian school of justice. Buckler (2000) argues that New Labour's version of redistribution in no way corresponds to patterned or outcome forms of distributive justice. Instead, New Labour follows a Rawlsian approach in that what is important are the distributive rules inhering in the basic social structure rather than constant interventions to ensure an end-state egalitarianism. This then explains why New Labour is committed to equal opportunities, social markets, education, employment and social inclusion. Although Buckler's interpretation of Rawls is occasionally shaky – tending to regard him as a prototypical Third Wayer – he does show that New Labour's is at best a *weak* egalitarianism (cf. Wissenburg, 2001).

What of reciprocity? More than anyone, Stuart White (1999, 2001) has established how and why the New Labour project holds to the basic principles of reciprocal justice. The essential reason for this lies in New Labour's insistence that rights and responsibilities should balance. I want to examine citizenship in more detail later on, but New Labour's point is that because social goods are the product of social cooperation, then those who share those goods are obligated to make a roughly proportionate contribution to the productive activities of that society or to demonstrate why they cannot. Hence the doctrine that has constantly informed their welfare reforms – work for those who can, security for those who cannot – and the implicit reliance not only upon need (security) but also upon desert: the proportionality between giving and receiving effected through work. According to White, reciprocal justice was rooted in the socialist and social democratic traditions as it articulated not only the collective nature of industrial modernity, but was also a means of criticising free-market capitalism and even capitalism *per se*. Since those who contributed most to the social product (the workers) were held to receive less than those who contributed the least (the bourgeoisie), then social justice required a 'politics of fair shares' and so either the substantial reorganisation of capitalism or its replacement altogether.

But although White is correct to observe that some commitment to both reciprocity and equality characterises Centre-Left traditions, we must not forget that the nature of this commitment may alter depending upon how the following two questions are answered. What is the proper combination of reciprocity and equality? What is the rationale for our chosen combination?

It seems clear that the NSD favours a mixture of weak equality and strong reciprocity. As indicated in the last chapter and already in this, New Labour is committed to a weak version of egalitarianism, of equal opportunities detached from any hint of outcome equality, where the objective is to arm citizens with the skills and assets that they need to prosper: the fishing rod rather than the fish. This is not to suggest that the NSD discards redistributive policies altogether, hence Tony Blair's pledge to eradicate child poverty in the UK by 2019 (Walker, 2000). But this is an opportunity-based conception of redistribution, where it is believed that unfair disadvantages can be eliminated with relative ease through various educational and labour market reforms (hence, New Labour speaks of unfair *advantages* much more rarely). What is downplayed is the necessity of a 'relativist redistribution' where the aim is to bring the top and the bottom closer together. New Labour insists that the most important aim is to raise the floor without worrying about the height of the ceiling: if the absolute position of the poorest is improved, then why worry about the relative position of the non-poor? Thus, a wealth of research and scholarship suggesting that equality *does* matter is largely ignored (e.g. Wilkinson, 1996; Phillips, 1999), matters because the status of the bottom depends upon positional comparisons with the top and deprivation is not only about what you hold, but where you stand in the scale of holdings (Hirsch, 1977). So as welcome as Blair's pledge is, much of the drop in child poverty may be due to less ambitious measurements than those applied in the past. Time will tell.[1]

Further, New Labour lays considerable stress upon reciprocity and associated concepts such as desert and duty. For the redistribution of opportunities to be successful, people must take up the opportunities on offer; they must either want to do so because of incentives, or must be made to do so through a series of disincentives and deterrents. Mutual obligations to the community are therefore emphasised without the old Leftist tendency to confuse communal standards with egalitarian criteria and without the conservative preference for judging obligations through the lens of the free market.

Yet this combination of weak equality and strong reciprocity leaves New Labour vulnerable to a charge of inconsistency and even hypocrisy. For, as White (1999: 171–3) also goes on to acknowledge, what is important is not so much reciprocity as *fair reciprocity*, where the nature of our participative obligations depends upon the background conditions that obtain. Simply put, to enforce an equality of obligation in a social environment which is profoundly unequal is to further victimise the casualties of that environment: the least well-off (Rose, 2000). Fair reciprocity therefore demands two stipulations. First, the state must perform the duty of guaranteeing socially just background conditions. This may require it to be the employer of last resort, to ensure that all jobs are well paid and that no-one is trapped at the margins of the labour market for very long – duties that appear to be more consistent with the old social democracy than the new one. Second, unless exclusion at the top is targeted as strongly and perhaps even more so as exclusion at the bottom, then the resulting imbalance allows the former to free ride on the deprivations of the latter.

Now, new social democrats are aware of these arguments and Giddens (1998: 66), for one, was initially enthusiastic for fair reciprocity. However, that enthusiasm has declined over time, bringing Giddens (2002a: 40–2) more into line with New Labour's policies. Three points explain this avoidance of fair reciprocity (cf. Wetherly, 2001: 161). First, the pragmatism of the NSD demands that social policies are strongly oriented to expediency and political strategies that adapt to electoral preferences which are held to be given and substantially unalterable (Heffernan, 2000: 119–38). Therefore, second, the electoral middle ground must be captured rather than reconfigured, by not alienating those who aspire to more affluence. The fear is that fair reciprocity would contradict the principle of meritocracy. Finally, the retention of unequal patterns of distribution is necessary since, otherwise, New Labour would be challenging the deregulated capitalism to which it has reconciled itself and from which it supposedly derives its appeal. So the New Labour antipathy to fair reciprocity is not an error that has yet to be rectified; it is essential to its identity: what Standing (1999: 317–19) refers to as asymmetrical or 'unbalanced reciprocity', where the poorest are mandated to join a society from which many of the affluent continue to abscond.

But if New Labour combines weak equality with strong reciprocity, and if this combination is undesirable, then does this condemn the NSD *per se*? Might more radical forms of NSD successfully combine strong reciprocity with strong equality also? To begin to answer these questions we must understand the merits of mixing equality and reciprocity in this way by examining three recent attempts to do so by White, Miller and Rawls.

The road to surfdom?

Although he believes fair reciprocity demands much more material equality than New Labour seems willing to countenance, White is insistent that the latter does not trump the former, since it is still the case that, . . . 'those who willingly accept the economic benefits of social cooperation have a corresponding obligation to make a productive contribution, if so able, to the cooperative community which provides those benefits' (White, 1997: 63–4; cf. 2000: 522). So if 1000 people agree to the formation of a public good (a lighthouse, say) and 100 then contribute nothing to its construction, this means that they free ride on the benefit-producing efforts of the 900. Therefore equality is not only material, it is also *civic* and civic egalitarianism requires that free riding be kept to a minimum through appropriate policies. So, for instance, this is what renders the proposal for an unconditional Basic Income (BI) unjustifiable (Fitzpatrick, 1999a), though White (1996) gives BI a qualified support nevertheless, because it may contain some reciprocity-friendly effects (cf. Elster, 1998).

Miller (1999: 234) argues that need cannot be the only metric of justice. The earth's resources are not manna from heaven, and so an equal share of them cannot be claimed, as resources must be produced and so shares must be earned: 'They are not simply waiting to be picked up and used . . . but have to be appropriated by labor [*sic*]: the deer must be hunted, the coal mined'. Social justice therefore requires reference to the principles of need, desert and equality, depending upon whether the social sphere in question is, respectively, one of communal solidarity, instrumental association or citizenship.

Finally, Rawls (1993: 15–22; 2001: 61–79) affirms that the difference principle is a principle of reciprocity, as the distributive implications of the former depend upon productive activity of which cooperation is the most important condition. This does not mean that people can be forced into particular kinds of work, since this would violate the principle of liberty, but it does make distribution dependent upon people contributing to the good of others by developing and deploying their 'native endowments'. So although the distributive pattern of society is determined on rational and impartial grounds through the original position (Rawls, 1972), each person's place within that pattern depends not upon their *possession* of native endowments (since possession is morally arbitrary and has nothing to do with desert), but upon the *use* to which they place their endowments within a fair system of social co-operation. Rawls (2001: 179) likes to use the example of the person who chooses to surf all day and so does not share the 'burdens of social life'. Is this person one of the 'least advantaged'? Rawls claims not. If we include 16 hours of daily leisure time within the index of primary goods, then we can see how the surfer gains an extra 8 hours of leisure per day compared to those who do work a standard day. As the surfer has chosen 8 hours of leisure rather than the equivalent income from a standard working day, then he cannot claim membership of the least advantaged and must support himself. The difference principle is therefore a principle of reciprocity.

White, Miller and Rawls all agree that strong equality must be balanced by strong reciprocity. To ignore this is to unbalance the egalitarian ethic and invite a society where those who are willingly uncooperative and non-productive free ride on the cooperative and productive efforts of others. Do these arguments stand up to scrutiny? If so, then might we have a firmer moral basis for the NSD? There are three main reasons for doubting so.

White argues that those who willingly accept the economic benefits of social cooperation have a corresponding obligation to make a productive contribution. However, in a society, as opposed to a voluntary association of some kind, there are economic benefits that we are free to accept and those that we are not. For instance, we each benefit from having a well-developed communications and transport infrastructure and short of hiking into the Scottish Cairngorms to live the rest of our lives in a cave and feed off the land there is little we could do to opt out of those benefits. So does the experience of involuntary benefits give rise to the same obligations as the acceptance of voluntary ones? To the best of my knowledge, White does not address this question (cf. White, 1999: 174–6; 2000: 521–2), but if the answer is 'no' this might suggest that a more complex approach to reciprocity is required, one where a certain degree of economic autonomy is the precondition of reciprocity, i.e. only when that precondition has been satisfied can the concern with obligation and free riding come into effect. This then resurrects arguments for BI on stronger grounds than White (2000: 529) perhaps imagines (Fitzpatrick, 1999a: 64–6; van der Veen, 1998).

Miller argues that we cannot claim an equal share of earth's resources because those resources must be appropriated and transformed. But whereas this may be an argument against *equal* shares, it is not an argument against equal *minimal* shares (Fitzpatrick, 1999a: 58–60). The existing stock of social assets is the result not only of living labour but also of natural and economic inheritances. If we assume that natural resources are subject to common ownership then everyone has a *prima facie* claim to a share of those resources (Cohen, 1995: Ch. 3). Although this cannot be an equal claim, as some will work harder than others to transform this inheritance into social assets, a minimal claim is not ruled out because it is nature rather than the labour of others which makes those resources initially available. What then gives substance to that claim is the idea that living labour only accounts for a small percentage of the labour which has transformed natural resources into social assets. It is our economic inheritance – dead labour, technological progress, advances in knowledge – which is mostly responsible for our stock of wealth. If it was our ancestors who sunk the coalmine, then although those who mine the coal have a greater claim than those who do not, this does not eliminate the claim of the latter for an equivalent minimal share, a BI for instance.

Finally, Rawls alleges that the surfer must support himself because primary goods include 16 hours of daily leisure time. Yet Rawls pulls this figure out of the air without explanation and it seems to conveniently treat labour market activity, i.e. an 8 hour day, as the source of our social obligations. But even if we define leisure time as a primary good, there is nothing to stop us making the relevant figure more consistent with the level of existing social wealth. What if the average working day was reduced from 8 to, say, 5 hours per day (cf. Gorz, 1989, 1999) and the difference treated as part of our economic inheritance? Even if the surfer then chooses to surf for those 5 hours he would still be entitled to the equivalent of 3 hours income (van Parijs, 1995: 96–8). In short, treating the difference principle as a principle of reciprocity may exclude the surfer from the category of the least advantaged, but does rule out the desirability of guaranteeing an unconditional minimal income for all at a level below that of the least advantaged.

To summarise. White, Miller and Rawls argue against the combination of weak equality plus strong reciprocity favoured by the NSD. They then present powerful arguments in favour of combining strong reciprocity with strong equality, a position more consistent with 'old' social democracy – though White (2001) suggests that it might also be consistent with more radical versions of the NSD than New Labour's. However, 'strong reciprocity' as they define it seems to contain certain weaknesses and fails for instance to exclude the possibility of distributing an unconditional minimal income to all. If equality therefore has to accommodate some notion of basic unconditionality, then this begins to take us in a post-productivist direction, i.e. one where productive activity is merely one of a series of badges of citizenship. The point of BI is to embody a principle of 'more eligibility'; unlike existing benefit systems where the aim is often to lower benefits to the point where claimants are effectively coerced back into work (less eligibility), BI stresses the advantages of a range of activities and lifestyles (Offe, 1993).

So my thesis is that social democracy should be taken in a post-productivist direction, a combination that I am here terming 'ecosocial welfare'. Ecowelfare is based not upon 'strong equality plus weak reciprocity', since the arguments for strong reciprocity remain powerful (though see the concluding section) (cf. Levine, 1999), but a combination of strong equality and *diverse* reciprocity. I return to this point in the section on citizenship. However, before doing so there are two perspectives on strong equality that we need to examine.

For strong equality to equality of powers

Even if it is strong equality that we favour, does this necessitate a substantial redistribution of income and wealth or might there be other 'metrics' of equality that are more compatible with the NSD? To address this question let us look at two influential contributions to the debate on distributive justice: Sen and Walzer.

Sen (1992) has long maintained that justice has to involve more than the just distribution of goods since a certain package of goods will equip different people with dissimilar degrees of freedom according to the varying levels of ability that they possess. The same package will bear completely different implications for John, a skilled able-bodied mechanic, than it will for Jane, a disabled and unemployed mother of two, because their capacities are different. Therefore to effect just distribution we should look not simply at goods, but at the relationship between goods and persons. Because of their differential capacities, people achieve different levels of functioning, i.e. what they can do and what they can be, and so what we must focus upon is a person's capability to undertake various functionings, implying not an equality of primary goods (Rawls) or of resources (Dworkin), but an equality of capabilities. So what this entails is a midpoint between primary resources on the one hand and the end-state of welfare and achievements on the other: an equal freedom to achieve. For our purposes Sen is important because he recontextualises income and wealth. He does not necessarily downgrade the importance of a primary resource such as income and wealth, but he does

insist that 'income inequality' is not the same thing as 'income inade-
quacy' (Sen, 1992: 109–12) since only the latter captures the idea that different capabilities will convert a low income into differential levels of
well-being.

While accepting the general thrust of Sen's critique there are nevertheless two objections we can make in order to defend the importance of
primary resources. First, there are the responses to Sen made by Rawls
and Dworkin. Rawls (2001: 168–76) insists that his list of primary goods
is far more flexible than Sen allows and that those both within the 'normal
range' of abilities and those below it are already catered for by his theory
of justice. Dworkin (2000: 299–303) similarly argues that his conception of
resources already includes the kind of personal capabilities that, by
placing them in a separate category, tempts Sen to fly too close to the sun
of welfare equality.

The problem with these responses though is that, having reaffirmed the
role of primary resources, they continue to neglect the importance of functionings. Rawls interprets falling below the normal range as a temporary,
contingent affair that requires no more than an *ex post* readjustment in the
goods being received. But what this does is to elide the deeper link
between goods and persons to which Sen draws attention, for what of
those who will never belong to a 'normal' range (Smith, 2001)? Dworkin
meanwhile treats resources and welfare as irreconcilable opposites. Circumstances shape choice, he acknowledges, but as long as the individual
identifies with the choice in question (though he excludes cravings and
addictions as examples of identification) then we need no more than
resource equality to be both endowment-insensitive and ambition-
sensitive (Dworkin, 2000: 287–99).

Yet if this represents an overestimation of the importance of free choice
in human affairs, as variously maintained by Arneson (1989), Cohen
(1989) and Roemer (1996), then we have a second, more convincing objection to Sen: focusing upon capabilities is all very well, but unless we
appreciate the extent to which capabilities are themselves shaped by
underlying circumstances then our conception of the person lacks a social
context. And it is not enough, *contra* Dworkin, for a person to identify
either with their capabilities and their choices, since this may derive from
nothing more than an adjustment to circumstances that the person falsely
perceives as necessary (adapted preferences) and excludes the possibility
of changing those circumstances (Roemer, 1998: 19–20).

What we have, then, is a means of bringing together functionings and
primary resources. What Arneson terms 'equality of opportunity for
welfare' and Cohen terms 'equality of access to advantage' is essentially
the convergence of three conditions: circumstances, capabilities and
choice. Distributive justice should compensate for that which is beyond

our control (circumstances and capabilities), but not for that which is within it (choice). Hence, Sen is correct in drawing attention to capabilities, but the role that involuntary circumstances (natural and social inheritances) play in the shaping of capabilities and choices still leaves a major role for primary resources and so for the substantial redistribution of income and wealth, if we are to compensate successfully for the moral arbitrariness of those circumstances. This is not to claim that such compensation involves *only* income and wealth redistribution, but there is certainly no reason to believe that it does not involve redistribution at all. Obviously, it is difficult to judge where circumstances, capabilities and choice each begin and end (cf. Steiner, 1998). The suspicion that circumstances are the key condition of the three certainly needs to be demonstrated and, even if this suspicion is correct, we still require some mechanism for guaranteeing bodily integrity if the slippery slope towards the redistribution of body parts and talents is to be avoided. Such a task is however beyond the scope of this book. So if primary resources are more important than Sen imagines, then his equality of capabilities can be rendered as an 'equality of powers', a definition of which follows once we have taken a brief look at Walzer.

Walzer (1983) is relevant because, like Sen, he also seems to recommend a recontextualisation of income and wealth that may be more palatable to the NSD. He asserts that money refers not to the entirety of what we mean by justice, but simply to one sphere of justice among a number of plural spheres each of which possesses its own distributive criteria. Therefore, justice requires not the redistribution of money, but ensuring that market-based inequalities in the ownership of commodities do not cross the relevant border and infect other spheres of justice, e.g. education and health care should not be distributed according to ability to pay.

Walzer's notion of 'complex equality' has generated a massive debate (e.g. Miller and Walzer, 1995), but the enduring problem with it concerns the suspicion that differential spheres are easier to maintain in thought than in reality. The objection to massive inequalities in income and wealth derives not only from a distaste for large inequalities in possessions, but also for the way in which material inequalities ossify into structural hierarchies of advantage (including, though not limited to, class). Does Walzer imagine that class advantages can be limited to the sphere of money? In which case, he needs to explain in far more detail how class could ever be so confined, given the experience of human history. Or is he suggesting that complex equality is itself a politics of classlessness? In which case, he needs to explain how material inequalities can be maintained without degenerating into relations of dominance (Miller, 1995; Swift, 1995; Arneson, 1995).

In short, although he proposes a differentiation of spheres, Walzer does not break away from the very logic that, in accounts of simple equality, he otherwise condemns. Indeed, he merely replicates that logic on a smaller scale. Thus, just as 'simple egalitarians' might assume a universality across all parts of the distributive sphere so Walzer seems to assume that what is fair in isolation will also be fair globally (Arneson, 2000). But if this is naive, if fairness and unfairness do not translate across all domains automatically, whether we are talking about one sphere or many, then what we require is a universal account of distribution (simplicity) that is sensitive to local variations in impact (complexity). So whereas Walzer only miniaturises the universalist logic of simple equality on a local scale, what we need is a simple equality that incorporates complex particularism within its universalist frame. Although this is another task too demanding to be attempted here, we can conclude that complex equality is implicit within simple equality, rather than being an alternative to it. If so, then the importance of redistributing primary resources is again reaffirmed (cf. Jayasuriya, 2000; Prabhakar, 2002).

The intention of this section was to elaborate upon what is meant by strong equality. If Sen and Walzer are wrong to underestimate the importance of primary resources like income and wealth, then we have a reason to side with the contributions to the debate made by Arneson, Cohen and Roemer. (It also implies that if social democrats are concerned with strong equality, then they have to make much greater room for income and wealth redistribution than that permitted by the NSD.) However, in contrast to the convoluted terms that they prefer (see above), I propose to refer to an 'equality of powers'.

By 'powers' I mean the ability to convert endowments into well-being through choice and ambition. However, if our endowments are undeserved because they are matters of social and genetic luck, and if they structure the opportunities to which we have access and through which we exercise choice, then powers are *relational*: my powers are not personal attributes, they are determined by and through the powers of those with whom I share a socioeconomic environment. If luck in the distribution of social and natural endowments therefore leads to an undeserved inequality of powers – and so to relations of social domination – and if egalitarian justice demands the rectification of undeservingness, then what we require is an equality of powers: *the equal opportunity to convert primary resources into sources of well-being according to one's capabilities and location within the distributional sphere.* Equality of opportunity therefore implies the equalisation of primary resources like income and wealth rather than the kind of weak equality favoured by new social democrats. However, the conversion of primary resources into well-being is conditioned not only by choice, but by the capabilities (Sen) and the complex location (Walzer) of the individual concerned.

Citizenship

The first component of distributive justice (equality of powers) is now in place and ready to be joined by the second: diverse reciprocity. I will make the case for diverse reciprocity through a critique of the kind of 'un-diverse reciprocity' that New Labour prefers. We will therefore not explore each and every aspect of diverse reciprocity in depth, though we will return to one significant aspect of it in Chapter 7. This section will also be much shorter than the previous one as the basics of my position should already be clear.

We have already reviewed the main ingredients of New Labour's approach to citizenship in Chapter 1. As stakeholders in a series of over-lapping communities, our primary duty is to participate in cooperative networks of trust and mutual endeavour. Citizenship is not a passive status where we are members of society simply by virtue of existing, it is an *active* form of contribution where individuals utilise their talents not only for their own sake, but for the ultimate benefit of all (cf. Ellison, 2000). Social inclusion is created not through rights and entitlements *per se*, but by tying rights to corresponding duties through various incentives, sanctions and moral injunctions. The space of duties centres upon the labour market and independence within that market is the best means of achieving citizenship. However, that space does not stop at the borders of the labour market, as it extends further into civil society and also needs to be expressed in terms of family, neighbourliness, caring, civic engagement, law abidingness, charitable donations and voluntary work (Turner, 2001). In short, reciprocity is at the heart of the NSD conception of citizenship in contrast to the Old Left's alleged emphasis upon unconditional passivity and the selfish consumerism of the New Right. The assertion that 'rights imply responsibilities' has been one of *the* distinguishing features of New Labour.

Is this correlation vulnerable to the kind of arguments presented earlier in this chapter: that reciprocity must mean *fair* reciprocity and that it must encompass diversity? There are four reasons to suspect so.

First, because it centres so heavily around the labour market, the correlation between rights and duties that New Labour favours takes a contractualist form where reciprocity is conceived almost as a type of market exchange (Jordan with Jordan, 2000). For if it is wrong to take without giving, the flip side of this doctrine is that it must be equally wrong to give without taking. Rights and duties are thereby tied together as forms of 'specific reciprocity'. But what this does is to eclipse and perhaps even degrade other sorts of reciprocity which are generalised and non-specific. For instance, if I accept benefits, tax breaks and support services by virtue of being a parent, specific reciprocity might demand that my parenting skills be monitored, e.g. through school/home contracts, child curfews and parental fines, in order to ensure that I am not wasting the assistance that society provides. By contrast, 'general reciprocity' adopts a more hands-off approach that does not impose top-down obligations at the point of receipt, but is content to receive the longer-term benefits to society that my child will provide. New Labour therefore regards entitlements as an expense that necessitates a corresponding fee if the ledger of citizenship is to be kept permanently balanced. But this cost–benefit approach ignores the age-old liberal idea that unless certain basic rights are defined as pre-social, foundational and *unconditional*, then interference in the lives of individuals and their associative relations is potentially unlimited. So the combination of communitarianism and commercialism that New Labour prefers treats liberal conceptions of citizenship as alien to the common good, rather than as inhering within it.

And this economistic, contractualist approach also degrades the wider, civic spaces of social participation. Take the example examined in depth by Barlow and Duncan (2000a, 2000b). New Labour inherits from conservatism the model of *homo economicus*, where individuals are taken to act according to a rational assessment of costs and benefits. What this excludes are other modes of rationality, of moral negotiations that occur in social contexts which are not quantifiable. One consequence is that when people make decisions that New Labour considers wrong they do not interpret this as deriving from alternative and equally legitimate forms of rationality, but because of (a) inadequate incentives, or (b) the person in question does not yet have enough information about the available incentives or (c) more sanctions and compulsion are needed. This model then exposes the tensions in New Labour's family policies: they want citizens to be both good workers and good parents. But how are these imperatives to be reconciled, especially given the time and effort that each activity requires? Through the traditional, two-parent family for which, with some pluralistic nods towards alternative forms of household, New Labour has habitually expressed a preference. The ambivalence towards lone mothers that New Labour has also repeatedly demonstrated is then explained because single parents expose the difficulties of said reconciliation. But rather than a substantial reform of the labour market, New Labour has preferred trying to modify individuals' decision-making. So their policies towards single mothers have emphasised incentives (stressing the benefits of paid work), information (experts to advise on job search and childcare) and sanctions (compulsory interviews intended to surmount the 'dependency culture'). What New Labour thereby ignores is the kind of moral decision-making which is much more sophisticated than its own cost–benefit model and so, perversely, it may if anything be *undermining* the very ethics of citizenship and communal solidarity that it professes to support but which are actually nurtured through public services and a welfare professionalism that effects social participation precisely by *not* subjecting individuals to a perpetual audit.

This productivist preference for the 'employment ethic' (the citizen as wage earner) carries over into the second objection to New Labour's version of reciprocity: its underestimation of caring. This is not to claim that Third Wayers ignore the importance of care, but even at the rhetorical level the support offered is often qualified by the insinuation that care work is not real work. Take, as one example, Glennerster's (1999: 37) observation that, 'Paid work brings dignity and respect. That does not preclude us from also giving dignity and worth to non-paid work. But to deny paid work or to encourage people to live without it is to deny a main source of dignity in our Western capitalist industrialised world'. What this does is to regard care work as equivalent to involuntary unemployment. When rhetoric is then translated into practice, the tendency to neglect care work becomes even more obvious. Although she does not examine the extent to which a feminist care ethic is ultimately reconcilable with the NSD, Sevenhuijsen (2000) condemns those such as Giddens for making simplistic distinctions between 'self-sufficient workers' and 'dependent others' since this downgrades alternative norms where citizenship is less about inclusion or exclusion from the job market and more about the giving and receiving of care (Fraser, 1997). Lister (2001b: 439) seems to suggest that this downgrading is almost a form of discrimination since it misrecognises the talents that unpaid caring involves and so places women, the main caregivers, at a further disadvantage. Williams (2001) goes further than Sevenhuijsen in arguing that a political ethic of care does represent a stark alternative to New Labour and the NSD ethic of employment. The paradigm shift from the latter to the former involves both autonomy and time: autonomy needs to be redefined as a form of interdependency rather than economic independence and a feminist ethic also necessitates a fundamental rebalancing of personal time, care time and employment time. Finally, Land (2002) finds that New Labour's emphasis upon formal care ignores and undermines the informal sector and abandons the right to work shorter hours on the grounds that this would be unfriendly to business and to UK competitiveness.

In short, many researchers insist that New Labour's espousal of the employment ethic narrows the accepted range of socially valuable activity and demoralises other forms of citizenship that do not orbit around wage earning, but which are equally valuable, if not more so. My argument is that this bias is not incidental to New Labour but is expressive of the NSD's productivism. By contrast, post-productivism subjects economic orthodoxies to a reassessment that, in its proximity to conservatism, is alien to the NSD. We will return to these arguments in Chapters 5 and 6, especially.

Defenders of the NSD may rush to condemn such radicalism as a return to the bad old days of unconditional and therefore hollow rights and there is a sense in which their suspicion is correct – though not their condemnation. To argue for diverse reciprocity is to argue that rights and responsibilities do not correlate, for the reason to be sketched shortly. Yet even if we accept the terms of the prevailing discourse, we do not have to imagine that rights and responsibilities must always carry an equivalent weighting. What duties does a recently born baby possess? Obviously, duties are owed *to* the child, but what is controversial about the 'rights imply responsibilities' mantra is not the philosophic point that the one must somehow somewhere imply the other – this is no more disputable than the assertion that 'up' must imply 'down' – but New Labour's insistence that they automatically correlate *at the level of the individual*: that for every right you possess you also possess a corresponding duty, and vice versa. This 'political' correlation does not follow inevitably from the 'philosophic' correlation, but by allowing the latter to slide into the former, the NSD cuts itself adrift from what I earlier called the age-old liberal idea that there are certain basic rights foundational to our persons and freedoms.

Yet at the same time as rooting itself in a liberalism of unconditional basic rights, diverse reciprocity also suggests that the NSD *does not even take responsibility seriously enough* – the third of the four reasons I am reviewing. For if there are no rights without responsibilities (Giddens, 1998: 65), then given New Labour's contractualism it presumably follows that there are no responsibilities without rights, a reverse correlation that conceals a very broad range of human concern. For instance, it could be said that we owe obligations to future generations, even though those generations do not yet exist to claim corresponding rights against us. By representing a post-productivist form of social democracy, ecowelfare treats the interests of future generations and the sustainability of distributive justice through time as being of central importance, in contrast to the short-term economic orthodoxy of the NSD. The details of the argument are delayed until Chapter 7, however, when we examine future generationalism in some depth.

The fourth and final reason for suspecting that the NSD's version of reciprocity is inadequate returns us to this business of correlation. The basic argument is simple and we anticipated it in Chapter 1: it is not *rights*

to which responsibilities correlate but *powers*. I have defined powers as
the ability to convert endowments into well-being and used this to define
an equality of powers. Responsibility is therefore generated in respect of
the voluntary elements of said conversion and not the involuntary ones.
But if it is endowments that structure our opportunities and abilities, if
(in the existing social conjuncture) those endowments are largely matters
of luck and if powers are distributed unequally as a result then the space
of voluntary action, and the corresponding space of responsibility,
expands or contracts depending upon your location within the distributional hierarchy. This is not to argue for a dutyless form of citizenship,
since only a minority of citizens (the very young, for instance) fail to
possess powers of any sort. However, it is to argue that the frequency and
intensity of responsibilities alters within the distributional hierarchy, i.e.
with the distribution of good and bad fortune in endowments. To put it
bluntly, the richer you are the more duties you possess because the luckier
you have been. (This risks penalising those who made good use of their
poor endowments and rewarding those who made bad use of their superior ones; however, something approximating Roemer's (1998) theory of
social types may offer a way of balancing equality with endowment-
sensitivity.) By focusing upon rights, New Labour's version of duty and
reciprocity assumes an equality of obligation that does not only camou-
flage distributional inequalities but, by loading more upon the poor and
less upon the wealthy, entrenches them. But if a right is simply a formal
entitlement to convert endowments, rather than the conversion itself, then
it is the actual powers available for conversion to which we should pay
attention.

We can therefore identify a contrast between the kind of reciprocity
favoured by new social democrats and the diverse reciprocity which takes
its place beside a strong conception of equality. For New Labour reciprocity has little to do with distributive justice, contains no notion that
rights are foundational, is individualistic in that rights are duties are
thought always to correlate at the level of the individual (necessitating
labour market participation in most cases) and is specific in the sense that
reciprocity is thought to follow the contractualist, rationalist logic of
cost–benefit analysis. By contrast, a theory of diverse reciprocity (1)
cannot be separated from the background conditions of social justice or
injustice, i.e. fair reciprocity demands material equality rather than simply
the inclusion of unequals; (2) regards rights as unconditional foundations
of the social self; (3) is social in orientation in that obligations are thought
to correlate to *powers* (the structures of social relations), rights and obligations do not always correlate at the level of the individual (we may
possess rights without obligations and vice versa) and wage earning
should not be regarded as the main badge of citizenship; (4) is 'general'

in that the equilibrium of social give and take is more effectively maintained by abandoning the model of *homo economicus*. This last point reiterates the idea that citizenship should not be reduced to a form of rational market exchange and we should adopt a hands-off approach to social participation where we are less obsessed with enforcement, surveillance and coercion.

There are therefore a number of reasons to suspect that 'undiverse reciprocity' does not offer a basis for an adequate account of citizenship. By preferring a 'Philosophy Made Simple' approach to citizenship, the NSD's sermons about duty and reciprocity are revealed to be largely simplistic and hypocritical.

Concluding remarks

This chapter has dealt with the questions of justice and citizenship and hopefully provided enough substance for the following definition of distributive justice:

> (1) equality of powers + diverse reciprocity
> = distributive justice

This definition diverges from New Labour's preference for weak equality plus strong reciprocity and so offers an alternative to the NSD *per se*. I have also hinted at a second equation that we will spend Part II of the book exploring more fully:

> (2) social democracy + post-productivism
> = ecosocial welfare ('ecowelfare')

Before moving on, however, there is one loose thread from this chapter that needs tying down.

I need to qualify the earlier assertion that diverse reciprocity is not the same thing as weak reciprocity. In fact, diverse reciprocity is both weak and strong, according to the diachronic dimension of progressive politics. Let me explain. Whereas Dworkin seems to assume a 50/50 cut between endowment-insensitivity and ambition-sensitivity, those such as Arneson, Cohen and Roemer (from a more radical Left-liberal position) suggest that luck and circumstance outweigh choice and ambition in determining patterns of distribution in contemporary capitalism. If the bar of undeservingness (or moral arbitrariness) is therefore high, then the springboard of ambition and achievements is correspondingly low. But rather than motivate a radical 'politics of fatalism' (where we accept the inevitability of those distributional patterns, but compensate the disadvantaged for their worst effects), it demands a radicalism which aims to lower the bar and raise the springboard over time. Therefore, if we are genuinely concerned with reciprocity, responsibility, ambition and achievement then we must work to avoid the avoidable elements of undeservingness in endowments, i.e. those that are either fully or partially social in origin. Reciprocity, responsibility, ambition and achievement can be regarded not as bourgeois fictions, but as values instrumental to the creation of strong equality. So as the bar of undeservingness is lowered we could expect the sources of well-being to improve in both quantity and quality: it would become easier to achieve a wider range of achievements because circumstances would not hold people back as much than they do at present. Therefore, an equality of powers is also a form of liberal perfectionism which aims to improve the sum of social welfare, not by promoting a single version of the good, but by expanding individuals' capacities to improve the available range of meaningful goods. This is another way of stating Tawney's (1931) point that when they are properly conceived equality and liberty can be seen to be inclusive.

So diverse reciprocity is both weak and strong: weak in the capitalist present (and so more concerned with compensation) but in conjunction with an equalisation of powers becoming stronger in the future (and so more concerned with cooperative participation) as the spaces of ambition and achievement become stronger. This relationship between equality and reciprocity corresponds to what White (2000: 522) calls 'threshold compliance' where obligations depend upon the social provision of a sufficiently high threshold of equal opportunities. It aims to reverse the trend of post-1970s politics where the wealthiest only recognise their duties, if at all, once the poorest have performed theirs. Reciprocity? Yes, if and only if it is a strategy towards egalitarian ends, ends of which reciprocity would then be constitutive.

To conclude, if you are genuinely concerned with reciprocity, responsibility, ambition and achievement, then you should be an egalitarian for only by lowering the bar of undeservingness can the spaces of freedom, well-being and authentic cooperation be promoted.

Note

1 Although after it emerged that in New Labour's first term child poverty was reduced from 4.4 million to 3.9 million, only half of its original target for the period 1997–2001, there were increasing signs that it *would* begin to measure child poverty differently.

3

The security state

Chapter 2 offered not only a critique of the NSD, but also sketched alternatives to its theories of justice and citizenship. I now want to examine two further debates that will not only refer us to back to some of the other critiques offered in Chapter 1, but will also act as a platform for Chapter 8 when we examine an important aspect of ecowelfare. Here, the intention is not so much to analyse the principles of community, meritocracy, reciprocity and inclusion as to understand the means by which the NSD seeks to secure and enforce these principles. The first debate concerns globalisation and I want to suggest that the NSD is congruent with a kind of globally-oriented state that possesses both conservative and social democratic features. This state corresponds particularly to recent developments in the UK and USA and so my analysis will draw upon a range of scholarship dealing with these countries. The second debate follows on from this and deals with information. My premise here is that the global information society is ordered around some familiar structures of power and domination that many accounts tend to neglect in their breathless enthusiasm for new technologies.

So we begin with globalisation and an account of what I shall call the 'security state'; this section aims to do nothing more than lay the ground for the following, longer discussion of information. We then return to other important aspects of globalisation in the next chapter. So as before the intention here is not to review each and every feature of these debates, but merely those that will allow a theory of ecowelfare to emerge.

Globalisation

With this last point in mind we can proceed to a brief overview of Bauman's account of globalisation, since Bauman captures very succinctly the kind of social and spatial polarities that are crucial to understanding the security state and so to understanding recent developments in the US and UK. I will be assuming that globalisation is an economic, political and social reality, but one that can accommodate a much wider range of ideological trajectories than those proposed by conservatives and new social democrats. For a defence of my stance on globalisation see Fitzpatrick (2001d).

Bauman (1998a, 1998b, 2001) describes the annihilation of spatial and temporal distances as a situation where the wealthiest are now able to free themselves from the localities that immerse the poor in immobility. To put it simply, the sites that are deterritorialised at the global level are reterritorialised at the local and economic inequalities have polarised space to the point of fracture (Harvey, 1996). This spatial polarisation is partly physical, as the public space of social interaction is replaced by 'interdictory spaces' that keep the polarities apart, and partly virtual: the electronic database centres itself within these exclusionary dynamics, e.g. credit ratings determine our degree of mobility/weightlessness or immobility/density (Fitzpatrick, 1999b). Globalisation therefore represents a structural distinction between two worlds that only appear to inhabit the same ontological field: the cosmopolitan elites (the tourists) live primarily in *time*, moving effortlessly through geographical and electronic borders; the excluded (the vagabonds) live primarily in *space*, weighted down in the immobile present by the monotony of meaningless time (Bauman, 1998a: 88–9).

A raft of policies is therefore brought to bear against vagabonds in order that the tourists' consumption of both their present and (likely) future status is stimulated. The increase in rates of incarceration is the most obvious way in which the privileged try to insure themselves against the insecurities that they misidentify as emanating from the excluded, and virtually the entire panoply of the security and surveillance industry can be interpreted as the refortification of class divisions and the criminalisation of poverty (Bauman, 1998a: 113–22; Short and Kim, 1999: 115–16), expressed most alarmingly in the ghettoisation of rich and poor areas (Body-Gendrot, 2000).

Bauman's account is not without problems (Warde, 1994), especially given his tendency to make sweeping generalisations that fit whatever metaphor he is captivated by at that moment. Even so, he is one of those whose approach is a welcome alternative to those who treat globalisation as a rupture in the historical condition (Giddens, 1991) and those who regard it as little more than an ideological fiction that inevitably functions according to capitalist imperatives (Bourdieu, 1998). The following exploration of the security state therefore follows the kind of lead that Bauman suggests.

The security state

Two caveats must be noted, however. First, this is not meant to be a general, all-purpose description of the globally-oriented state. States around the world are following a variety of trajectories according to the political and economic strategies adopted and the institutional background at work. Indeed, Chapter 4 will suggest that 'old' social democracy is far from dead, precisely because there is far more heterogeneity than accounts of the investment state, or the competition state, or the workfare state, or whatever, normally allow for. Even so, I neither want to underestimate the degree of state convergence that globalisation implies and the 'security state' is a working hypothesis that I apply to the UK and USA, two countries in which the NSD has arguably been most influential. Second, however, this is not to insinuate that the security state is a product of the NSD; indeed, it would make more sense to reverse the relation and argue that the NSD is a product of the security state. More accurately, the NSD and the security state can be regarded as aspects of one another. The UK and the USA are two countries within which conservatism arguably took the greatest hold so that, in reworking the welfare state and then, in turn, being reworked by the more limited social democracy of Clinton and Blair, conservatism has fashioned a political agenda that we can understand through the intellectual convergence of social policy and criminology. Therefore, the security state and the NSD are both consequences of conservative hegemonisation. I will therefore draw a picture of the security state in outline and then indicate why New Labour's main welfare and criminal justice reforms to date are consistent with it.

The state's job on the domestic front has traditionally been to weave order out of chaos: to prevent anarchy, to ensure historical continuity, to suppress revolution, to scapegoat minorities, to balance the fluctuations of economic supply and demand. As global capital becomes *apparently* unmanageable, as the polity and the economy detach after a century of alignment, the state can only now prosper if, in addition to weaving order out of chaos, it facilitates and manufactures much of that chaos in the first place in order to remain attractive in the eyes of capital. As the maintainer of order at the national level, the state has traditionally been the guarantor of stability (whether through constitutional or authoritarian means); under contemporary conditions it is just as often the instigator of instability and disorder by colluding with, failing to prevent or even generating global market forces – think of the World Trade Organisation (WTO), the Multilateral Agreement on Investment and the General Agreement on Trade in Services. So the chaos that the state now gives order to is often a chaos of its own making. As the state increasingly submits to the dominant logic of global capital, so it must socially and discursively construct threats that only it can address through what Jordan and Arnold (1995; Jordan, 1998: 183) call a 'politics of enforcement' (graphically illustrated by the reaction of the Genoa police to anti-WTO protesters in 2001). It helps to create the spatial polarisation that Bauman draws attention to and then represents itself as the principal means of depolarising and restabilising the resulting conflict (Zukin, 1991; cf. Hughes, 1996). The security state consists of a series of punitive responses to the chaos it has facilitated.[1]

Therefore, the state that withers away is only the macro-interventionist state, rematerialising at the micro-social level through a series of state, semi-state and non-state interventions (Cohen, 1994), criminalising those such as beggars, street-level entrepreneurs, claimants, the low paid, single mothers and teenagers (Cook, 1997: 131–52; Pavarini, 1997; Dean, 1999; Parenti, 1999). The state extends its reach by relaxing its grip. So although social spaces are polarised, they are also simultaneously subjected to a regulatory gaze where freedom and governance merge in new technologies of control (Rose, 1999; Garland, 2001): '. . . technology-based contexts of interaction that regulate, organise or monitor human behaviour by integrating it into a pre-arranged environment, built upon a conception of "normality" or "regularity" that all subjects are expected to reproduce' (Lianos with Douglas, 2000: 264).

But if these 'pre-regulated' spaces encompass both rich and poor territories, the asymmetries of power *between* those territories alter the means of reproduction *within* them (Fitzpatrick, 2001d). In the affluent territories the periphery consists of marginal people who must be both excluded and endlessly reimagined. Reproduction therefore consists of a constant vigilance against potential threats; otherness represents a source of victimisation and so must willingly subject itself to surveillance. If it does not, then because that which is non-monitored is equivalent to lawlessness then punitive measures are entirely justified. In the poorer territories, the periphery consists of wealthier lifestyles that are omnipresent and so must be emulated through recurrent debt and processes of 'clearance', constant proof that you are worthy of entry. These 'prudential' or 'actuarial' spaces enforce gestures of normality upon those the wealthier can no longer recognise *as* normal, i.e. as resembling themselves.

The security state therefore presides over a patchwork of preregulatory spaces that are polarised socially and symbolically between a series of alternating peripheries. Struggling to meet the basic needs of social security, it can reconfigure those needs as basic fears by operating as the simultaneous origin and resolution of *global security risks*. Once the gatekeeper who tried to protect against post-war turbulence; now the state invites the global turbulence to storm through the national economic and political walls that it generously offers to maintain. By engendering economies of risk and flexibility, globalisation demands both the collective enforcement of the duty to work (see Chapter 2) and the dismantling of the workplace regulations that threaten international competitiveness (Jordan, 1998: 82–3). And so we are collectivised into an active acceptance of our own passivity. This duty appears under several guises: as the overworked 'presenteeism' of the securely employed, as the on-call insecurities of the marginally employed and as the compulsory submission of unemployed claimants to the demands of the benefit system. Correspondingly, social entitlements are now based less upon having a voice within the workplace and more upon the capacity (though only for the lucky ones) to flee *between* workplaces: entitlements are possessed by 'job consumers' rather than cooperatively-organised workers. Thus, under pressure from global capitalism, the state assists in the individualisation of rights and the collectivisation of duties (Fitzpatrick, 1998a): the privatisation of common fate and the collectivisation and control of individual autonomy. Hence what I referred to in Chapter 1 as the desocialisation of society. Yet the security state's work is, literally, never done. The more obsessed with safety we become, then the less safe we feel because the more we monitor (in order to reduce our fears) then the more dangerous the non-monitored begins to appear. The security state therefore perpetuates itself infinitely.

Developments within the benefit system, both pre- and post-New Labour, illustrate this transformation (Fitzpatrick, 1998a). The principle of social insurance came to embody the commonality of fate by having both a spatial dimension (universality) and a temporal dimension (cradle to grave) and so was oriented both to the past, in the form of work-based contributions, and to a knowable, predictable future. Social insurance was therefore suited to an age of working-class ascendancy (the commonality of fate) and to a widespread acceptance of the desirability and feasibility of planning (temporal continuity). A naive acceptance of free market globalisation (see Chapter 4) has undermined both of these conditions. Consequently, the income inequalities which the NSD refuses to challenge substantially make the idea of *social* insurance redundant: the affluent can afford to insure themselves whereas the poor can be helped with targeted forms of assistance. Systems of universal coverage crumble and the life-cycle fragments and splits: in insuring ourselves against risk, it is no longer 'we' who work forward from the determinate past, but 'I' who works backwards from an indeterminate future as the solitary entrepreneur of my personal fate (O'Malley, 1992). This is what the 'Americanisation' of social security implies and New Labour has gone even further than its Conservative predecessors in introducing workfare, benefit sanctions, in-work means testing and 'single gateways' which treat all new

claimants the same, whatever their work record. The affluent are effectively opted out into the private insurance market, especially with regard
to pensions and personal security; the poor become subjected to means
testing and to forms of control that are benignly authoritarian: the discourse of paternalism becomes indistinguishable from that of control. The
movements and schedules of claimants become part of a process of negotiation between themselves and appointed experts; accents, gestures and
sartorial appearances (clothing, hairstyles, jewellery, cosmetics) become
subject to official scrutiny (Marx, 1995: 228).

Thus the benefit system, never the most benevolent of institutions to
begin with, embodies a strategy of 'anticipatory deterrence': whereas it
used to be largely re-active, reacting to problems once they had occurred,
it is now increasingly *pre-active*, defining problems in advance and clamp-
ing down on any hints of abnormality. The nakedness of this strategy has
been most in evidence in the case of asylum seekers and refugees, the
internationally homeless, for whom any distinction between social and
criminal policy has long become meaningless and when the histories
of New Labour are written, their treatment of asylum seekers may well
prove to be their greatest shame.

What all of this means is that we do not return to the workhouse of the
pre-welfare state, nor do we advance to a post-welfare state of last-resort
safety nets; instead, we experience a security state where welfare institutions paternalistically prod and encourage us into deregulated and flexible labour markets (Rose, 1996, 1999). The ethic of state welfare and basic
needs is not abandoned; instead, what we need is redefined away from
entitlement to material goods towards a duty-led ethic of emotional
belonging and social inclusion enforced, where necessary, by the globally-
oriented state (Culpitt, 1999; Kemshall, 2002). 'Security' encompasses
'welfare' in order to transcend it. This is the ethics of 'market collectivism'
(Fitzpatrick, 1998a). If we do not volunteer to keep ourselves socially and
morally fit, ready for the opportunities that the global economy might
scatter in our direction, then the state will be on hand to volunteer us
instead. The collectivisation of duties occurs because duties are now
thought to be orientated to the global; the individualisation of rights
occurs because it is assumed that the global cannot accommodate
common rights. Citizenship attenuates between two spaces. The *social*
space recoils upon itself despite various compensatory efforts to knit these
shrinking spaces into an integrative patchwork, e.g. the European Union;
the *global* space inflates into an immense, vaulting arena, big enough both
to amplify the shouts of the angry and drown the cries of the powerless.
Being an attenuated citizen now implies localised training for global
responsibilities.

These developments have also been visible within the criminal policies of New Labour's first term and some have argued that by the 2001 general election there was no effective distance between Conservative and New Labour policies on law and order (Downes and Morgan, 2002). Putting to one side forms of electronic surveillance and control (dealt with below), those policies have been characterised by the following four main characteristics.

First, New Labour accepted the 'prison works' philosophy of the Conservatives, the belief that incarceration for *individuals* is the best way of resolving *social* problems. The continuities in this respect between Michael Howard and Jack Straw as, respectively, Conservative and Labour Home Secretaries are obvious. By 2002 England and Wales had a higher proportion of its population in jail than China, Saudi Arabia or Turkey, the second highest rate in the EU behind Portugal (Travis, 2002). And although this is still only one-fifth of the rate of incarceration to be found in the USA, it nevertheless represents a similar trend towards a punitive individualism in the context of unjust social inequalities (Christie, 1994; Reiman, 1998).

Second, there has been a preference for targeting repeat offenders and for zero-tolerance campaigns, the 'broken windows' strategy imported from the USA of coming down hard on minor examples of law breaking in the belief that these, if left unattended, will multiply into major incidents through their impact on victims, perpetrators (if left unpunished) and the civic capital of the local community. This zero tolerance has also affected other aspects of civil order with New Labour partly collapsing the distinction between terror and civil disobedience. Again, there is no solid evidence that such strategies work, but they have served the purpose of fuelling tabloid paranoia about the imminent breakdown of society (Garland, 2001).

Third, New Labour has promoted the use of curfews and exclusion orders in order to keep troublemakers either at home at certain times of day or away from certain urban districts altogether. Naming and shaming persistent troublemakers is a means not only of exclusion, but of inclusion: by 'keeping out' we also 'keep in' the law abiding and hard working, so reaffirming norms of civic, communal and familial identification (Braithwaite, 2000). That these powers have been actually deployed much less by local councils and police forces than the government would have liked reflects the belief that pandering to the fear of crime is different to addressing the actuality, not least because perceptions of risk almost always diverge from the reality of risk, with the public consistently overestimating the extent of crime, misidentifying the victims of crime and underestimating rates of incarceration (Pantazis, 2000).

Fourth, the evidence has struggled with ideology to influence government policy. Civil liberties arguments have been repeatedly denounced as the chatterings of middle-class liberals comfortably separated from the working-class communities where crime palpably affects the quality of life. Therefore, the fear of crime needs addressing, even when those fears are naive or unrealistic (Young, 1999; cf. Taylor, 1999). Targeting 'the criminal' is so important that it can only be infrequently left to juries, 'liberal' judges (hence the need for minimum mandatory sentences) or defence lawyers. But what this populist stance then does is to feed an hysteria that can never be satiated. When paranoia is pandered to rather than challenged, then there is no need for self-limitation, since the politicians and press always say you are right. If asylum seekers are dispersed and given vouchers, then racism is given an official stamp and you can riot; if the courts and prisons are soft then the enemy is always within and you can intimidate a few paedophiles (and settle some old scores along the way); if immigrants are not integrating – otherwise why else would they need language classes? – then there is no need for British identity to change. Ironically then, the separation between civil liberties and social justice not only backfires on New Labour's more liberal tendencies, but leads to a situation where crime seems to be ubiquitous and so quality of life in the very communities New Labour professes to support is always undermined.

This is not to accuse all New Labour's policies of being unremittingly foolish. Just as a preference for targeting has allowed rises in some benefit levels, so the government has been able to sneak in some welcome reforms below the populist radar, e.g. to drug laws and to the police (through the Macpherson Report). It has also resisted the worst excesses of anti-paedophile hysteria and the outcry over the Bulger killers' release in 2001. Nevertheless, both social and criminal policies have been willing to reconfigure welfare and need in terms of security and risk, effecting a convergence of conservatism and social democracy around the imperatives of a security state. The distinction between criminal and welfare policies is now less clear than at any time since the nineteenth century.

To summarise, the security state arises as a result of two processes: the conservative assault on the social democratic welfare state, followed by a more limited version of social democracy (the NSD) later accommodating itself to the conservative settlement. The security state is therefore characterised by: (1) large amounts of social inequality, increasingly manifested as spatial polarisation, regulatory instincts, the loss of a commonality of fate and fewer communicative and symbolic interactions between richer and poorer; (2) a pathologisation of social problems where those at the social edges are blamed for their marginalisation, criminalised for being unable or reluctant to become risk takers in the global environment that the security state engenders; (3) supply-side reforms where the excluded are to be supervised and remoralised as a condition of their reintegration into the social mainstream, whether through rationalist incentives, normalisation, surveillance or punitiveness. The security state represents not the dismantling of the welfare state, but its incorporation within a punitive ethic of risk and fear. The consolidation and growth of the security state can then be witnessed in the bulk of New Labour's social and criminal policies, and the ways in which those disciplinary boundaries are flimsier than ever. As a last word I suspect that, without a substantial change of direction, New Labour's eventual replacement in power by the Conservatives will produce no greater discontinuities than the replacement of the New Democrats by Bush junior's Republicans in the US.

Information

We now move on and explore the NSD's relationship to the information society by applying the above lessons. My basic thesis will be that New Labour has conceived of information as being asocial and contextless (reflecting the individualisation of social problems), as commodified (reflecting the hegemony of conservative economics) and as a source of surveillance (reflecting a criminalisation of the supply side). The argument is made through the following four sub-sections. I shall first set out my analytical stance by applying critical theory to information society debates and then review the above characteristics in turn.

Cyber-criticalism

As perhaps the key contemporary figure in information society debates Castells makes an effective startingpoint. Castells (1996: 470–4) underlines the point that networks are not structureless webs demonstrating no hierarchical features, but grids that flow according to logics of power. Networks may consist of nodes, but some nodes are more powerful than others, exerting a greater gravitational force on the relations that stream around them. He talks of networks being connected by 'switches' that are the privileged instruments of power, i.e. global flows of financial capital, ensuring that the network society is a capitalist society of 'decentralised concentration'.

Having reached this point, however, Castells (1996: 469) then veers towards a postmodernist reading (though he might not accept the description), insisting that '. . . the power of flows takes precedence over the flows of power.' In short,

> above a diversity of human-flesh capitalists and capitalist groups there is a
> faceless collective capitalist, made up of financial flows operated by electronic
> networks. . . . This network of networks of capital both unifies and com-
> mands specific centers of capitalist accumulation, structuring the behaviour
> of capitalists around their submission to the global network. . . . While capi-
> talism still rules, capitalists are randomly incarnated . . . (Castells, 1996: 474)

So although capitalism has triumphed, it is potentially vulnerable to
changes within the electronically-mediated 'global capital network'. Yet
what this does is to remove capitalist agents from capitalism, to treat it
as an agentless system where capitalists must submit to their 'random in-
carnation'. The reason for this move – first recognising power and then
emptying it of agency – is because Castells wishes to contrast the 'power
of flows' with the 'power of identity', defining the latter as the cultural representations and codes of information around which socially-
significant mobilisations can form. What Castells (1998: 348) eventually
makes clear is his belief that there are no more stable power elites because
culture is now the source of power, of capital and therefore of the information age's social hierarchies.

From a critical theoretical perspective, the kernel of truth here masks
the fact that when oppositional movements mobilise against global capitalism they do so not only in terms of cultural identities but also in terms
of the *materiality* of the global network that Castells dissolves into informatic signs. Therefore, although he offers hope to oppositional movements, it is the hope of an identity politics divorced from the great
economic and ideological struggles of modernity (Castells, 1998: 359). So
as well as underestimating the power of capitalist agents, Castells enjoins
us to abandon the ideological reference points and strategies that provide
such struggles with long-term direction. That most of the social movements he celebrates are perversely unwilling to do so, that ideology may
actually motivate micro-political struggles is not something he seems able
to accommodate.

One consequence of this is that his observations regarding surveillance
practices are too simplistic (Castells, 1997: 299–303). For although he is
correct to identify the enhanced surveillance capacity of corporations,
Castells seems to believe that this renders forms of centralised surveillance impossible, due to the declining power of the nation-state. But what
this analysis does is to neglect the points made above, namely that the
security state attempts the reregulation of the micro-social within a global,
free market economy. According to this thesis, and as we shall see below,
state and corporate forms of surveillance are conjoined in a network
where centres and peripheries continually fold into one another.

Cyber-criticalism, then, offers a richer account of surveillance because
it does not imagine that the power of flows has overwhelmed flows of

power. Therefore, the application of critical theory to information society debates requires us to understand how and why traditional hierarchies of power *adapt* to new technologies, allowing themselves to be reconfigured by them, without being substantially undermined in the process. Cyber-criticalism therefore characterises the work of a number of authors (Sardar and Ravetz, 1996; Perelman, 1998) who identify hierarchical struggles (as always, including class but not limited to it) as a defining feature of 'informatic capitalism'. Let us quickly review two principal contributors.

Herbert Schiller (1981, 1984, 1989, 1996) works with three basic premises. First, informatic capitalism is riven by inequalities between the information rich and poor. This does not mean that the poor are excluded from information *per se*, merely that ICTs constitute a positional good so that informational inequalities will always be reproduced, even as access to informational networks spreads. Second, that information is subject to market criteria such that the most valuable information is that which can be bought and sold. Increasingly, this implies not information about the goods and signs to be consumed, but information about the audiences who will do the consuming. In short, the marketisation of information engenders the next stage in the capitalist commodification of the self. Third, the advent of informatics strengthens corporate capitalism (van Dijk, 1999). So Schiller lays down the three characteristics of information that I listed earlier: asociality, commodification and surveillance.

Dyer-Witheford (1999) offers a similar but more optimistic reading, relocating cyber-criticalism in an interpretative context that stresses the power of excluded agents to resist and challenge the growing hegemony of informatic capitalism. He cites numerous struggles by class and social movements around the world as evidence that, although the frontiers of information are expanding, the interior spaces of those expanding horizons are vulnerable to opposition and reconfiguration in the direction of radical alternatives.

Therefore, cyber-criticalism agrees with Castells that information networks are significant, but is less ambiguous than Castells appears to be about the political economy of this shift. It treats the information revolution as a revolution *within* capitalism and not a revolution *of* capitalism, so that although information flows, it either flows up or down a gradient that, like all stages of capitalism before it, continues to be defined by the state–market nexus (Wyatt *et al.*, 2000; cf. Slevin, 2000: 204–7). Informatic struggles therefore occur between those who use technological systems to assemble peripheries around multiple centres of information flow (call it the Bill Gates approach) and those who exchange and/or disrupt information to resist the state–corporate nexus by peripheralising the centre and breaking it open to the public gaze (Fitzpatrick, 2002c).

So we can define 'information systems' as the technological infrastructures that form the principal conduits of the informational web, as the flows of power of informatic capitalism, as systems that are also potential sites of both submission/repression and resistance/liberation. I now want to explore those information systems in more detail, relating them to the NSD along the way, in order to explain why the latter offers only a myopic vision of the information society. The next three sections therefore explore the three characteristics already mentioned, focusing more upon examples of submission than resistance.

Asocial information

Now this is not to claim that New Labour omits any reference to social contexts in its approach to ICTs, as it appears to be fully aware of how social inequalities affect the access to, and use of, information technology. However, having made the link between social inequality and access New Labour has been driven to a series of technological fixes to repair what it sees as the gap between the two (Selwyn, 2002; Hudson, 2003). Its reasoning seems to resemble the following: if we now live in a post-industrial service society and if the job of government is to facilitate social inclusion through the provision of opportunities and assets, then access to ICTs not only requires a technological fix but a fix that *is itself a means of addressing social inequalities* (Leadbetter, 1999). This reasoning has had several tragicomic results.

For instance, in his 1999 budget Chancellor Gordon Brown set aside £15 million to provide 100,000 computers under a Computers Within Reach scheme (Humphries, 2002). The scheme's intention was to supply, through the voluntary sector, low-income individuals and families with cheap, secondhand PCs, software and printers. The scheme proved to be fairly disastrous, partly due to poor administration and partly due to recipients lacking the financial resources that would enable them to exercise their intended role as consumers. The scheme was quietly shelved in 2002. Even with the best of intentions, therefore, New Labour missed the point repeatedly made by researchers (e.g. Hellawell, 2001; Nixon and Keeble, 2001) that the digital divide is so embedded in social divides that improving access to technology requires more old-fashioned social policies than the government has been able to contemplate, due to its inability to regard egalitarian redistribution as essential to social justice. This inability has consequently influenced its entire approach.

As articulated by its 1999 White Paper, New Labour has interpreted the ICTs revolution as providing innovation, empowerment, choice, greater convenience and improved opportunities for all. Any problems relate to the difficulties of implementation alone so that 'information exclusion' is attributed to a lack of knowledge and skills, with inequalities in socio-economic resources being pushed into the background; what is largely ignored is the danger of ICTs reinforcing existing power imbalances and injustices. So the White Paper (HMSO, 1999: section 3.19) heralds the arrival of teleclaiming (submitting benefit claims electronically) in terms of an enhancement of efficiency, accuracy and speed in the processing of claims, but ignores, and may implicitly welcome, the possibility of the technology subjecting claimants to bureaucratic harassment, disciplinary sanctions and conditions, and relentless observation of their habits, lifestyles and sexual partnerships. With 'independence' constantly being confused with 'wage earning', the potential disadvantages of integrating administrative systems and databases is wilfully overlooked. In short, what is constantly emphasised in the White Paper is the right of tax-payers to know that their taxes are not being 'wasted' and so, ultimately, it is the taxpayer who is being empowered by ICTs, not the claimant. At one point, the White Paper (HMSO, 1999: section 5.14) does acknowledge the dangers that ICTs can pose through the 'inappropriate transfer of data' and states that government must commit itself to data protection. But who decides what is inappropriate? Is data pertaining to a claimant to be as secure as that pertaining to a non-claimant? The government's obsession with targeting and benefit fraud suggests that it will not. Therefore disasters such as the Computers Within Reach scheme are not accidents, but are rooted in New Labour's hostility to strong equality.

To treat information as asocial, to underestimate the influence of offline upon online environments (Fitzpatrick, 2000), to prioritise national competitiveness and to reach for technological fixes is to reconstruct the citizen as the 'massless citizen'. The 'massless citizen' is the ghostly inhabitant of the information society and the term is meant to conceptualise the fact that with the integration and comparison of computer files, we each have an electronic shadow or *doppelganger*, a 'data-self' (Lacy, 1996: 162–3; Fisher, 1997: 120). Sometimes this virtual self is nothing more than a cyber-reflection of the real person; increasingly though, the flesh and blood person is being treated as an inferior version of their data-shadow, as in the case of a credit check or a CCTV scan. It all depends upon whether *we* possess our data-selves or are possessed *by* them. So, somebody does not have to be logged into the Internet to become massless: in a society of information systems, even the most computer-illiterate person is a massless citizen in that they have an online virtuality which is sometimes a simulation of, and sometimes simulates, their offline realities. We are all massless citizens because we are all caught and implicated within the informational webnet of the state–market nexus. So, whereas the term 'digital citizen' focuses simply upon online–offline interactions, 'massless citizen' is meant to encompass both digitality and social hierarchy: the 'digital hierarchy'. Masslessness implies both virtuality – streams of data that are without mass (photons) – *and* post-collectivism, i.e. a society where the masses are no longer said to exist; and despite its communitarian discourse, by accepting the post-collectivist settlement of conservatism, it is precisely this shift to an individualist society of social polarities and pathologies that the NSD has perpetuated.

So what New Labour's actual and proposed reforms to social security, health care (Keen *et al.*, 1998) and education add up to is a 'self-service welfare state' where the individual performs many of the functions and roles traditionally performed by administrators (Loader, 1998; Fitzpatrick, 2003a). It also implies a one-stop system where individuals interface with government at a single point as a range of public services become electronically available (Frissen, 1997). Self-service welfare may only enhance a process whereby the state penalises those who demonstrate an inability to look after themselves by enforcing a strong market dependency in a deregulated global economy. In a digital version of the Poor Law, the state may say: here is the information and the technology needed to access it, now solve your own problems, or else!

Information as commodity

New Labour also has little to say regarding the commodification of information about both employees and consumers (Fitzpatrick, 2002c). With power having shifted towards employers and large corporations, and with New Labour having consolidated that hegemony, employees and consumers are reduced to information bits that are then conceived in terms of profit and loss. The simple, productivist logic of many employers and managers says that since they are paying employees a set rate to perform a job, then they need to know whether they are getting their moneys worth. Unfortunately, workplace surveillance tends to be a one-way system (Sewell, 1996; Marx, 1999; Miller and Weckert, 2000; Moore, 2000). The monitoring of emails and Internet activity is extremely simple, mini surveillance cameras are increasingly prevalent, background checks on employees and job applicants are now easier to run because of data-matching techniques and genetic screening is on the rise, especially in the USA (McCahill and Norris, 1999). Call-centre workers are assessed upon simple, quantified criteria (how long it takes to dispose with each caller), through teleworking it becomes easier to monitor workers at home and dial-in facilities erode the distinction between job and non-job sites. Employees are increasingly judged upon what they *may* do rather than what they have actually done (Lyon, 2001: 41).

In short, electronically generated information tends to act as information always acts in a market; it is information about the relatively powerless that flows to the relatively powerful. So although there is some capacity for good in such surveillance, e.g. to prevent sexual harassment, this is more than outweighed by the dangers of misuse on the part of those who control the systems in question.

Consumption betrays similar preregulatory characteristics (Sklair, 1995) and again New Labour has said little about the inherent dangers here given its reluctance to challenge the conservative agenda substantially. Demand is now increasingly managed through practices that constantly predict future behaviour, based upon past behaviour. As every purchase is logged or every credit card scanned, and as consumers miraculously find their favourite brands on the supermarket shelves in just the right quantities, so the windows of consumption begin to narrow. Demand is matched to supply not only through mass advertising, but because we become our own market researchers. The loyalty or reward card is only the most individualised manifestation of networking technology: the encoding of the purchaser and not just the purchase. ICTs help us to consume more efficiently, but also close off non-consumerist spaces, both because of the allurements of frictionless consumption and because those same databases easily become means of surveying those who will not or cannot browse the shelves.

Furthermore, the body is no longer a simple appendage to the machine, but what some like to call a terminal plugged into the informatic circuitry. The cyborg is neither just a metaphor (Haraway, 1991) nor a physical assemblage of machine and organism, but a risk processor that increasingly simulates an informational system by relating to its environment as a series of dichotomous zeroes and ones: threatening/non-threatening, insider/outsider, same/other (Fitzpatrick, 1999b).

Nor does net surfing allow us to erase the traces that we leave behind us. Our own computers store data about us through 'cookies' that can be accessed by commercial interests (Lyon, 2001). Though apparently conducted in secret, journeys in cyberspace emit visible electronic trails that can be accessed by those with the means and the software to do so. Such electronic information is generated for the ultimate benefit of capital accumulation and permits the ideology of exchange value to invade personal areas of life, e.g. leisure time, with greater ease than ever before. And because the information available to consumers remains limited (not revealing, for instance, the impact that the production of goods may have had upon the environment or upon the lives of workers in the developing world), then it acts as something of a barrier to anticonsumerist forms of social interaction and political mobilisation.

Information as surveillance

But if surveillance is generated by a logic that fetishises market commodities, it is also driven by the security state itself (Fitzpatrick, 2002c).

As information systems make it theoretically easier for people to gather information upon those who rule them, both commercially and politically, so it becomes easier for the latter to justify the gathering of information on the former (William and Webster, 1999: 129). Convenience and accessibility become the watchwords of both the commercial and political worlds: the frictionless flow and instantaneous exchange of information. Of course, possession of information about the governed is an inherent feature of governance and over the last century, the welfare state was instrumental in accelerating the gathering of information. Cradle-to-grave provision requires the tagging and monitoring of the employment, contributory, educational, marital and medical histories of its citizens, a bureaucratic and administrative machine that files, catalogues, indexes and processes you in hundreds of ways (Lyon, 1994: 94–6). But as the welfare state mutates into the security state, as needs are reconfigured as risks and fears, so policy-makers propel surveillance into new realms.

The most obvious example of covert surveillance is the spread of CCTVs. 'Covert' not in their visibility (which is deliberately prominent, though people still underestimate their prevalence), but in their insidious effects upon the public sphere: the will to govern strengthens as the macro-state shrivels (Smith, 2000). Those effects are being chartered by an increasing amount of research and scholarship (Coleman and Sim, 2000; Williams and Johnstone, 2000) and so Norris and Armstrong (1999) are not alone in concluding that CCTVs are used in accordance with the existing structures of social power: by and large, the cameras are there to defend commercial and affluent areas and camera operators survey those they perceive as being socially excluded according to popular prejudice. CCTVs may be popular with local politicians and administrators, due to the need for cities to maintain social order, so that they may advertise themselves as desirable objects of global investment (Sassen, 1991) within the security state. With such attitudes in place the way is clear for surveillance cameras to be increasingly computerised so that images (faces, behaviour, licence plates) can be scanned, digitised and compared to various databases. This has already led to the blanket scanning of public areas and the technological presumption of guilt in crowds of post-anonymity. CCTVs enable databases to grow which, in turn, justify the use of CCTVs, and so on. Cameras do not see people, they see classifications into which digital images may or may not fit and some allege that ever more sophisticated, algorithmic forms of surveillance are imminent in order that those categories can be multiplied and applied indefinitely (Graham and Wood, 2003).

But as well as facilitating covert surveillance, New Labour also operates more overt forms. Let us take two recent controversies. The Regulation of Investigatory Powers Act (RIPA) came into force in the UK in October 2000 (Calleja, 2000). The Act sets out the procedures by which the security services and the police can monitor and access electronically-mediated communications. For instance, they are now able to track communications data – the websites and newsgroups individuals visit and the addresses of their email correspondents – through the use of 'black box' technology, effectively transforming service providers into wiretappers for the state. If criminal activity is suspected, then the security services can apply for a warrant to intercept and decode the actual content of such Internet traffic. The original bill was particularly draconian and came under sustained attack. Critics were able to argue that New Labour was allowing its authoritarian instincts to dominate and allowing 'gee whiz' technological determinism to shape the agenda. This opposition was successful, but only partially so.

So even though the RIPA is preferable to the preceding bill, its powers invade privacy to a far greater extent than previous interception procedures and the criteria for the release of warrants is not as stringent as it should be. Additionally, if that content is encrypted then the individual in question is required to surrender the encryption keys or face a jail sentence of up to two years – or even five years if they reveal to a third party that the surveillance warrant exists. Initially, the burden of proof was entirely on individuals to establish that they had lost or forgotten their keys, i.e. that they were guilty until they could prove themselves innocent. The government backtracked and the Act requires the prosecution to prove that individuals have not done all they can to recover a key. However, critics like Liberty and Stand allege that the burden of proof in UK law has been undermined and that, bizarrely, those whose criminal activities would otherwise attract longer jail sentences can now opt for a shorter sentence by refusing to surrender their keys.

The second controversy concerns New Labour's foray into biometrics. Biometric technologies are those that employ the body as a site of identification and surveillance (Nelkin and Andrews, 1999; Andrews and Nelkin, 2001) where we are identifiable through our physical characteristics: voice, face, eyes, fingerprints, palmprints and DNA. Increasingly, then, existing forms of identification are likely to merge with biometric technology, with the latter protecting the information contained on smart cards and credit cards and such cards being used to store biometric data. So biometrics has a wide range of applications, from welfare institutions such as the benefits and health-care systems through to the criminal justice system. DNA fingerprinting is an obvious form of biometrics that is now a commonplace procedure (Krawczak and Schmidtke, 1998) and many are now calling for the expansion of DNA registers and databases (Blume, 2000).

Those who worry that biometric technology may encourage an increase in institutional coercion, error and alienation (Lyon, 2001) were not reassured by New Labour's expansion of biometric surveillance. In January 2001 New Labour presented to Parliament the Criminal Justice and Police Bill. Receiving the Royal Assent in May 2001, this was to allow the police to retain fingerprints and DNA profiles from individuals suspected of a crime, even when they are not subsequently prosecuted or when they are acquitted of a crime. DNA samples will also be retained when they have been volunteered during a mass screening programme by the police. Written consent from the donor must be obtained but, once given, *that consent can never be revoked*.

New Labour offered five main justifications for this extension of police powers. First, that it will help to fight crime, especially crimes perpetrated by habitual criminals, because the DNA of those individuals will already be on record. Second, it will help to eliminate innocent people from suspicion and law-abiding people in general have nothing to fear from extensive DNA databanks. Third, safeguards to prevent abuse will be ensured. Fourth, a DNA profile is an 'objective form of evidence' which should no more be thrown away than other pieces of evidence, e.g. interview notes – the quote comes from Home Secretary Jack Straw in the Commons on 29 January 2001. Finally, too much time and expense is wasted in reprofiling those who have already been profiled in a mass screening programme. Do these reasons bear scrutiny?

If fighting crime is such an overwhelming priority, then why not require everyone in the country to provide a DNA sample (including newborn babies)? Politicians who claim that large DNA databanks are popular know that they are not *this* popular. Yet even if they were there can be no mandate for the abandonment of basic civil liberties and even those politicians who disagree might hesitate to compel millions of non-compliers to surrender DNA samples. Much easier then to allow the databanks to be built up from those who come within the purview of the police since, as is well known, it is individuals who commit crimes and not social conditions! This is a pathological argument which overlooks the extent to which crime is socially and discursively constructed. Almost inevitably, such databanks will contain a disproportionate amount of DNA samples from the poorest and most vulnerable.

The endless refrain that the innocent have nothing to fear is the usual Orwellian means of neutering the civil liberties argument that the proper distinction is not between the innocent and the guilty, but between the relatively powerless and the relatively powerful. In fact, the relatively powerless *do* have something to fear whenever the presumption of innocence shifts towards a presumption of guilt. Yet in denying this what the Orwellian refrain does is to employ an actuarial logic where individuals are required to obey the norms that define them as moral/insiders rather than immoral/outsiders. Yet since there is no system that is immune to abuse and errors 'the innocent' do have something to fear and only a naive technological determinism can pretend otherwise.

The claim that a DNA profile is an objective piece of evidence is even more disturbing. Not just because a piece of evidence is objective only in conjunction with other pieces of evidence (a DNA-yielding hair found at a crime scene may have been planted), but because Straw's claim reduces DNA to the status of an interview note rather than as something that yields vital personal information about us. The commodification of society that Schiller warns against has engendered the *criminalisation* of society for, as Bauman (1998a) notes, those who cannot or will not be seduced by the commodity form are immediately suspected as being threats to it. Therefore the commodification of the body also engenders the *criminalisation of the body* as its logical extension: what I earlier referred to as the security state's criminalisation of the supply side. After all, why not treat genetic tissue and body parts as just another processable piece of matter if crime is of such overwhelming concern?

Finally, what of the idea that, once given, written consent for the retention of DNA samples taken during mass screening programmes cannot be revoked? As the then Home Office minister Charles Clarke pointed out, if consent can be revoked at a later time, then we have barely changed the current situation where samples are automatically destroyed. Clarke was actually being quite honest: a managerialist logic that values centralisation, efficiency and cost effectiveness above liberty and autonomy is one that demands the non-revocation of consent.

Conclusion

I warned you earlier that we would be examining the repressive rather than the liberatory aspects of information systems and it is worth repeating now that the worrying trends identified above do not mean that we are sinking inevitably into a one-dimensional society of surveillance. Surveillance, even in some of its less appealing roles, can have socially beneficial effects if, say, it helps to reduce traffic congestion or protects children from abuse – mobile-phone robberies notwithstanding! Further, ICTs also permit forms of counter-surveillance and counter-hegemonic activity through which the gaze of employers, corporations and the security state is redirected (Fitzpatrick, 2002c). Yet these qualifications aside, I have wanted to stress New Labour's role in promoting an information society that is drifting towards some disturbing ends. Sometimes covertly and sometimes overtly, sometimes consciously and sometimes not, New

Labour is ushering us towards a society where civil liberties, like social justice, are constantly on the defensive.

In the previous chapter I outlined New Labour's preference for weak equality and strong reciprocity and in this chapter I have wanted to suggest that, by tipping the balance away from redistributive rights and towards duty-led inclusivity, this preference both derives from and further engenders a security state. As an amalgamation of conservatism and social democracy, the security state has not replaced the welfare state, but subsumed it within a society (1) of social and spatial polarities; (2) where social problems are pathologised; and (3) of punitive supply-side reforms. These dimensions are then visible with New Labour's approach towards ICTs, where information is conceived as asocial, as commodified and primarily as a source of surveillance. Along the way, I have hinted at an alternative approach, one that I termed 'cyber-criticalism'. Like the theory of distributive justice offered in the last chapter, we will now put this to one side until Part II.

So we are almost ready to proceed to Part II and to the outline of ecowelfare contained there. However, before we can do so there is one highly important and influential defence of the NSD that we have not yet considered at any length.

Note

1 Although I am focusing upon global developments throughout the 1990s, I believe that developments since 11 September 2001 help to confirm my hypothesis, since the most extreme and hysterical reactions to the attack in the West have occurred in the paradigm examples of the security state, i.e. it is in the USA and UK that civil liberties have been subjected to the greatest threat. People (if governments and newspapers are to be believed) appear more willing than ever to sacrifice freedom (their own and that of others) in exchange for security. And this security often takes the form of pre-emptive intervention against the Other, no matter how remote or improbable the imagined threat.

4

Social democracy in Europe

The NSD's defenders have quite a devastating card up their sleeve, one which I mentioned in the introductory chapter. Whatever the merits of the last three chapters' criticisms – and they would no doubt reject all or most of them – there is an argument which potentially trumps them all.

It does not matter whether equality of powers or diverse reciprocity or whatever triumph on the page, what matters is what we can do in the real world, according to existing circumstances. And if you look at the present social, economic and political conjuncture, you will see that the circumstances are not propitious. Even *if* the world is bad, it is both self-indulgent and harmful to the least well-off to refuse to adapt yourself to it. The old social democracy ran its course and conservatism altered the agenda in ways that we have to acknowledge and work with. This is what almost all countries have been doing: neither to praise the welfare state nor to bury it, but to *save* it! Like it or not, the NSD is the best we can do in a bad world.

This argument has an undoubted persuasive force. How should we respond to it? The premise of this chapter, and so of the book, is that this argument is not a trump card for two reasons. First, it is at best a simplistic interpretation of post-1970s developments. Conservatism has certainly been in the ascendancy and the political Centre has certainly shifted towards the Right, but this is only a broad brush caricature of a very complex situation. Conservatism may have set the agenda in several countries, the UK included, but its influence elsewhere has been contested more effectively and so we must be sensitive to details and nuances that the above account overlooks. Second, therefore, we should not all be sheltering beneath the umbrella of NSD as older traditions continue to hold sway throughout Europe and the 'old' social democracy continues to thrive, even if with some difficulty, in the Nordic countries.

So our aim here is to establish that social democracy is more robust than defenders of the NSD imagine. A further aim of this chapter and the next is to suggest that the difficulties it faces are best addressed not by the productivist form of social democracy but by a post-productivist one. We begin by examining strong and weak versions of the 'social democracy is dead' argument and reject both in turn. We then examine the health of European social democracy and diagnose general good health, though with several ailments that are cause for concern. We finish with an initial contrast between productivist and post-productivist responses to those ailments and conclude that the case for the latter deserves to be made.

Globalisation again

There are two versions of the argument that social democracy is dead: the strong argument (SA) and the weak argument (WA). The SA asserts that globalisation and certain 'endogenous factors' (demographic pressures, technological costs, changes to families and households, taxpayer revolts) have made social democracy redundant and that it only continues to exist as a residual after-image that will eventually fade. The WA asserts not that social democracy *per se* is finished, but only those versions that are socialistic, collectivist, egalitarian, corporatist, Keynesian and welfarist. Something resembling the NSD is therefore appropriate. Let us examine the SA first of all.

The strong argument

The SA has been proposed most often by conservatives on a variety of grounds though we will here confine ourselves to the economic ones.

The economic case revolves around the supposed superiority of free, flexible and deregulated markets. Evolving in various stages throughout the 1970s and 1980s, the basic allegation is that an expensive, comprehensive welfare state puts a country at a competitive disadvantage in a globalising economy where capital is mobile and where endogenous factors already create enough internal pressures for reform. Nations that therefore refuse to deregulate and privatise will fail to attract investment and so will undermine their own welfare states anyway once the economy eventually begins to haemorrhage.

This argument was heard constantly in the early to mid-1990s following the final discrediting of command economies and an explosion in financial markets and, popularised by the IMF (1991), the OECD (1994) and the World Bank (1994); it still articulates the background assumptions of negotiations in and around the G8 and the WTO. The discourse has become less extreme than that heard in the early 1990s and there are fewer calls to dismantle state welfare than there are to reconstruct it as a series of safety nets that would underpin and facilitate economic productivity on the grounds, not of austerity-for-austerity's-sake, but because this would be the best way of preserving the well-being of the poorest (OECD, 1999). (The argument is usually extended on a global scale in assertions that only *free* trade can assist the world's poor.) Does it stand up to scrutiny, though? There are three main reasons to suspect not.

First, there is enough empirical evidence to show that comprehensive and expensive welfare states are not at a competitive disadvantage at all (Leibfried, 2001; Pierson, 2001a; Huber and Stephens, 2001; Sykes *et al.*, 2001; Taylor-Gooby, 2001). For example, with some reforms (see below) the Nordic countries are weathering the global economy fairly well for various reasons. The high degree of protection that Nordic welfare states provide *assists* productivity by allowing the economy to absorb shocks, by making people less risk-averse and by encouraging agreement among the social partners (government, employers, unions) for mutually-beneficial reforms. This evidence could be disputed by arguing that globalisation actually does its work quite slowly so that the debilitating effects of state welfare have yet to be fully felt. Time will tell, though this retreat makes the SA resemble those people who predict the immanent destruction of the world because they are actually quite looking forward to it.

Second, the SA focuses upon competitive cost at the expense of competitive *quality* (Hay, 2001). One way of undercutting your competitor is to do what he does cheaper, or better or to create a new demand. The SA advocates a 'race to the bottom' – under cover of anticipating one according to the 'iron laws of globalisation' – because it overemphasises the importance of competitive cost: to make your labour force attractive, you must reduce relative wages, reduce the burdens on business (red tape and employers' insurance contributions) and make the social protection system less passive and more flexible. The failure of this race to materialise on any significant scale indicates that the social cohesion and stability which welfare states can engender is as important to the maintenance of competitive advantage as cost.

Third, globalisation and endogenous factors are not homogenous entities but are differentiated across time and space. One reason for this is what the 'new institutionalists' refer to as 'path dependency' (Myles and Pierson, 2001). Globalisation affects different countries differently according not only to the political responses they make to it, but to the environment upon which it impacts and through which it is inevitably mediated: a complex of institutions, structures, practices and relations are socially and historically embedded to the point where they *affect* exogenous forces as much as they are affected *by* them. Context matters. Globalisation is therefore dialectical (Palier and Sykes, 2001), meaning that it is constructed differently on a variety of local, national and regional levels.[1] Similarly, endogenous factors vary across time and space, so there is no such thing as *the* demographic time-bomb or *the* family crisis. The SA is insensitive to these variations.

The weak argument

But if the SA fails what of the WA? This is an altogether trickier proposition, not least because it is promoted by those who say they come to save social democracy from itself. The WA can be identified in the work of Giddens and Merkel, New Labour and Ramesh Mishra – for a variety of additional arguments for and against social democracy see Chris Pierson (2001: Ch. 4).

Giddens nowhere provides a substantive argument in support of the view that globalisation is sweeping all before it. He accepts the interpretation of Hirst and Thompson (1996) that recent developments resemble a rerun of the international economy between 1870 and 1914, but insists that what is really important is the dissimilarity with the 1945–75 era of the Keynesian welfare state; he also accepts that globalisation is not a 'force of nature' because it has been engendered by a series of state and non-state actors (Giddens, 1998: 29–33). Yet despite these acknowledgements of the importance of agency (the agency that constructed the welfare state and the agency that has challenged it) he still characterises ours as a 'runaway world' that renders old forms of social democracy unviable (Giddens, 1999, 2000). He does not accept globalisation uncritically, since without coordination it threatens a kind of market fundamentalism that must be resisted, but because Giddens believes communication technologies to have sliced open the closed economies upon which the post-war welfare state allegedly depended, social democracy has to mould itself around the open economies of global finance, investment and trade through what he calls the 'social investment state' that nurtures social and human capital rather than egalitarian redistribution.

There are a number of criticisms that have been made of Giddens's approach to globalisation (Hutton and Giddens, 2000). First, the distinction between closed and open economies is overdrawn, since all economies embody relative degrees of closure and openness and one of the criticisms of the WTO is that it allows affluent nations to impose upon developing ones an openness that they do not always practicse themselves. Nor is it the case that the welfare state depended upon economic closure: some welfare states did and some did not; indeed, Rodrik (1998) and Garrett (1998) maintain that high social expenditure is more consistent with economic openness. Secondly, to the extent that post-war economies were stable vis-à-vis one another this was due to collective agreement through the Bretton Woods System, an agreement that eventually broke down as a result of *political* action and inaction rather than due to any economic law of nature. But what Giddens does is to allow just enough agency into the picture to justify the NSD, but no more. Yet there are no grounds for this and so no grounds for denying that a substantial global regulatory system could be reconstructed. Thirdly, citing the obstacles presented by ICTs is not enough. As we saw in the last chapter, governments are perfectly willing and able to regulate when it suits them. Indeed, markets always depend upon regulation of one form or another: it is not a question of *whether* markets are regulated but *in whose interests* (Standing, 2002: Ch. 2) and so 'deregulation' is something of a myth. An inability to regulate market exchanges is therefore due not to technological determinism but to a lack of political will. Finally, Giddens welds 'Keynesianism' and 'old social democracy' too closely together. This is something that many social democrats have done (see the introductory chapter) but because Giddens does not want social democracy to postdate Keynesianism, he has to erase any suggestion that the former *pre*dated the latter also (Pierson, 2001: 88–9). So even if Keynesianism is finished then the case for the NSD is not automatically made.

Nevertheless, the view that this case is done and dusted has been prominent in recent years. Wolfgang Merkel (1999) offers one of the shrewdest accounts by claiming that there is not one Third Way but many: the British, the Dutch, the Swedish and the French.[2] We will be taking a closer look at recent Swedish and Dutch welfare reforms later on in this chapter and in the next, but we can immediately raise a number of criticisms. Essentially, like Giddens, Merkel depends upon an overdrawn series of distinctions between the 'golden age' and the present:

Old welfare state	New welfare state
Statist corporatism	Market facilitation
Redistributive egalitarianism	Equal opportunities/supply side
Industrialism/homogeneity	Post-industrialism/heterogeneity
Dependency-inducing passivity	Activation and flexibility
Rights	Responsibilities
Universalism	Selectivism targeting the needy

It should be pointed out that Merkel is by no means uncritical of existing Third Way politics. Even so, his motive is to favourably contrast the NSD both with the old social democracy and with conservatism. Doing so, however, leads him to homogenise all three schools of thought. First, it can be said that the old welfare state incorporated elements that are grouped under the new (work-search requirements, citizenship duties, means testing) and that what Merkel calls the new welfare state inherits key aspects of the old, e.g. corporatism and egalitarianism have not been abandoned in countries like Sweden. Second, in order to distant it from the NSD Merkel identifies conservatism with free markets and the minimal state. But this characterisation is simplistic. Echoing the point just made, conservatism does not so much deregulate as reregulate in favour of the already-powerful; nor does it minimise the state, but allow it to invade more and more aspects of social and cultural life in order to ensure that the 'free' market is protected. Therefore, if the distance between the NSD and conservatism is not as great as Merkel imagines, then the relevance of the old social democracy may be more compelling than he seems to believe (Moschonas, 2002: 80–1, 202, cf. 228–31).

So Merkel does not make either a conceptual or normative case for the NSD. As argued in this book, the NSD describes a few countries like the UK and has influenced various others, but to regard it as describing *all* of the recent developments within social democratic movements and governments is to stretch the portrayal too far (see below). The conclusion of Chapter 1 was not that the NSD is conservative, but that it represented the social democratisation of conservatism, reintroducing some old themes (justice, solidarity) but failing to pull away from the conservative hegemony.

But if Giddens and Merkel at least make an effort to kill off the 'old' social democracy before interring it, New Labour just buries the victim under cover of darkness (Jordan, 1998; Wetherly, 2001). What is exorcised from their position is any suggestion of causal structure. For whereas Castells observes capitalism without capitalists (see Chapter 3) New Labour lives in a world of *capitalists without capitalism*. It constantly refers not to capitalism but to 'the market' and so is able to score cheap points off those who do not believe in 'the market'. Fairclough (1999: 23–30) underlines the point that, in its speeches, newspaper articles and White Papers, New Labour reifies the processes and effects of globalisation, treating it as if it popped into existence from nowhere. Since it is reluctant to challenge capitalism to any great extent, and since globalisation is in large part the newest phase of capitalist development, one that contains many harmful features, New Labour is consequently reluctant to offer a substantive critical analysis. And without a convincing account of structure, its conceptualisation of politics is hollowed out also. Politics is inserted into the picture only once this global economy of capitalists without capitalism is in place as a *fait accompli*; we are free but we must use our freedom responsibly to compete, to train and retrain, to adapt ourselves to 'changes', or else be left behind in the global economy. So, this global environment is regarded as empty of structural conflicts (Brown, 2000), such that those who engage in conflict must therefore be ideological dinosaurs who have failed to adapt and recognise the positive-sum nature of the new economy. Globalisation is therefore monolithic (economistic, exogenous, unregulatable, inevitable, omnipresent) and government's role is to shape society to those external pressures by enabling business to innovate and by requiring the labour force to do so.

As indicated in Chapter 1, what we are faced with here is ideology masquerading as pragmatism. New Labour regards the free movement of capital as inevitable and beneficial, whilst insisting that the migration of labour needs to be carefully regulated lest it offends national borders and identities: thus the gulf between (genuine) asylum seekers who are fleeing persecution and (bogus) immigrants who are coming here for 'economic' reasons. The consequence of New Labour's discourse is that people are justified in being outraged at 'bogus asylum seekers', requiring their symbolic exclusion through dispersal policies and supermarket vouchers, but have to accept the inevitability of global forces.[3] That New Labour is rarely consistent on this last point, that it is shocked and upset when companies decide to disinvest, e.g. BMW in 2001, signifies those moments when it is faced with the inadequacies of its position, when agents act according to structural imperatives that New Labour has airbrushed from its perceptions. Furthermore, upset turns to fury when the structural conflict that is supposed to be dead suddenly reappears, when another set of actors, the anti-corporate movement, turns up on the doorstep of those agents who are determining the shape of this 'unregulatable' globalisation. But rather than address the contradictions of this position – other than a constant reassurance to listen to the protestors next time – it is easier to condemn those who unreasonably force the local police from Seattle to Genoa to act brutally.[4] In short, the NSD is not justified because of the advent of globalisation (New Labour's view); instead, globalisation is constructed in a certain, conservative way because the NSD needs justification.

Finally, Ramesh Mishra (1999) insists that globalisation is one more nail in the coffin of the post-war, classic welfare state. Our job, he says, should be to identify and secure the best form of capitalism available: one that does not sacrifice the 'social' in the name of the 'economic'. So although the category of *social rights* is redundant, being no longer acceptable to either governments or electorates, it is still possible to imagine *social standards* being formulated through some form of communal consensus, standards that would be relative to that community's level of economic development. These standards could then establish the rules according to which global capitalism would be regulated.

The problem is that Mishra's defence of social *standards* is premised upon an epitaph for social *rights* which is without substance and uncritically translates the experience of countries like the UK to other developed welfare states. There is no real analysis of this argument, though, and Mishra is reduced to rehashing old ideas about social rights being unattractive because (unlike civil and political rights) they depend upon public expenditure. Yet if, as Plant (1993) argued long ago, this distinction is specious then, according to the logic of Mishra's argument, we would either have to bury civil and political rights also, or else allow for the reconstruction of *all* rights and entitlements, including social ones, at the global level. Mishra would presumably dislike the first alternative, whereas the second is one that he nowhere considers.

We have therefore reviewed three versions of the WA that, whilst being nowhere comprehensive, indicate that rumours of the 'old' social democracy's death are somewhat premature. But even if arguments for the NSD fail on these grounds, does this mean that everything is hunky-dory in the welfare states of traditional social democracies? Not quite.

Family resemblances

If it is simply incorrect to portray the old social democracy as finished, as having metamorphosised into the NSD along the lines suggested by Merkel, it would be equally misguided to overlook the cuts and bruises it has received since the early 1990s. Whether the cause is globalisation, or the attempt to fulfil EU convergence criteria, or a series of domestic pressures common to all countries, or problems with social democracy itself (Glyn, 1998), or political mismanagement, or recession, or some combination of these, social democracies are no longer the laboratories of socialism that they were once assumed to be. If we take Sweden as our exemplar, research identifies the following five trends (Callaghan, 2000; Kosonen, 2001; Timonen, 2001).

First, Sweden's welfare system has become more employment-oriented than before. Although it has always operated with activation policies on job search and what might be called the social democratic version of workfare, those policies were joined in the 1990s by cuts in unemployment benefits and sickness benefit. Benefits have also been made more earnings related and linked to contributions, more people now draw assistance benefits, and eligibility criteria were tightened to discourage fraud. Second, Swedish corporatism is now based less upon social criteria, aimed at the maintenance of social solidarity, and more upon market criteria and the need to maintain competitive advantage. Third, taxation and wage policies are also more closely oriented around market criteria. Incentives have been accorded more importance than before, leading to support for the creation of low-paid service jobs and lower marginal rates of taxation at the upper level. Fourth, the growth of public sector employment has long since levelled out and has been reduced in line with social expenditure cuts. Finally, pensions have gone through a number of reforms, e.g. a change from defined benefits to a defined contributions system, that will make pensions less expensive in the future than under the old system.

However, these trends can only be fully understood if they are seen in context (Lindbom, 2001). Swedish society is still highly egalitarian. Despite the pressures it has faced, especially in the early 1990s, income inequality barely changed throughout the decade (though it did increase slightly towards the decade's end) and there are few voices demanding its dilution. And universalism is still the operating principle despite the increases in means testing, due to its beneficial affects upon both equality and solidarity (Korpi and Palme, 1998; Rothstein, 1998). In short, Sweden's welfare reforms have defended traditional social democracy rather than replaced it with an alternative (Pennings, 1999; cf. Ryner, 1999; Feld, 2000). Its cuts and bruises have not required major surgery. The other Nordic countries reveal similar ambiguities: some evidence of retrenchment and dilution, yet set against a background where social democratic principles and practices are still healthy and widely supported. This reiterates a point made in Chapter 1: conservatism is more likely to fail to alter the existing settlement wherever social democracy has laid down substantial social roots.

But perhaps the defender of NSD could accept the picture just sketched and yet nevertheless identify NSD as *the* trend in those countries which are less committed to traditional social democracy. Two examples. Welfare reform in the Netherlands predates New Labour and, indeed, goes far beyond it in its passion for a more targeted and conditional benefit system that is offset by a spectacular growth in employment. By applying NSD-type reforms, the Dutch Disease of the early 1980s had been replaced by the Dutch Miracle of the mid-1990s. In France, the Jospin government talked Left but acted Right. For example, its programme of working-time reductions appealed to socialist aspirations but, as worked out in practice, embodied a doctrine of market flexibility that employers in other countries might envy. So here, too, the NSD can be identified. In short, the NSD signifies a trend across a range of West European nations that are trying to create American-style employment growth without replicating American levels of poverty: flexibility and security, 'flexicurity'.

This is another powerful argument that draws upon the path dependency thesis that we earlier used in defeating the SA. For if it is true that different historical and social environments blunt the local effects of globalisation – so that the global economy does not hollow out national contexts as the hyperglobalisers imagine (Held *et al.*, 1999) – then it is equally true that path dependency militates against traditional social democracy for all but those few (Nordic) countries that possess strong institutional and cultural roots in that direction. Therefore, egalitarians in those countries that are not social democratic are far better off supporting a NSD that is consistent with those nations' long-standing support for market capitalism. This is exactly what New Labour, the 'Purple Coalition' and the *Parti Socialiste* were doing even if, respectively, UK, Dutch and French versions of the NSD are not identical. So, for instance, to try and introduce the old social democracy into a conservative context is a non-runner for precisely the same reason that the SA was a non-runner: to be successful reform has to go with the grain.

A full response to this interpretation of the path dependency thesis will be delayed until the next chapter, since it bears considerable implications for post-productivism. What can be pointed out here is that the above argument, even in making concessions to the continued strength of the old social democracy, still works with blunt conceptual tools. For if it is true that the old social democracy is still thriving, albeit with some dilutions, it must be equally true that it manifests itself in non-Nordic countries also. In short, the above argument achieves its effect by distinguishing too sharply between social democratic and non-social democratic nations and does not capture the extent to which social democratic traditions, as well as being fairly heterogeneous, are to be found within and across a much wider range of welfare states. Therefore, 'going with the grain' may be an argument as much *against* as *for* the NSD since, in any one country, there are several grains, i.e. multiple paths that could be followed, since each is consistent with that country's values and institutions.

This is precisely the problem with regime theory and so much of the comparative analysis upon which it is based (Esping-Andersen, 1990): in grouping nations according to ideal-types (regimes) it misses the complexities, the nuances, the conflicts and contestations to which all nations are inevitably subject – a particular criticism of feminist researchers (Sainsbury, 1999). Even in a conservative country like the USA, there is no reason for 'old' social democrats to thrown in the ideological towel since there are many aspects of American values and conventions that support it. 'Going with the grain' does not mean we are locked into the paths that have dominated in the past.

So let us return to the above examples. Although they are broadly supportive of its reforms, Hemerijck and Visser (2001) resist depicting the

Dutch 'Polder' Model as Third Way since they regard this as too much of a broad-brush description. Green-Pedersen *et al.* (2001) *are* willing to identify a Third Way across a range of European countries like the Netherlands and Denmark, but argue that this represents *continuity* with old, egalitarian social democracy rather than discontinuity. Goodin *et al.* (1999) go even further in depicting the Netherlands rather than Sweden as the archetype of (old) social democracy. Finally, Clift (2000) argues that the Third Way does not translate into a French context at anything other than a superficial level – though Jospin spent the last two years of his incumbency trying to imitate it, an attempt that contributed to his unceremonious defeat in April 2002. In short, the path dependency argument for the NSD does not succeed. The old social democracy has had to adapt and reform itself, but those reforms can be interpreted as a defence of traditional objectives and values rather than as a capitulation to the NSD.

None of which is to deny the salience of the NSD – otherwise I would not have spent the previous three chapters arguing against it – but it is to deny the geographical scope that Blair, Giddens and those such as Merkel attribute to it. What we find in Europe is not a crude distinction between the old and new social democracy, and certainly not a situation where the former must give way to the latter, but a mosaic of social democratic movements, some of which hegemonise the country in which they are found and some of which do not. Drawing upon Wittgenstein's notion of family resemblance, we could identify overlapping clusters of European social democracies. In the UK we find a representative form of NSD that has accommodated itself to substantial aspects of conservatism; in Sweden we continue to find a form of old social democracy that has more or less resisted the sirens of NSD; and in between there is a range of nations within which both old and new social democrats contend with each other and with other political traditions and ideas. What unites these social democracies is commitment to social solidarity and opposition to *laissez-faire* markets, but to imagine that they can all be described in terms of the NSD is to eclipse other countervailing traditions. NSD may have stretched towards the Right, but this has elongated the social democratic family rather than having encircled it.

Yet if these arguments stand then far from establishing a case for post-productivist social democracy, they seem to support the familiar, productivist type. For it is only by proving its compatibility with national prosperity, investment, competitiveness, productivity and employment growth that social democracy has been able to persist under such unfavourable conditions. To replace productivist social democracy with a post-productivist variant would therefore be inherently risky. It is to this criticism that we now turn. My argument in the next chapter will be that social democracy already finds itself at the door of post-productivism and throughout Part II I will maintain that it should start to push that door open.

Post-industrial equality

The last section proposed that, although the SA and the WA fail, European social democracy finds itself in an ambivalent position. It is still prospering in both its old and new forms, but has received some bruises since the early 1990s and its electoral strength by 2002 looked less impressive than just 5 years earlier. Its welfare systems continue to attract popular support but have been subject to various degrees of retrenchment in differing countries. The divergence of European welfare regimes has therefore not collapsed and there is no convergence around a single welfare model – the NSD or anything else. Nevertheless, some kind of paradigm shift has occurred and the divergence of welfare states may well have been reconstituted. As such, some are concerned about the future viability of social democracy within this new paradigm. Bonoli *et al.* (2000: Ch. 8, 160) foresee the greater use of private provision, widening inequalities and the subversion of 'welfare objectives' to the imperatives of competitiveness. Europe, they say, therefore faces a future of 'divergence within convergence'.

This notion of divergence within convergence, or what we might call 'relative reconvergence', is articulated most forcefully by Bob Jessop (1994, 1999, 2002) in arguing that the Keynesian Welfare National State (KWNS) has gradually been replaced by a Schumpeterian Workfare Postnational Regime (SWPR). The KWNS incorporated four dimensions. First, it secured the conditions for full employment through a demand-side management of the economy. Second, economic and social policies were closely attached to citizenship rights. Third, it subordinated local, regional and international states to national economic and social priorities. Finally, it was statist, in so far as the mixed economy was shaped and guided by state institutions. Despite its successes, though, an ongoing paradigm shift, ultimately due to the transformation of Fordism into post-Fordism, can be traced to the 1980s, whereby the KWNS has been gradually transformed into the SWPR. Jessop is at pains to point out that the latter is as characterised by divergence as the former, so that this shift took a number of complex and multiple paths. Nevertheless, he claims that those paths have led us to a new paradigm: the SWPR.

First, it is Schumpeterian and so is characterised by a permanent revolution of innovation and flexibility in the name of competitiveness. Economic and labour market instability therefore becomes the organising principle. Second, the SWPR is concerned with workfare rather than welfare, in that social policy is subordinated to the demands of competitive flexibility. The needs and rights of individuals take second place to the needs and interests of business, as paid employment is widely assumed to be the main source of well-being. Social policies become less concerned with demand-side interventions and more with improving the supply of labour by equating 'citizens' with 'workers' and remaking the latter into dynamic, risk-taking entrepreneurs who embrace market insecurity. Those at the bottom of the income ladder can then be assisted with workfare policies (King, 1995, 1999). Third, policies become postnational as the nation-state is 'hollowed out': upwards towards international agencies and interstate forums, downwards towards regional and local levels and sideways towards cross-border forms of governance. Finally, the state plays less of a role in the SWPR. Or, rather, the state must enter into a variety of partnerships with the private and voluntary sectors in a 'mixed economy' of social welfare provision.

Therefore, in order to survive the demise of the KWNS, liberal, conservative and social democratic regimes have transformed themselves into liberal, conservative and social democratic versions of the SWPR. Although Jessop has been criticised for being too economistic, his analysis does capture the fears of many contemporary social democrats. For it is not that social democracy is on the slippery slope towards a conservative ditch, since social democracy may be as compatible with post-Fordist globalisation as conservatism, if not more so, but that the upward trajectory of social democracy has vanished. Post-war social democracy depended upon an expansion in social expenditure, the public sector and the hope of some that, if taken far enough, welfare capitalism would give way to welfare socialism. But if, as Paul Pierson (2001b) insists, we have entered an era of 'permanent austerity' then we face not necessarily the contraction of social democracy but a politics of compromise whereby aspirations for a post-capitalist society have been closed off forever. Put simply, the horizons of the SWPR are narrower than those of the KWNS and social democracy may find it harder to breathe within this confined space than its liberal and conservative alternatives.

What shape might this politics of compromise take?

The problem

Whereas Jessop's account draws upon the post-Fordist debate, I want to answer this question through the lens of a different but not dissimilar debate, that of post-industrialism.

One of the most influential post-industrial accounts is provided by Iversen and Wren (1998) drawing upon the ideas of Baumol (1967).

Baumol argued that productivity increases in manufacturing were always likely to outstrip those in the service sector, since the latter is inevitably labour intensive. Whether it be public services or private ones, we consume services precisely because of the labour involved: computers may supplement but can never replace the teacher or personal tutor; and you go to a restaurant precisely in order to be served by a waiter. Baumol predicted that although service prices would therefore remain high, the demand for those services would also remain high so that the service sector would absorb the jobs lost in the more efficient manufacturing sector. With more and more workers employed in the service sector, the economy would face reductions in productivity and so reductions in the rate of economic growth with inevitable knock-on effects: lower growth means less growth in wages which therefore means less revenue from taxation and payroll contributions. The fiscal basis of the welfare state is consequently undermined. In a demographically static society this might not matter, but since all societies face ageing populations, then the demand for health care, elderly care and pensions rises as the state's ability to fund that demand declines.

According to Iversen and Wren (1998), these post-industrial changes lead us towards a 'trilemma' where we must trade-off between employment growth, wage equality and budgetary constraint: we can achieve two of these objectives but not all three. Conservative societies prioritise employment and budgets. According to conservatives, the answer to the trilemma is a strong private sector with employment growth at the low-wage end of the labour market, benefit reforms to prod the unemployed into that labour market ('a low wage is better than no wage') and the privatisation of large parts of the welfare state, e.g. the shift towards private and occupational pensions in the UK in the 1980s. The price is a massive degree of income inequality and the individualisation of risks and costs.[5] Corporatist welfare states prioritise equality and budgets. High payroll costs offer workers an impressive degree of protection through high replacement ratios, but public sector expansion is contained. The problem is a gulf between labour market insiders and outsiders, leading to high rates of unemployment amongst the latter and the conservative allegation that generous social insurance systems are inflexible, inefficient and so unaffordable. Social democracies prioritise employment and equality. The public sector provides a large degree of employment and wage equality, but the problem is that depends upon very high levels of social expenditure.

None of these responses to the trilemma is economically superior to the others, they each have advantages and disadvantages, such that our preference is ultimately a matter of politics, morals and (if we take path dependency seriously) historical inheritance. The problem for each welfare regime in the future is in coping with its 'excluded objective'. Can conservative societies contain the social pressures caused by income inequality? (The attempt to decrease income inequality without destabilising employment growth and budgetary constraint is precisely what characterises the NSD.) Can corporatist ones reduce unemployment? Is social democracy still affordable? Many social democrats therefore worry not that its resolution of the trilemma is logically weaker than the others, but that high social expenditure is becoming harder and harder to maintain.

Of course, much of the above can be disputed. Leys (2001: 90–5; Mahon, 2000: 34; cf. Schwartz, 2001) argues that Baumol underestimates the extent to which, given capitalism's propensity to commodify anything and everything, productivity increases in the service sector are possible. Nevertheless, and whatever the timescale involved, the evidence supporting Baumol's thesis is impressive (Huther, 2000; Iversen, 2001). How then might social democracy best cope with its excluded objective? How do we maintain employment growth and wage equality whilst keeping social expenditure within high but nevertheless acceptable limits?

Possible solutions

These are the questions with which contemporary social democrats are wrestling. There is no space here to review all facets of the debate and the contributions made by those such as Leisering and Leibfried (1999) and Gershuny (2000) will be placed to one side, though we will make passing reference to Goodin *et al.* (1999) – for a critique of all three, see Fitzpatrick (2003b). However, there are several suggestions that I would like to examine and we shall do so in the form proposed by Huber and Stephens (2001: 324–31).

First, Huber and Stephens make the point that what matters is less the ageing of the population and more the ratio of the economically active to the economically inactive. In this respect social democracies are better equipped to meet the demographic challenges of the future, for whereas conservative countries also have an impressive record of job creation, the low wages of the latter displace rather than address the demographic problem. High labour market participation rates, of women as much as men, are therefore the *sine qua non* of social democracy.

Second, domestic investment has to be encouraged and they suggest this be done through social insurance funds. However, because these funds would quickly become the 'dominant owners of stocks, bonds and money markets' (Huber and Stephens, 2001: 326), and because it is necessary to prevent the kind of backlash that killed the Meidner plan in the 1970s, those funds should own and be owned 'passively'. Moreover, continued wage restraint is necessary, especially if investment is to be emphasised above profits. The insurance funds could be invaluable in this respect also, since by improving the share of capital that accrues to wage earners, workers would have a built-in incentive not to drain the resources needed for investment.

Third, payroll contributions should be reduced so long as employers agree to deploy the revenue for investment purposes rather than profits or dividends. This would then boost jobs at the lower end of the pay scale, requiring some kind of tapered benefit scheme to improve the resulting incomes of those who take such jobs. What they are hinting at is a Negative Income Tax (NIT) (Scharpf, 2000). Furthermore, those entering the labour market at the lower end need some kind of additional protection if they are not to be trapped in such jobs permanently. Esping-Andersen (1999: 178–84) recommends a 'mobility guarantee' that would limit the amount of time each individual was forced to remain in low-waged, unrewarding jobs.

Finally, social democracies need to follow the Dutch example in creating more 'part-time jobs, opportunities for job sharing, and flexibilization of work schedules' (Huber and Stephens, 2001: 327). This in turn requires a scheme of benefits for part-time workers. Furthermore, greater flexibility in hiring and firing is desirable so long as generous compensation and retraining programmes are available for those workers made redundant.

The justification that Huber and Stephens (2001: 184) offer for the above proposals involves a reformulation of decommodification, defined by Esping-Andersen (1990: 21–2) as occurring 'when a person can maintain a livelihood without reliance upon the market'. But if this implies 'freedom from the market' then social democracies have never been based upon this as an operating principle. Instead, they have been, and must always be, based upon a strong level of participation *in* the market. Decommodification captures the idea that people should have entitlements to an adequate standard of living when involuntarily separated from the labour market, but for Huber and Stephens the key social democratic principle is active participation. This goes some way to meeting the feminist objection to Esping-Andersen's formulation – that it ignores the patriarchal effects of decommodification for women – and offers what Orloff (1993: 318) calls a 'right to commodification'.

If these proposals define a productivist future for social democracy, then what can we say against them? Why should we even try when they appear eminently desirable? Let us run through them again.

First, the distinction between active and inactive is simply too crude. The implicit premises are that employment equals activity and unemployment equals inactivity. Yet there are relatively few people who are economically inactive. If, for example, a retired grandfather looks after his granddaughter for several days a week then the net gain to the economy is obvious, since this is work that neither his child's employer nor the state now has to perform. Undoubtedly, lower levels of activity do correlate with old age (especially after the age of 80) and with certain conditions like unemployment and sickness, but a simple active/inactive dichotomy does not capture this complexity.

Furthermore, what is important is not so much 'activity' as 'value'. High-activity employment that is environmentally unsustainable may be of less long-term value than low-activity non-employment which is eco-logically friendly. So although social democracies are rightly regarded as environmental pioneers (Andersen and Liefferink, 1997) even their record is mixed (Grant *et al.*, 2000: 118, 140–1), as we shall see in the next chapter, and it may be that a new conceptualisation of value – one that interprets economic health in terms of environmental health – is needed.

Second, the idea that insurance funds should own and be owned passively, merely as sources of investment and wage restraint, resembles the kind of asset egalitarianism long championed by Meade (1995) and implies that participation in the economy is active so far as the labour market is concerned, but passive when it comes to the structural and insti-tutional *foundations* of the labour market, i.e. the distinction between wage earners and profit earners is maintained, though to the greater benefit of the latter. This would certainly represent an improvement on existing cap-italism, even social democratic variants, but somewhat gives the lie to the equation of social democracy with active participation. In truth, social democracy is active with regards to the labour market, but relatively passive in terms of democratic participation in the economy.[6] So as with activity/inactivity, the active/passive dichotomy is constructed according to some familiar and quite conservative orthodoxies.

Third, what of NIT plus a mobility guarantee? The problem with NIT – and with the tax credit schemes that are working towards it (Jordan *et al.*, 2000) – is that it derives from the orthodox constructions that the last two paragraphs have queried: that activity and active participation need greater incentives than the 'incentives' of inactivity and passivity – the attractions of the latter are usually assumed by NIT advocates rather than explained. NIT and BI are administratively and financially similar, yet by being *ex ante* the latter provides a degree of security and risk taking that the *ex post* provision of the former cannot match (van Parijs, 2000). NIT also represents an 'Oliver Twist' form of citizenship ('please, sir, can I have some more?') that elides the apparent equity between those who would and those who would not need to draw it (Fitzpatrick, 1999a: Ch. 5).

The initial problem with Esping-Andersen's mobility guarantee – apart from the fact that it is based upon a superficial rejection of BI – is that it saves social democracy by destroying part of it, i.e. by proposing that the maintenance of budgetary constraint requires greater income inequality, and does not explore other potential sources of value and revenue. This 'equality within inequality' approach is justified by giving it a temporal rather than a social dimension: social equality is to be maintained through occasional periods of low wages and insecurity. But is this distinction plausible? Esping-Andersen states that the time limit on those periods is to be guaranteed through effective education and retraining schemes – rather than through the guarantee of public sector jobs, presumably because this would reintroduce the budgetary dilemma. This seems to indicate that the risks of inequality would fall upon the individual and, more likely than not, *disadvantaged* individuals: 'skills are the single best source of escape from underprivilege', he states (Esping-Andersen, 1999: 183). Yet Esping-Andersen avoids the implications of his recommendations by quickly substituting the reference to 'underprivilege' with that of 'unpleasantness'. Risks will not fall disproportionately upon the poorest, he implies, because 'many of us will experience a spell of unpleasantness'. Yet if this rhetorical slip from underprivilege to unpleasantness means anything, it means that Esping-Andersen is concealing (perhaps from himself) the true import of 'equality within inequality', for it is not unreasonable to anticipate that the 'unpleasantness' will continue to fall most frequently and most catastrophically upon the least well-off. In short, temporal stratification is a manifestation of social stratification and not its replacement (Fitzpatrick, 2003b).

Finally, Huber and Stephens recommend more part-time jobs, job sharing and work flexibility. Here I am in agreement, but this still leaves open the question of civic context. Goodin *et al.* (1999: 225–36) also praise the Dutch model as coming close to the ideal of 'combined resource autonomy' where individuals have enough income to meet basic needs and enough free time to make use of that income. However, this embodies a rather hollow, negative conception of free time (freedom from employment) rather than the more positive conception of informal, civic engagement that Gorz (1999) and Jordan with Jordan (2000) discuss. So free time is as much about quality as quantity and, because quality requires socially just background conditions, we are again referred back to the kind of institutional reforms that the social democratic principle of 'active labour market participation' (productivism) only touches upon.

From productivism to post-productivism

Huber and Stephens's critique of decommodification is therefore relevant but limited. It captures a productivist conception of social democracy, but ignores the possibility of a post-productivist alternatives. By incorporating the notion of 'involuntary separation' from the labour market it retains a pathologised view of socioeconomic interdependency and reaffirms the 'employment ethic': the assumption that employment is and should be *the principal means* for achieving wellbeing (Fitzpatrick, 1998b). This is not to define post-productivism, as Goodin (2001) unhelpfully does, as 'welfare without work' but it is to detach wellbeing from employment to a greater extent than most social democrats seem presently willing to contemplate.

Post-productivist welfare therefore agrees that the challenge of the postindustrial trilemma needs to be addressed, but suspects that productivist dichotomies of activity/inactivity and active/passive divert us away from sources of social and ecological value that are deeper than those captured by the principle of 'active labour market participation'. Social democratic versions of productivism are preferable to conservative and infinitely preferable to conservative ones, yet risk ossifying into another end-of-history ideology unless we can push through towards post-productivist institutions and relations. Let me underline this last point.

Post-productivism is opposed to the *ideology* of productivity, not the practice. If productivity implies *increases in the transformation of natural resources into sources of wealth* then post-productivism insists that those increases be assessed according to moral criteria that do not derive from the discourse of production itself (criteria specified in the next chapter). There is little point in supporting an economic system where the only end of productivity is the search for more productivity. Social democratic productivism has thankfully generated high levels of well-being, but the ultimate end of social democracy should be the maintenance of those levels without having to live in an employment society where we are required to spend so much of our lives being 'active' in this narrow sense. For instance, Huber and Stephens (2001: 326) talk about more income accruing to wage earners but neglect the issue of time accumulation. Indeed, unless productivism aims at its own demise then the moral (as opposed to the economic) case for social democracy is undermined. If we could start society again from an original position we would have three options: (1) to avoid productivism altogether, (2) to use and then transcend it or (3) to perpetuate it forever. The third option is meaningless. If social democrats do not realise this then, to misuse Bevan, they are proudly displaying the medals won in the battles that they have already lost.

Conclusion

In this chapter we have seen that social democracy is much more robust than either conservatives or even new social democrats suppose.

Although some parties and countries have moved identifiably towards the Right, others have been able to weather the storms of social and economic changes without abandoning the core precepts of the old social democracy. However, this is not to claim that post-war welfare states can simply be resurrected with a wave of the political wand and when looking to the future social democracy (old and new) undoubtedly faces some hefty challenges whether we characterise this in post-Fordist terms (Jessop) or postindustrial ones (Iversen and Wren). According to those such as Huber and Stephens (and Esping-Andersen) social democracy can meet those challenges by re-emphasising its productivist principles and institutions. However, I have introduced several reasons why the case for a post-productivist social democracy deserves to be made. We will pick up these themes again in Chapter 5.

We are now ready to define, theorise and explore post-productivism in more detail and this is the task for Part II.

Notes

1 We examine path dependency below and return to it again in Chapter 5. However, I want to explain at the outset that although it is a useful tool for criticising the SA it, too, carries conservative implications in that it risks ossifying the existing political environment and so underestimating the potential for radical change (Gray, 1998). Therefore, path dependency is a useful tool with which to criticise the hyperglobalisers, those who would hollow out all local contexts in the name of the global economy, but is not necessarily an accurate depiction *of* those local contexts.
2 A position close to that I expressed in Chapter 1 when arguing that there are multiple political Centres.
3 Vouchers were eventually curtailed in 2002, but not before the Government's discourse had effectively legitimised the attitudes of the British National Party and done so at the very time when the far Right was on the move across the rest of Europe.
4 Though note how New Labour's response to employers' revolts, e.g. the Fuel Protestors in 2000 or the Countryside Alliance in 1999–2000, has been far more muted and respectful.
5 2002 brought additional evidence that private pensions are not the panacea that Conservatives and New Labour imagine them to be, with many private schemes shifting towards the defined contributions or money-purchase model that provides less security in old age for many.
6 I say *relatively* passive because I am aware of social democracy's favourable record in achieving social partnership and cooperation. Nevertheless, this corporatism still falls short of the kind of economic democracy that is the ultimate rationale for Centre-Left politics.

PART II

5

Productivism and beyond

In Part I, we began by outlining the main principles of the NSD, using New Labour as our exemplar. I outlined the major criticisms and argued that the main problem with the NSD is that, although it should not be equated with conservatism, it fails to establish a distinct and convincing alternative to the conservative hegemony. Chapter 2 began to substantiate this position, defining the NSD as support for weak equality and strong reciprocity, in contrast to an alternative theory of distributive justice (equality of powers plus diverse reciprocity) that I believe a more radical politics should aim towards. Chapter 3 argued that the NSD derives from and embeds a security state that has remodelled the welfare state and reconfigured needs as risks and fears; the security state was then further explored in terms of New Labour's approach to information and ICTs. In the last chapter I then questioned the scope of the NSD, showing that 'old' social democracy is still very much alive, though not without difficulties. However, I also suggested that productivist reforms are not the only potential solution to the post-industrial dilemmas that social democracy faces.

We have therefore laid the ground for Part II where our focus shifts from the NSD to what I call 'ecowelfare'. Since ecowelfare is a post-productivist form of social democracy, theoretical and practical hints of which can be found lurking within existing social democracy itself, then our first task is to define and justify what is meant by post-productivism. This then leads into a model of ecowelfare. Rather than expose you to an overlong chapter, we will here focus upon post-productivism and then use Chapter 6 to explore ecowelfare.

Productivism and post-productivism

Robert Goodin (2001) offers an interesting purchase on these ideas. He categorises welfare regimes in terms of the relationship between welfare and work: conservative welfare states are based upon the ideal of 'work *not* welfare', corporatist ones are based upon 'welfare *through* work' and social democracies are based upon 'welfare *and* work'. In other words, whereas conservatives interpret welfare and work as crowding each other out, social democrats regard them as being complementary and conservatives adopt a middle position between the two. On this basis, Goodin defines the ideal of post-productivism as 'welfare *without* work' and identifies the Netherlands as the embryo of a post-productivist welfare system. Yet as suggestive as Goodin's formulation is, there are at least three problems with it.

First, as a description of the relationship between work and welfare *policy* it is reasonably accurate, but it says little about welfare in the more philosophical sense of well-being. Second, by gathering both waged and unwaged labour under the heading of 'work', Goodin confuses work with employment, although he is undoubtedly aware of the distinction, and intimates that attitudes towards unwaged work can be read off from attitudes towards waged work, though feminist researchers have argued for years that things are not so simple (e.g. Lewis, 1992). Third, Goodin's encapsulation of post-productivism is a hostage to fortune, since it is hardly realistic at present to imagine an employmentless society and certainly not a *work*less one! Nevertheless, so long as these points are remembered we can use Goodin's formulation as a starting point for understanding the contrast between productivism and post-productivism.

The common denominator for each of these welfare regimes is waged work. They may disagree on the nature of citizenship rights and duties, and on the relation between formal and informal labour, but the commitment to employment is pivotal to all three. This commitment derives ultimately from the view that underpins all developed societies: something is valuable proportionate to the extent to which it contributes to productivity growth, i.e. social value is primarily *economic* value. This does not mean that activities which do not contribute to, or even subtract from, productivity growth are necessarily devalued, but it does mean that they are *undervalued*, that the farther we stray from economic criteria then the harder it is to justify non-economic sources of value. There is, we could say, a kind of 'economic gradient' by which moral, aesthetic, emotional and natural values must constantly struggle to overcome the event horizon of the economic. This gradient tends to be more severe in conservative versions of capitalism than in social democratic ones, as the cash nexus is more prominent in the former, but although social democratic capitalism has reduced the gradient, it has nowhere near eliminated it, due partly to the fact that the traditional labour movement has sought to distribute social goods more widely rather than reconfigure the meaning of social value. Productivism is therefore the insistence that employment is the principal means by which growth in productivity can be effected because it is easier to increase capital stock, and therefore output, through formal than through informal activity, since the former involves more specialisation, more division of labour and a greater potential for substituting labour with capital. So just as social value largely signifies economic value, so work revolves around the norms of employment.

Before defining post-productivism, I should indicate how the above account differs from some other recent theorists. Holliday (2000: 708–9) characterises productivist welfare as an alternative to Esping-Andersen's typology and identifies it as an East Asian regime for which 'social policy is strictly subordinate to the overriding policy objective of economic growth'. He therefore interprets productivism as the subordination of 'state policy' to economic growth, a subordination that even liberal and conservative systems avoid. Yet this is too narrow a conception of productivism, since economic growth is everywhere the *sine qua non* of social policy and although welfare states may differ in the degree of subordination they embody, none has sought to invert it. Holliday imagines that decommodification implies freedom from the labour market when, in practice and as indicated in the last chapter, it offers only relative freedom. This is not a mistake made by Dahl *et al.* (2001: 301), though even they too tend to interpret productivism as activation policies rather than as a logic that underpins modern welfare. It is Offe (1984: 296–99; 1993: 67–72) who manages to trace that logic through the ontological and cognitive frames of modernity, regarding it as that through which a complex of political and cultural practices constructs as natural, desirable and self-evident activity which is most conducive to the commodification of well-being.

Although there is no space here to critique Offe's approach in any depth, he does suggest that there are at least two counterpoints to the reduction of social to economic value and of work to employment. First, there is carework, most of which is unwaged and most of which continues to be performed by women. Carework possesses obvious economic value, in that it involves the performance of activity that neither the capitalist market nor the state have either the inclination or the ability to remunerate fully (Waring, 1988), which is exactly why public carework services have been established almost everywhere in recent decades. Indeed, there have been various attempts to estimate the shadow value of carework, i.e. the extent to which it would increase GDP. However, although carework possesses economic value, economic value is not its primary rationale. We do not have children in order to populate the future economy, or look after us in old age; we do not care for elderly relatives in order to make a profit.[1] The value of carework does not derive from our willingness to pay for it in a market. Therefore economic value is a consequence of carework, but not its motivation; some carework can and should be performed as waged activity, and should be factored much more closely into social and economic policies than at present, but most carework will always remain informal, performed for reasons of emotional belonging. In short, carework is largely non-employment work and a form of value captured by the term 'emotional labour'. We will return to these points in Chapter 6.

Second, there is the ecological value of the environment. Greens have long pointed out that, whatever your ideological interpretation of it, economic value depends upon and feeds off an environmental substructure (Henderson, 1981; O'Connor, 1998; Douthwaite, 1999; cf. Brennan, 2000, 2001). The resources we mine and the ecosystem we pollute once those resources have been utilised are the origin of economic value. Locke's definition of property, as the mixing of labour with the fruits of the earth, gave rise to the labour theory of value where labour is implicitly defined as 'active' and nature as 'passive' leading, whether subsequently cloaked in capitalist or Marxist costume, to an emphasis upon labour rather than the nature that labour converts into commodities. For Greens, by contrast, the environment's value may be quantified to some extent (Pearce, 2000), but ultimately transcends the economic. As argued in Chapter 6, to convert each and every aspect of nature into the commodity form is the preferred solution of productivism, but one that is ultimately self-defeating. Most Greens therefore argue that no economic system is fully capable of preserving the environment: it is certainly necessary to 'Green' the economy, but even a Green economy could not perform all of the work of sustainability that needs to be done. For this, a wider conception of social activity and participation is required. In short, sustainable work takes us beyond the employment society in order to preserve the intrinsic essence of ecological value.

These counterpoints resemble each other in that both are concerned with the emotional and ecological conditions of economic value, but conditions that can be only partially nurtured by the employment society, given the dominance it accords to economic value (the economic gradient). At the end of the last chapter I mentioned the importance of devising criteria that do not derive from the discourse of production. What I now propose is that we regard the above emotional and ecological conditions as providing us with such criteria, the means by which productivity (the transformation of emotional and natural resources into sources of wealth) should be judged. I therefore propose to incorporate emotional and ecological value under the heading of 'reproduction'. Reproductive value refers to the emotional and ecological foundations of economic value, that upon which economic value is founded, but which it can never fully incorporate or commodify, since care and sustainability imply forms of activity so extensive that they can never be completely quantified or reduced to economic criteria. Reproductive value and economic value therefore share ambiguities vis-à-vis one another. Economic value depends upon the reproduction of its conditions, but cannot acknowledge this dependency, since no economy is wealthy enough to fully compensate for the emotional and ecological costs that it creates: the ethics of affluence and growth are undermined the moment we render visible the foundations upon which they rest, because it is these foundations which they are gradually eroding. Reproductive value is the ultimate source of economic value, yet it is the destructive effects of affluence and growth which now provide us with the reflexive skills and resources needed to preserve reproductive activity. Reproductive and economic values therefore push both away from and towards one another.

Productivism is that which would subsume reproduction within the sphere of production, insisting that the costs of the employment society *can* be incorporated within an economic logic, e.g. by insisting that care-work and sustainability are job and therefore growth friendly. Post-productivism is that which would subsume production within the spheres of reproduction, insisting that those costs are beyond the capacity of the employment society to fully recognise and absorb, so that we must alter our conceptions of value and so of affluence, growth and work. Post-productivism is therefore a doctrine of 'reproductivity', whereby productive activity is justified if and only if it can be demonstrated that the emotional and ecological sources of production are enhanced. Reproductivity does not, then, deny the importance of productivity, but subjects it to 'non-productivist' criteria, i.e. it is opposed to the ideology of productivism but not to productivity *per se*, since productivity growth *may* be crucial to the maintenance of reproductive value – though the extent to which this is true cannot be judged theoretically. Of course, productivists will argue that productivity is *never* an end in itself and that economic growth is pursued not for its own sake, but to improve human well-being. Post-productivists answer that this ideal no longer prevails (if it ever did) and that the well-being we are allowed to experience has narrowed to an economistic range upon which it is consequently dependent. Rather than economic growth serving improvements in well-being, it is the narrowing of well-being that serves the pursuit of economic growth. For post-productivists, therefore, it is increasingly necessary to foreground emotional and ecological values that underpin the economic, but which are not reducible to it.

This contrast between productivism and post-productivism may throw light on the faultlines in radical politics. Many within feminism, environmentalism and on the Left advocate the productivist route (Midgely, 1997;

Bowles and Gintis, 1998; Gough, 2000: Ch. 8). 'Wage-earner feminism' prizes Orloff's right to commodification and says that gender equality is best delivered through dual breadwinning households; ecological modernisers insist that Green reforms are ineffective unless they promote productive activity; the labour movement has long argued for better ways of creating and distributing, rather than reconstituting, economic growth. However, others advocate what we here call post-productivism on the grounds that productivism undermines the sources of its own value and so is ultimately self-defeating. Some feminists point to the disadvantages of dual breadwinning, e.g. that it predicates gender equality upon the repertoires of masculinity; many Greens argue that ecological modernisation is a short-term solution at best; the post-industrial Left calls for approaches that do not try to beat capitalism at its own game.

So should we base our radical politics upon productivism or post-productivism? The strongest support for productivist radicalism can be found in social democracies, for here we witness not only distributive justice, but also a large degree of gender equality and the gradual emergence of sustainable economics.

Feminist researchers nearly always praise social democracies, though they also acknowledge the incompleteness of the social democratic record. Plantenga *et al.* (1999) note that the Netherlands idealises the equal sharing of time between waged and unwaged work and between men and women. However, although women's labour market participation has increased, there has been no corresponding increase in men's care participation and so women are still the secondary earners in a 'one-and-a-half-earner' model (Lewis, 2001). The Dutch system salutes part-time employment as the means of combining employment and care, but it is primarily women who take such jobs and so the government has not yet created a 'twice-three-quarter' model where both men and women are in the labour market for approximately 4 days per week. Policies still favour breadwinning and thus the privatisation and feminisation of care. According to Tracey Warren (2000), Denmark too pulls away from the male breadwinner model, but only half successfully as unwaged work remains underemphasised and, as in the Netherlands, because the substitute for *male* breadwinning is regarded as *dual* breadwinning, then considerable remnants of male breadwinning nevertheless remain as women are concentrated away from the core jobs that men have little incentive to vacate. There is a similar pattern visible in Sweden: high rates of female participation in the labour market combined with generous childcare and parental leave policies. The price, though, is a labour market with some of the most sexually segregated divisions to be found anywhere, with women grouped into public sector jobs and the one-and-a-half model also visible here (Sainsbury, 1999).

Is the ambiguous record of social democracy due to relatively simple policy failures that await rectification? Or might those policies be perfectly consistent with the productivist logic that underpins them?[2] Productivist logic demands either lots of waged breadwinning or lots of unwaged caregiving (or preferably both): the former facilitates economic growth, since improvements in output are easier to achieve through formal activity; the latter is consistent with economic growth so long as employment levels are reasonably high. Conservative and social democratic nations depend upon high rates of breadwinning, though the former prefers low-wage jobs in the private sector, whereas the latter prefers high-wage jobs in the public one. Corporatist welfare states by contrast have strong insider/outsider markets and so have low rates of female participation and therefore high levels of unwaged caregiving. What the productivist logic cannot countenance is lots of *remunerated caregiving*, since this seems to subtract from growth by being neither inexpensive nor oriented to productivity increases. In a productivist economy, then, employment (labouring for another) *must* be promoted over carework (labouring for others).

So the ambiguous successes and failures of productivist social democracy is no accident. Whereas social democracy is able to pay women to enter the labour market, and so expand the very caregiving services that those women need, it cannot pay men to leave, it since this would strain social expenditure to bursting point. This is not to decry social democracy's record on gender equality, nor to predict that future improvements will not be made, but it is to observe that there are productivist limits to the feminist agenda: male breadwinning can only be reduced if it is replaced by dual breadwinning, though evidence shows that the latter retains considerable residues of the former.

Similarly, evidence also suggests that social democratic societies are the Greenest (Lafferty, 2001). We hinted at this in the previous chapter and, in the mid-1990s, then Swedish Prime Minister Goran Persson was talking of creating a Green welfare state and society (quoted in Lundqvist, 2001a). Action, though, has languished behind the rhetoric and, because of the stress upon international market competitiveness, the emphasis has been placed upon technological, end-of-the-pipe fixes, top-down managerialism rather than grassroots democracy, a win–win philosophy that avoids the difficult questions of trade-off and a legacy whereby Swedish industry has developed through environmental exploitation (Jamison and Baark, 1999) – Sverrisson (2001) suggests that this is for reasons of pragmatism. Environmental concerns have not been integrated into the wider array of economic, social and welfare issues, unless to justify a 'business as usual' approach (Eckerberg, 2000, 2001). Jamison and Baark (1999: 217) find that Denmark's record is better, but that, even here, environmental policies have not been integrated in the social lifeworld, such that they are easily abandoned when they become too costly – a risk also noticeable in Finland (Niemi-Iilahti, 2001). In the Netherlands and Norway, the environment tends to be brought into the decision-making picture only when it benefits, but does not challenge, economic orthodoxy, e.g. job creation in the waste management industries (van Muijen, 2000; Langhelle, 2000).

Again, this is not meant to sound petulant, as social democracies already offer a model for other nations to follow, but it is to insist that just as there are productivist limits to feminism, there are similar limits to environmentalism. There are many aspects of the environmental agenda that can assist productivity, growth and efficiency: where, say, sustainable technologies can reduce the costs borne by the transport infrastructure or health care systems, releasing expenditure that can be invested elsewhere. But just because there can be sustainable growth, it does not mean that all forms of growth can be rendered sustainable and costs to the environment that are inherent within a productivist economy tend to be ignored. For example, without a reduction in many types of consumption and without the localisation of production, the shift towards cleaner technologies and recycling is likely to resemble the habit of jamming one foot on the brake and the other on the accelerator (Douthwaite, 1996). Yet such reduction and localisation point in the opposite direction to consumerist, cosmopolitan capitalism and would mean bringing onto the economic stage values and criteria which are of no obvious or short-term benefit to the actors involved. Only a democratic, ecological state can direct the action across a longer timespan, but that requires the kind of political rationality that is barely visible even in social democracies, where the imperatives of global competitiveness hold sway (Lundqvist, 2001b).

So although the strongest support for productivist radicalism can be found in social democracies, that radicalism has taken social democracy to the door of post-productivism. In terms of both caregiving and sustainability, social democracies have gone further than other countries in incorporating reproductive values into their socioeconomic institutions and policies. Yet they are bumping up against the limits of productivism because the economic gradient makes it harder to achieve more than modest (though still welcome) forms of gender equality and sustainability. And, I would argue further, if social democracies are therefore poised between productivism and post-productivism, then path-dependency arguments finally fall by the wayside.

Path dependency and post-industrialism revisited

This is an argument that I hinted at in the last chapter when addressing the criticism that if path dependency disproves the hyperglobalisation thesis, then it also rules out the possibility of all but a few countries pursuing the social democratic path. I suggested that this depends upon a simplistic conception that neglects the extent to which political traditions are to be found across a range of national contexts. Indeed, if this were not so then hegemonic struggles could not occur as there would be no oppositional forces to hegemonise!

But if so, then it is also the case that political traditions are not one thing or another. Within the hegemonic battlefield they are spread across diverse lines of attack and defence. So just as there are multiple paths within a particular nation, there are also multiple paths within a particular tradition. In short, the path-dependency thesis explains nothing unless we understand (1) the extent to which traditions are 'overdetermined' (Laclau and Mouffe, 1985), i.e. each tradition incorporates multiple versions of itself within a multilayered domain, and (2) the means by which traditions hegemonise in the process of being hegemonised. This means that version of the tradition that prevails is not the real or only one, but the version which dominates within a given conjuncture according to contingent circumstances. But that conjuncture and those circumstances not only fluctuate constantly, but do so as a result of hegemonic struggle, both within and between traditions. So just as the distinction between social democratic and non-social democratic nations is overdrawn, so the distinction between productivist and non-productivist social democracy is overdrawn. Those who therefore say that the future of social democracy *must* be productivist, because this is the path that has already been set, are ignoring the idea that any path is a multiple overdetermination of itself within a contingent field. Counter-hegemonisation may be difficult to achieve, depending upon the conjuncture in question, but is never impossible. This is reason why I have defined post-productivism, not as opposed to productivity, wealth, etc., but as a doctrine that, consistent with feminism, environmentalism and the post-industrial Left, recontextualises those goals at a layer deeper than that of economic value.

What this also does is to throw a new light on the trilemma that we discussed in the last chapter. In fact, the trilemma might be regarded as an example of social democrats limiting their horizons by refusing to think outside the productivist box. The trilemma holds if economic and employment growth not just *are* but *ought to be* the objectives of any welfare system. However, we have reason to question both of these aims. What of economic growth, first of all?

Let us dispense with two perspectives, both of which insist that growth and sustainability are mutually exclusive (Dryzek, 1997). The first perspective insists that sustainability must prevail, even at the risk of economic contraction (neo-Malthusianism) and the second insists that sustainability can be made consistent with existing forms and rates of growth (the Procrustean Bed argument). Neo-Malthusianism diverts too radically from contemporary expectations and neglects the possibility that social (if not always personal) affluence can be a force for good; Procrusteanism is simply dangerous wishful thinking. We are therefore faced with two further options. One is to introduce environmental criteria into GDP/GNP measurements and the other is to regard economic growth as only one among a much broader range of indicators. In short, the productivist orthodoxy defines us as wealthy according to the size of GDP and as productive according to the rate at which GDP wealth grows (cf. Coates, 2000: 265–73). Post-productivism defines us as wealthy according to the enhancement of the reproductive conditions underpinning GDP growth and as productive according to the rate of reproductivity. What are the respective merits of these options?

Those who defend Green GDP/GNP do so on the basis that the environment can be treated as a form of capital for which we must pay the appropriate charge and what follows from this is support for the 'substitution' of natural resources for their manufactured equivalents (Choi, 1994). The first of these premises risks being superficial. Nordhaus (Nordhaus and Tobin, 1972), for instance, estimated that the USA should commit no more than 2 per cent of its annual national income to environmental investment. One problem with this is that to make estimates of ecological value according to (a) economic standards and (b) existing market preferences is to confuse price with value and to regard the environment as equivalent to other goods when it is in fact much more fundamental (Douthwaite, 1996: 38–9). Another problem is that economists usually favour a 'market discount rate' rather than a 'social discount rate' in comparing future costs and benefits to present-day ones, precisely because the latter is less amenable to purely economic calculation. But if economistic calculations are too narrow, then the market rate is misleading (see Chapter 7).

The second premise of Green GDP/GNP tracks back to the assumptions that neo-classical economists were making in the 1970s, namely that capital can substitute for natural resources. Daly (1997a, 1997b), following the lead of Georgescu-Roegen (Perrings, 1997), argues that this is to underestimate the importance of nature, the entropic effects of growth (at least on a local scale) and to overestimate the possibility for converting resources into capital, since this does not overcome the ultimate problem of scarcity and ecological finiteness. In response, one of the architects of those neo-classical assumptions conceded that substitution has only an 'intermediate' usefulness (Stiglitz, 1997); the other architect (Solow, 1997) does not address the essential critique. The merit of a Green GDP/GNP, then, is that it ties in with existing practice and offers a short- to medium-term solution that, through substitution, can slow down the rate of environmental degradation. The problem, as Stiglitz acknowledges, is that although substitution can reduce the resource amount needed to produce one unit of output, it cannot ever halt the depletion of resources. The problem of scarcity and finiteness is simply deferred.

The implication is that Green GDP/GNP must eventually be superseded by less productivist conceptions and measurements of wealth such as that articulated by the Index of Sustainable Economic Welfare (ISEW), an overview of the debate being provided by Jackson (2002). According to research cited and conducted by Jackson, because we have reached a threshold beyond which the benefits from growth no longer outweigh the losses of environmental degradation, then the quality of life is permanently stalled. This is true even in social democracies, though here the ISEW scores began to diverge from GDP scores more recently and less dramatically than in other nations. In short, Green GDP/GNP can be effective in the short-run *if* it is used to turn our economies away from their present course towards conceptions of wealth captured by the ISEW though Jackson concedes that even the ISEW may need to be superseded in the long term. To put it another way, productivism must gradually abolish itself in favour of post-productivism.

These considerations also relate to the second assumption of the trilemma, that concerning employment growth. If we need much broader ideas of wealth, then we may also need a much broader notion of what is and is not valuable work and an acceptance that unwaged activity may often be preferable to employment. As noted in the last chapter, if it can be demonstrated that unwaged work contributes to sustainability more than its employment-based equivalent – by being more local, involving more self-reliance and less orientation to profit, for instance – then we can no longer afford to devalue it as most productivists continue to do, e.g. recall the dichotomy between employment/activity and non-employment/passivity that Huber and Stephens expressed in Chapter 4. Employment growth is essential *only if* 'the active' are interpreted as subsidising 'the passive', since the passive would otherwise be without purchasing power (income). But if this distinction is too crude, then what we need is a kaleidoscope of social activity that contributes to reproductivity, a *mutual service society* of both waged and unwaged service provision which operates on the basis of diverse reciprocity.

On one level this is a now-familiar call for an expansion in the 'Third Sector' or 'social economy'; yet remember that almost everyone supports

the Third Sector and almost everyone disagrees about its practical implications (cf. Mertens, 1999). For conservatives, it is frequently an alternative to state provision (Green, 1993), while for new social democrats it
complements state provision in the form of not-for-profit associations and
faith-based organisations offering welfare services (Jordan, 2001). For
post-productivists, it implies an expansion in land trusts (and ecotaxation), welfare associations, communal self-management, democratic social
investment funds, stakeholder firms, basic and participation incomes,
informal exchange systems (whether based on currency or time) and local
banking (Offe and Heinze, 1992; Offe, 1996: Ch. 7; Douthwaite, 1996;
Benello *et al.*, 1997). What this Third Sector would do is capture and
harness the wealth that we already create for ourselves, and upon which
productivism already depends, directing it in more socially reproductive
ways (Jordan and Travers, 1998).

   None of this is to deny the difficulties that social democracy faces. In
fact the post-industrial trilemma actually *underestimates* the obstacles
ahead because, by focusing upon budgetary constraints, it neglects not
only environmental constraints but also the familial constraints that Dean
draws attention to (Dean, 2002). Yet the characterisation of our future
as one of permanent austerity does not capture every aspect of our condition, since productivists also underestimate the natural and social
resources to which we have access and which can be re-engineered to
meet these constraints if we can break free of simplistic notions of growth
and affluence. It may well be that post-productivist welfare would require
an increase in the *absolute* amount of wealth dedicated to common goods,
yet this increase may actually represent a *relative decrease* as a percentage
of the total stock of available wealth compared to existing social expenditure levels.[3]

Concluding remarks

Tying up the loose ends of this and the previous chapter leaves us with
three points to make.

   First, productivist social democrats will continue to appeal to *realpolitik* by observing that post-productivism in one country, or even several,
is far from being a realistic option, given the shift towards global free trade
in the 1980s and 1990s. Path dependency implies that enough space exists
for variations around the productivist model, but not for an ideal that
appears to violate international constraints. Even *if* Nordic countries are
poised at the brink of post-productivism, international constraints ensure
that at the brink is where they will remain.

   This objection is well taken and because post-productivism recommends the greater localisation of economic activity, such localisation is

unlikely to occur on any worthwhile scale unless the national and inter-national structures are in place to facilitate it. Yet this dualism is not some-thing to which the Green, anti-corporate and women's movements are oblivious (Cohen and Rai, 2000; Houtart and Polet, 2001; Rowbotham and Linkogle, 2001) and in fact the campaign for alternative forms of globali-sation operates with a much more sophisticated vision of local/global interactions than the apologists for global free trade will ever achieve. Therefore, productivist social democrats have to decide whether they are on the side of the free traders or the fair traders. If the former, then how are they to take account of the familial and environmental constraints that we have discussed above? If the latter, then why not argue for more local production, trade and consumption, as post-productivists recommend? In short, because international constraints are an omnipresent feature of any political strategy, then productivists have to make a *moral* case for the superiority of one type of international order over another. *Realpolitik* is no more than a refuge for the lazy.

Second, Chapters 4 and 5 have hinted more than once at the limitations of the concept of decommodification if this implies 'freedom from the market', since such freedom is only ever partial and highly conditional, even in terms of health and education systems.[4] Huber and Stephens are correct to point out that in practice decommodification refers to 'active participation in the labour market' and so implies a contributive form of autonomy and satisfaction that social democracies have come closest to embodying: freedom *within* rather than freedom *from*. However, although a complete freedom from market exchange is unrealistic, the more impor-tant questions are 'what kind of market?' and 'what kind of informal activity, are possible?' Post-productivism addresses itself to both of these questions, implying markets that are geared towards reproductive value and activities outside the formal economy that are similarly concerned. In short, the aim of radical politics should not be decommodification *per se*, but the post-productivist versions of both commodification and decom-modification. This idea is partly captured by Room's (2000) redefinition of decommodification as self-development, where creativity, learning, self-actualisation and *critical* participation are regarded as much more important than at present. Room offers this as an alternative to the standard notion of decommodification for consumption, where Esping-Andersen and his intellectual descendants set out to measure the extent to which living standards are maintained during periods of labour market absence.

Yet although Room's variables are more subtle and varied than those usually run through the statistical cruncher, he too remains with an employment-centred paradigm that valorises human and social capital. To be fair, Room does so to operationalise self-development and it has to be conceded that, by relegating the kind of variables that render productivist societies quantifiable, post-productivist societies would be difficult to measure and so could make thousands of social scientists unemployed (I suspect I've just lost half my audience). Fortunately, those social scientists would not find themselves trapped between the pincers of employment and non-employment, for the rationale of post-productivism is not that it frees us from 'the market', but that it multiplies the number of social spaces within which meaningful social interaction and exchange can take place. Therefore post-productivism is not an alternative to decommodification, but it *is* an alternative to the productivism that collapses decommodification back into the employment society where our primary role as citizens is to earn, shop, save and pretty much shut up.

Finally, I have associated post-productivism strongly with social democracy. But does this mean that conservative societies cannot provide a launch pad to post-productivism? If so, this would imply that the only route to post-productivism is through social democracy and how realistic does that make post-productivism in anything shorter than the very long term?

However, the answer is 'no', social democracy is not the only launch pad and it *is* possible to envisage conservative and corporatist variants of post-productivism. The former would perhaps resemble a situation where reproductive values are attended to through an extreme form of social stratification, i.e. ecological and emotional conditions depending upon heavy doses of inequality, coercion and moral conditioning. The corporatist version would be more solidaristic, but might still make reproductivity depend upon a strict distribution of fixed roles across a conditional, hierarchical and familialist set of social relations. In short, just as there are free-market, corporatist and social democratic versions of productivism, so there could be free-market, corporatist and social democratic versions of post-productivism.

Yet just as social democracy is the preferable version of the former, so it is the preferable version of the latter given its core commitment to egalitarian universalism. Therefore, and especially within conservative contexts, productivist and post-productivist social democrats need to do what they usually do already: make common cause in favour of universalism, distributive justice and social citizenship. The dispute about the relative merits of the productivist and post-productivist models cannot be deferred forever, obviously, and clearly affects the counter-hegemonic strategies adopted in nations where social democracy does not dominate. Nevertheless, such compromises are possible and the faultine in radical politics can be overcome and has been on numerous occasions. To conclude, post-productivists and traditional social democrats have more to gain from one another than they have to gain from alliances with others:

social democracy needs post-productivism, and vice versa. Such is the premise of this book.

Notes

1 Though some of these economic reasons may have been stronger in the past.
2 I am not intending to analyse the concept of patriarchy. I assume that patriarchy and productivism are not the same – indeed, wage-earner feminism insists otherwise – but that they *are* mutually reinforcing. So although there is no logical contradiction in the idea of non-patriarchal productivism, it is unlikely ever to emerge for the reason about to be given.
3 However, I offer this assertion tentatively and it is another hypothesis that cannot be demonstrated theoretically and so awaits empirical proof or disproof.
4 I specify 'limitations' because my intention is not to reject commodification either as a concept or an indicator (and recall that we made use of it in Chapter 3), but simply to observe that it has to date been caught within the productivist discourse that I have now spent more than a chapter challenging.

6

A model of ecowelfare

Post-productivism is therefore opposed to the social dominance of waged work, as this involves neglecting the reproductive value of emotional and ecological labour. As such, productivism has begun to reach the limits of itself because of its increasing inability to reproduce its own conditions. Like a dying star, productivism survives by consuming the waste that it has produced, it absorbs the consequences of too little care and too little sustainability by attempting to convert them into further sources of productivity. But these waste products are no substitutes for a proper ethics of care and sustainability, ethics that guide us beyond the employment society of endless GDP growth and endless productivity, so that this process cannot last indefinitely. Productivism does not necessarily reach a crisis – there is nothing historically inevitable about post-productivism – but it does implode into a cycle where productivist solutions are more and more ephemeral, re-inverting into further social problems at an ever-accelerating rate. It is the disease that purports to be the cure.

So, over the last couple of chapters I have stressed the importance of care work and sustainability, on the basis that these continue to be underemphasised by social democrats, old as well as new. In addition to distributive justice, these are the philosophical foundations of an ecowelfare politics, of a post-productivist social democracy. We have already addressed the main features of distributive justice in Chapter 2 and so our task here, in the following two sections, is to give an account of care and sustainability. I will then provide a simple model of ecowelfare and explore the main points of creation and tension between its three principal components.

Recognition and care

For reasons that will become clear, I want to treat care not in isolation, but in relation to the principle of recognition (cf. Daly, 2002: 263). Recognition has become an important and controversial topic in recent years and may represent the single most important contribution that postmodernism, post-structuralism and the 'cultural turn' have made to radical politics. However, my argument will be that recognition is incomplete without reference to distributive justice and to an ethic of care. In turn, the deficits of this ethic can be repaired by relating it to that of recognition.

I first want to dispense with those who would either replace distributive justice with recognition or at least subvert the former to the latter. This is the position of Iris Young (1990) and Alex Honneth (2001) for instance.[1] Young (1990: 15–16) wants to displace the distributive paradigm on the grounds that it is concerned with the distribution of material goods and social positions and so is too inert to be extended to social goods that are non-material and culturally dynamic. Honneth (2001: 53–4) insists that both recognition and distributive justice derive from the demand for social esteem so that, for instance, unemployment represents the denial of social esteem, because the unemployed person is left less able to engage in social cooperation than before.

The problem with Young's formulation is that although she is correct to cite potential problems with the distributive paradigm – the insensitivity of its abstract universalism to particularity – she then wants to shift paradigms altogether without considering the possibility of resiting distribution upon a more sophisticated universalism. So, although Young acknowledges the importance of distribution, by abandoning universalism altogether she leaves herself unable to reconcile distribution with difference and so continues to prefer the latter.

The problem with Honneth is that although unemployment may deprive an individual of self-esteem, this is a consequence of unemployment and *not the motivating factor*. Employers do not issue redundancies in order to reduce self-esteem, but as a response to market imperatives. Contrast that action with the racist joke. Of course, such instances may overlap, as when the employer makes only his black employees redundant, but although distributive injustice can take a cultural form, this does not mean that culture reaches 'all the way down' the system of production. Honneth might reply that such capitalist acts derive ultimately from the impulse to gain power over others by 'misrecognising' their moral worth, i.e. conflict within capitalism involves struggles for recognition rather than, as for Marx, the recognition of (economic) struggle (Honneth, 1995: 145–51). But by giving such weight to recognition, Honneth seems to propose that as recognition implies justice so injustice must imply misrecognition. Yet although this will often be the case (see below), this does not mean that injustice is no more than a form of misrecognition (*A* may imply *B* but *B* may imply both *A* and *not-A*) and so Honneth neglects the possibility that we can have injustice even where we have recognition.

This is precisely what is at stake in arguments about capitalism. Does recognition require (a) the equalisation of resource ownership, (b) equal opportunity for ownership or (c) an opportunity (however remote) for ownership? Because each may imply a recognition of equal worth, depending upon your social premises, adjudicating between them requires a theory of justice that cannot be reduced to 'moral feelings of indignation'.[2]

But if a politics of recognition is not enough, then should we be satisfied with a politics of distribution? Brian Barry (2001) has launched a wide-ranging attack on the political theorists who champion multiculturalism, minority rights, difference and recognition, accusing them of fashionable incoherence at worst or, at best, of saying nothing that cannot be accommodated within a philosophy of egalitarian liberalism. Barry's is an effective attack against those who would either abandon liberalism or else substantially reconstitute it around a differential politics of identity. At the extreme, this leads to a social morality of group separatism that was effectively satirised by Lukes (1995) and which Rorty (1998) and Klein (2000) condemn as having sent the American Left down the blind alley of political (or, more properly, 'cultural') correctness. The problem is that Barry tends to conflate these positions (anti-liberal multiculturalism and liberal multiculturalism) with a third that we can term 'multicultural liberalism'. His critique is therefore at its weakest when it is rejecting those who extol this third position.

For instance, Barry (2001: 138) presents Kymlicka as believing that 'self-governing national minorities should not be constrained by measures imposed by a liberal state to prevent violations of liberty and equality', in the course of outlining a liberal theory of group rights that substantially replicates that offered by Kymlicka (1995) himself.[3] Similarly, Nancy Fraser is condemned for imagining that homosexuals need anything more than 'equal legal rights' (Barry, 2001: 274–9), a kind of don't-frighten-the-horses argument that neglects the varied reasons why the walls of gay and lesbian prejudice are gradually falling. I do not want to pick a fight with Barry, since he offers many ideas that are themselves consistent with a multicultural liberalism. Nevertheless, he often manages to simply invert the simplicities that he otherwise condemns in multiculturalism; as when, for example, he equates cultural identity with expensive tastes, or when he treats preferences as if they exist in a socio-cultural vacuum, or when universalism is presented as having to make no concessions to group differences (Barry, 2001: 34–5, 65, 114).

It is perhaps Fraser who therefore has come closest to outlining a liberalism that is both multicultural and distributive (1997, 2000; Fraser and Honneth, 2001; cf. Okin, 1989). Fraser (2001) notes how distributive justice and recognition are usually treated as incompatible, because the former is regarded as a question of 'the right' (Kant's notion of universal rules) and the latter as a question of 'the good' (the *Sittlichkeit* or ethical judgement that Hegel attributed to the embedded self). But Fraser's argument is that recognition, too, involves justice claims so that it can rescued from an identity politics which, in valorising group identity, everywhere risks a repressive and non-material communitarianism. Instead, recognition implies social status and participation on a par with others and is therefore opposed to the 'misrecognition' that is generated through institutional exclusion and forms of subordination. Challenging misrecognition therefore means ensuring a 'parity of participation' by distributing material resources in such a way that economic structures are just and through an equal respect being accorded to all social participants. Fraser observes that a certain pragmatism is required in judging who does and does not warrant recognition and whether recognition should imply universalistic or particularistic strategies. It is *not* the case that all groups deserve equal recognition. For instance, by denying participative parity to others, racist groups could be said to exclude themselves from equal social participation. Equal respect should therefore be accorded to all those who would not deny participative parity to others. In short, by elaborating upon a philosophy of right, Fraser offers a liberalism that is multicultural, without according equal value to all groups indiscriminately, and which can also encompass the economic, non-cultural dimensions of distributive justice. She steers a course between those who would either subvert distribution to recognition (Honneth), i.e. the economic into the cultural, or those who would collapse recognition into distribution (Barry), i.e. the cultural into the economic.

While agreeing substantially with Fraser, I would point to several potential weaknesses in her argument. First, to acknowledge that recognition involves justice claims does not commit us to the view that justice claims are *all* it involves. For instance, in a brief discussion of environmentalism, Fraser argues that the dispute between ecologists and anti-ecologists can be resolved with reference to the needs of future generations, needs of which only a Kantian, deontological approach can conceptualise. But, as I will argue in Chapter 7, although deontology is the most useful starting point for discussing future generations, any such discussion has to take account of the contingencies of the present and near future. Our conception of future generations will alter, depending upon whether ecological catastrophe is assessed as being 50 years away or 500 years. Therefore, although there are some future generations whose interests we should recognise, there are others (presumably in the more distant future) to whom we should be fairly indifferent. Yet this 'recognition' is such an integral part of the deontological equation that it cannot be determined by that equation itself.

So the second potential weakness is that although Fraser makes room for pragmatic judgement, she perhaps underestimates the role that such judgement will have to play. Participative parity is an important benchmark but, unless we are to restrict our notions of 'participation' and 'parity' to some kind of all-purpose universalistic denominator, then contextual contingencies again become important. In the ecological example, there may be some future generations to whom we should be paternalistically accountable, but who cannot be said to enjoy parity with more immediate generations. Finally, Fraser (2001: 36–7) acknowledges that it may be necessary to turn to *Sittlichkeit* but, she insists, not until deontological reasoning has been exhausted. However, if the above criticisms are valid then the 'turn' cannot be delayed for very long, which is another way of saying that deontology cannot *be* exhausted without contextual judgement entering into it as an equative factor. Fraser's account of reasoning (deontology then *Sittlichkeit*) is too linear and dichotomous.

So although Fraser is correct to root both distribution and recognition in the 'right', we also have to make greater room than she allows for practical judgement (Bauman, 2001: Ch. 6). This practical judgement is what I here term 'care', defined as a means of negotiating between abstract justice claims and context-sensitivity. I am not going to spend much time defining care as this is covered thoroughly in the literature referenced below (also Kymlicka, 2002: 398–420) – see also the discussion of New Labour and care work in Chapter 2.[4] In essence, though, care involves the following key features.

Care implies *interdependency*, i.e. an alternative to the independence/dependence distinction that infects social policy with all it implies for those not perceived as being willing to be productive by labouring for another in the formal economy. Interdependency implies a relational, dialogical concept of the self in contrast to the possessive self that pervades both economic and political markets. It refers to the solidaristic lifeworld which is our ultimate source of well-being. Care is therefore an expression of, and a means of, nurturing the webs that we weave around and through one another, often without knowing it; interdependency returning endlessly to itself in a loop we call society. Care is also an *other-directed practice*, in that both the giving and the receiving of care are gifts. Care cannot take place without action (whether in speech or gesture) directed towards others, yet because of the interdependency of which the self is made, 'gifting' should not be confused with 'giving'. Receiving is as much an act of gifting as is giving: to gift is to give by receiving and receive by giving. Love is the most perfect example of gifting in that the acceptance of another is a means of nourishing the other.[5] Care is therefore not the same as charity. For whereas charity is unidirectional at best (or enlightened self-interest, at worst), gifting is multidirectional; charity fragments the self that gives from the self that receives, in line with Protestant individualism, where gifting unites the receiving and giving selves as an interdependent bond. Care is directed towards *needs*. While preferences are expressed as bargains and satisfied through exchange, i.e. a trade that satisfies both partners by confirming their separateness, needs are expressed as calls that can only be satisfied through interchange, the contraction of separation. Preference items are things to be ingested where need items are emotional harbours into which we can moor: the former *takes in*, the latter *takes itself to*. The calls of the needy are answered not to augment the needed, but so that it and the needy can mutually belong. That even our needs are so often institutionalised as demands, claims and entitlements is a sign of how far our moral cultures have lost themselves within productivist mazes. Finally, care implies *attentiveness*, meaning an empathy for multiple perspectives and sympathy towards interdependent others. It is an openness to all voices, especially those that normally go unheard, and a willingness to respond. The responsibilities of care are not primarily reciprocal, they are not triggered by an equivalent stimulus and do not take the form of exchange for visible, productive effort. First and foremost, responsibility involves listening for sounds of the invisible, the quiet screams of the vulnerable.

But if this is what care *is* then how is care to *proceed*? It is here that we part company with those who would have care proceed either religiously or conservatively through the world, as if care is too fragile to sustain categories and boundaries. The problem is that for every Simone Weil (1987) there are thousands for whom pain and suffering is to be welcomed either as a opportunity to share in divine grace or as an opportunity to demonstrate, through charity, the ultimate benevolence of capitalist inequality. Care must therefore proceed *politically*. Although the reservoirs of care may be infinite because, as imperfect social beings, we cannot draw from those wells quickly or simultaneously then caring is not a costless activity. Political conceptions of justice are therefore needed as guidance to how and why those costs should be borne.

We can first dispense with those who would exclude care from considerations of justice. Jaggar (1983), for instance, says that in order to adjudicate between different and competing interests we need a degree of objectivity and rationality that a care ethic, immersed as it is in the contingencies of particularity, cannot supply. In anything less than a world of harmonious interests a care ethic cannot suffice. But this runs up against an objection similar to that noted against Fraser, above: admitting that care cannot *substitute* for the justice perspective is not the same thing as *excluding* care from that perspective altogether. Imagining that the necessity of exclusion follows from the impossibility of substitution risks neglecting the perfectly legitimate features of adjudication that a purely rationalistic approach may overlook.

We should also dispense with those who would separate care and justice out into separate moral epistemologies and/or gendered ontologies (Elshtain, 1981; Gilligan, 1982). Here, the problem consists in recontextualising the elements that have been so sharply divided out. If care and justice co-exist in parallel epistemological worlds, then how are we to travel consistently and effectively between those worlds? One solution is to propose that the dividing lines are gendered: care is what women do best in the private sphere and justice is what men do best in the public. Feminist politics should then try to achieve parity between male breadwinners and female caregivers (Fraser, 1997: 55–9). But apart from the latent contradictions within this position – how can parity ever be achieved if our epistemologies are so gendered? – its coherence depends upon sacrificing considerable elements of social identity; to put it simply, women are called upon to suppress their need for public participation and men are called upon to suppress their need for caregiving and receiving. Such parity would be a perverse reflection of existing inequality.

The best recent work on care therefore attempts to bring care and justice more closely together. Take the following examples. Tronto (1993: 166–75) insists that care and justice should not be separated out into what she calls 'false dichotomies', as a justice perspective reveals the many problems that an exclusivist care ethic would involve. For Sevenhuijsen (1998: 59) care and justice are extensions of one another. Meyers (1998: 143) regards a care/justice distinction as antithetical to feminist politics and political theory. Noddings (2002: 22) insists that 'care supplies the basic good in which the sense of justice is grounded'.

Yet having reached this point the above authors are still neglecting an important aspect of care. Tronto (1993: 153) writes that, '. . . any attempt to posit a universal moral theory of care would be inadequate . . . If all we can do is to determine universal principles about the need for care, then we will not be able to understand how well care is accomplished in the process of realising it.' Yet this stance is confusing. Tronto begins by stating that the attempt to posit a universal theory would be inadequate, but then immediately proceeds to acknowledge that although the attempt *could* succeed, the actual realisation of care is not the same as its theoretical formulation as a set of universal principles. But although it would be impossible to universalise each and every aspect of care, precisely because life is too messy and chaotic, to be both motivated and assessed, actions must be referred back to a universalist background in order to negotiate a way through the vagaries that are used to justify a care ethic in the first place. Should I first help the driver or the pedestrian when the latter has been more badly injured in an accident, but had stumbled out of a pub obviously drunk? Such dilemmas cannot be decided in some kind of court of moral universalism, but because when we act we act *with* principles, rather than leaving them behind, it is best to be clear about what a universalist reasoning reveals those principles to be.

Sevenhuijsen (1998: 64–8) goes even further than Tronto, adopting what looks like an anti-universalist position or rather a post-structuralism that treats universalism only ever as an ephemeral construction which is glimpsed occasionally through the storms of dialogical contestation (Butler *et al.*, 2000). The problem here is that, in abandoning the 'liberal distributive paradigm', Sevenhuijsen leaves herself making a distinction between power and domination without any real explanation of where the distinction lies, without an account of why domination is non-distributive and without an exploration of anti-universalists' inability to either supplant or properly assimilate universalism (Fitzpatrick, 2002b). In order to avoid an overhasty marriage of care and justice, Sevenhuijsen risks an overhasty divorce that collapses back into the epistemological dichotomies that I criticised above.

Meyers (1998: 147) comes closer to explaining what a non-distributive form of domination means: it consists of some depriving others of the power that comes through interdependent relations. But, as above, what this depends upon is a separation of principles from practices and an insistence that morality involves sympathy for the disadvantaged (Meyers, 1998: 166–8). This is fine if we possess an acute moral sense of desert and disadvantage; the problem is when we remember that our moral sense is tutored in societies of conflicting needs, demands and interests for which an indiscriminate, all-embracing sympathy, cut adrift from principled frames of reference, is likely to be inadequate. Meyers attempts to address such objections by discussing the teaching of moral sympathy in schools, but does not explain why Professor Hume would be less biased in this respect than Professor Kant.

Finally, Noddings (2002: 24–31) regards caring for as the primary, natural state from which justice (caring about) derives and upon which it is dependent for its efficacy. She insists that to try and base justice upon rationalist foundations, as Rawls does, is to search for laws that do not exist. Natural care (affection, inclination) precedes justice claims, though natural care requires cultivation in families and schools, i.e. it is a virtuous disposition rather than a biological essentialism.

Noddings is correct to some extent, as the problem of defining justice and erecting just systems is only a problem for those who are virtuous enough to recognise the pull of justice in the first place. The problem arises when Noddings attempts to relegate rationalism to a subservient role. A social ethic of care, she says, revolves around the psychological instinct to 'stand with one's own', at which point a theory of justice is needed to ensure that this instinct does not work to the detriment of others. The trouble with this is that if moral boundaries are first drawn through psychological instinct, then any subsequent theory of justice is likely to reflect this bias and so may provide inadequate recognition of what is and is not harmful. Noddings allows for the possibility of justice tempering care (cultivation), but not of challenging it. Basing care upon 'neighbourly affectation' is to assume that the identification of one's neighbours is unproblematic, yet this assumption is dangerously myopic. Justice may sometimes need to work *with* the grain of psychological instinct and sometimes *against* it; justice may sometimes follow the lead of care but, when the care instinct proves to be parochial and prejudiced, it may also need to precede it. In short, what Noddings excludes is the possibility of an ethic of grounded universalism, an ethic of both justice and care that *can* identify moral laws based upon considerations of luck, disadvantage, responsibility and domination.

What the above theorists are doing then is either ignoring or downgrading a universalistic ethic of care, as if care is too fragile to cross the universalism-particularism borders. So whereas Fraser delays for too long the turn towards context, pragmatism and *Sittlichkeit*, for those such as Tronto the turn cannot come quickly enough. Therefore what is being missed here is an ethic of recognition and care that while grounded in a universal frame of reference is also sensitive to particularism. Not a universalism and *then* recognition/care – as Tronto (1993: 148) seems to imagine in her quip about universalists treating care as a 'moral fill-in' – but recognition/care that is simultaneously universal and particular. Fraser (1997: 59–62) is hinting at this kind of move in her ongoing work on the 'universal caregiver model' and, while bearing the above criticisms of her in mind, it is this which may represent the best platform for future reflection.

For the sake of convenience, I propose to group recognition and care under the heading of 'attention'. Attention implies 'attending to', that is, we have a responsibility to recognise the diversity and difference out of which one's own identity is shaped; it also implies 'being attentive' or caring for the damage that is an ineluctable part of social and emotional relationships; finally, it also possesses a locutionary force (as in 'stand to attention!') that implies a systematic approach to justice and care, which avoids treating all groups or all care claims as being of equal moral worth.

Sustainability[6]

The key principle associated with environmentalism is that of sustainability though, like any key concept, this migrates around the political spectrum, reappearing in a number of ideological guises. This means that like its counterparts – 'equality', 'liberty', etc. – sustainability is overused to the point where it has become less rather than more precise. In its most famous definition, sustainability implies meeting '. . . the needs of the present without compromising the ability of future generations to meet theirs' (Brundtland Commission, 1987: 8), yet this apparently simple definition is contested and contestable. What do we mean by 'needs', 'the present', 'compromising', 'ability' and 'future generations'? The many possible answers to this and to numerous other questions are due to the sheer diversity of environmentalism.

Essentially, environmentalists identify a disjunction between what we demand of the world and what the world is capable of supplying. If the demands we make are infinite, yet the resources upon which we can real-istically draw are finite, then ours is an unsustainable existence. Sustain-ability therefore refers to the process of reducing human demands and/or increasing resources, so that that disjunction is reduced.

Yet how can demands and resources be made to conjoin? This is where the controversies really begin to kick in (Dobson, 1998). One way is to expand the stock of resources, perhaps by replacing renewable resources, by substituting for non-renewable ones and by searching for technologi-cal solutions to the problems of depletion and pollution (Weizsacker *et al.*, 1998). Let us call this approach one of 'weak sustainability'. A second way is to revise the demands that we make on the world so that, for instance, we consume far less than we do at present. So, rather than adapting the world to suit ourselves, we adapt ourselves to meet the finitude of nature. Let us call this approach one of 'strong sustainability'. A final way is to navigate somehow between those two approaches; call this 'moderate sustainability'.

Now I assume it is uncontroversial to state that since the Rio Confer-ence of 1992, governments have preferred the 'weak' version of sustain-ability and have struggled to operationalise even this, the least ambitious of the three objectives just sketched. It would be surprising had weak sustainability *not* been the priority since sustainability is a collective action problem that both governments and electorates are notoriously slow both to recognise and to address. Policy-makers have thought it best to work from within the existing institutional forms of market and state and so the emphasis, to put it simplistically, has been upon changing the world, i.e. making resources go further, rather than changing society (Mol and Sonnenfeld, 2000). This form of 'ecological modernisation', an approach based upon the regulated market, has prevailed even in social democra-cies (see Chapter 5) with the insistence that the economy can be Greened without challenging its fundamental precepts. What is more surprising is the general lack of progress that has been made towards even weak sustainability. To some extent this has been due to the obstinacy of the USA yet, according to many Greens, it is also due to the inadequacies of ecological modernisation and the modesty of the weak sustainability at which it has aimed. The World Summit in Johannesburg in September 2002 is a useful illustration of this point. Corporations dominated the agenda, ensuring that voluntary guidelines rather than binding regulations would prevail. Poor countries were urged to make themselves more hospitable to inward investment, tying ecological policies into an agenda for privatisation and deregulation. Consequently, the summit concluded with only one major achievement (a sanitation target designed to halve the number of people without basic sanitation by 2015, the lack of which kills 1.3 million children a year) and a long list of failures.

If these criticisms are valid then what alternatives do Greens propose? As should be already clear, no simple answer to this question can be given since there are as many schools of Green thought as there are of socialist, libertarian, feminist thought, etc. Nevertheless, we might with only some distortion group those various schools under the headings already mentioned, the disagreement being fundamentally one of temporal scale and ecocentric range. For some, moderate sustainability should be the aim. This means working with a timeline of several centuries, where human and non-human interests are balanced in an ethic which is humanistic without being anthropocentric, and supporting a more radical adaptation of existing state and market practices. For others, this is still too modest an approach and we should be thinking across an even longer timeline that necessitates not piecemeal, techno-administrative reforms, but a root-and-branch restructuring of socioeconomic relations. Human interests are important (for all but a minority of anti-humanists), but only if those interests are recontextualised within a new biocentric ethic that does not centre around the human. This is the option of strong sustainability.

I am going to assume that moderate sustainability is the preferable path and a justification of this stance has been offered elsewhere (Fitzpatrick with Caldwell, 2001). For the time being, then, we assume that 'piecemeal, techno-administrative reforms' are appropriate even though this is regarded by the prevailing orthodoxy as too utopian and by the advocates of strong sustainability as not utopian enough. We do not have to spell out the full implications of moderate sustainability here, merely those that relate to social policy. So, what are the main critiques of state welfare made by the school of moderate sustainability and where might those critiques lead us?

Critiques and proposals[7]

First, environmentalists oppose social policies and welfare systems that are unsustainable and argue, as we have already seen in previous chapters, that indiscriminate economic growth is at the heart of all unsustainable practices. Despite this, economic growth is one of the logics of modern society whose value is usually unquestioned. It is the economic expression of the Enlightenment vision of historical progress and social development and, as such, almost all political philosophies have incorporated that productivist logic into themselves. Consequently, economic growth has become a form of meta-ideology, such that environmentalists often attract a kind of vitriol that productivist ideologies do not reserve for each other.

On these grounds, social policy leaves itself open to the criticism that existing welfare systems are *dependent* upon productivist practices that are ultimately unsustainable and that social policies *contribute* to unsustainability. The unifying factor here is the commitment to GDP growth that we have already explored. In essence, moderate sustainability therefore advocates a reconceptualisation of the economy and of economic activity that does not necessarily abandon the ethic of growth, etc., but certainly regards as inadequate the introduction of a few Green indicators into orthodox measurements and discourse.

This leads to the second Green critique of social policy, that it is too heavily based upon wage earning, whether as a source of material security, self-identity or social participation. Again, I do not want to revisit arguments already, made but there is one question that we have not addressed. Given the prevalence of productivist assumptions, is it not the case that environmentalists are arraying themselves against a series of opposing forces that they can never hope to defeat? Yet environmentalists are not quite as isolated as they first appear and it is precisely this post-productivist coalition that I am articulating in this chapter. Moderate sustainability does not argue for the abolition of employment, but for a recognition that security, identity and participation derive from a far wider range of sources and activities than the current orthodoxy admits. In this respect, ecologists side with those feminists who redefine flexibility towards employment, unpaid work and leisure away from restrictive masculinist conceptions of economic well-being. Indeed, since both ecologism and feminism argue for what I have here called 'reproductivity' (though the former stresses ecological labour and the latter emotional labour), then the scope for further convergence between these ideas is considerable. It is not the case that *all* forms of either feminism and environmentalism converge beneath the umbrella of post-productivist social democracy, since some will prefer productivist solutions and some will eschew social democracy altogether, but there are considerable numbers of those who challenge the employment-centred society (and includes many who might not identify themselves primarily with feminism or environmentalism, e.g. post-industrial socialists), so that the ecowelfare constituency may be very large indeed.

The third main critique made by environmentalists towards social policy concerns the degree of control and autonomy currently possessed by individuals. The allegation is that existing forms of social organisation and welfare provision underestimate the extent to which citizens can be self-organising and most Greens are dissatisfied with the degree of centralisation that currently prevails. The state is interpreted largely as too distant and impersonal a set of institutions. Representative democracy is thought to encourage a passive, consumerist attitude towards the common good, one that minimises the level of political participation and organises participation around party machines that are top heavy (Doherty and de Geus, 1996). The assumption is that although most people care about the environment, this concern has barely registered on the mainstream political agenda since the party system embodies a *status quo* that is immensely slow to respond to new developments. And even where the Greens have had some success (*Die Grunen*, for instance), they have had to compromise to such an extent that their ideological distinctiveness is eclipsed.

In terms of social policy, this state centralisation is thought to encourage the 'clientalisation' of welfare, where well-being is something we receive from other sources (experts, bureaucrats) and rarely something that people collectively generate for and through themselves (Fitzpatrick, 1998b, 2002d). The price of paternalism and basic needs satisfaction has been an overarching collectivism that allows little space for bottom-up provision. Greens therefore tend to support not an ethos of Victorian self-help or the decentralisation of the market, but a new welfare settlement where the state provides a universalistic framework of regulation, accountability and basic service provision, but where greater room is made for civic associations (Hirst, 1994), decentralised policy communities (Ellison, 1999) or cooperation circles (Offe, 1996) that would control funds and allow the 'recipients' of welfare to become their own 'producers' (Barry and Proops, 2000: 93–4). We return to this debate in Chapter 9. In short, Green social policies seem to require a greater degree of 'decentralised collectivism' and the emergence of a new welfare citizen.

These Green critiques of social policy – focusing upon growth, employment and centralisation – are not exhaustive, but they do capture the main criticisms of social policy implied by moderate sustainability. As to where we go from here, well, the need is to design a doctrine that represents an alternative to ecological modernisation that is not only desirable but also viable. Again, I do not want to use space replicating arguments that have been made elsewhere (Fitzpatrick with Caldwell, 2001), but it is worth saying something here about what I call 'ecological radicalisation' (see Fitzpatrick, 2003c).

If modernisation is essentially reformist, then radicalisation is more ambitious regarding both the means and ends of social transformation. This does not mean that radicalisation abandons reformism, but it does mean that reformism need not be limited to modest and relatively conservative objectives. Therefore, although radicalisation may overlap with the more ambitious aspects of ecological modernisation, it regards modernisation as the beginning rather than the end of social reorganisation (Christoff, 1996; van der Heijden, 1999). Consequently, rather than burying welfare reform within a broader concern for economic and public policies, social policy comes much more to the foreground. As noted in the introductory chapter, the job of this book does not involve offering a menu of policy reforms. Even so, given the fact that ecological radicalisation has to be both practical and ambitious, we perhaps need some idea of what it translates into. There are four key proposals worth mentioning in this context.

We have, first, already said something about BI in Chapter 2. A BI would be received by every man, women and child periodically (whether on a weekly, monthly or annual basis) as an *unconditional right of citizenship*, i.e. without reference to marital or employment status, employment history or intention to seek employment (van Parijs, 1992, 1995; Fitzpatrick, 1999a). What makes it appropriate for ecological radicalisation is the fact that BI represents the further evolution of the existing tax and benefit systems – and so of developments within that system towards tax credits – but also contains a potential for further social reorganisation, depending upon the form that a BI would take. In Chapter 7 I will suggest why a BI should be attached to the socialisation of substitutable resources and the reform of land taxation, an attachment that could satisfy both the Green and the socialist preference for the common ownership of, respectively, natural and social resources.

The second aspect of ecological radicalisation has already been touched upon in Chapter 5 and involves the demand that informal exchange and activity play a greater role in the ways in which we conceptualise and utilise reproductive value. One example of informal exchange that has attracted much attention in recent years is Local Exchange and Trading Systems (LETS). LETS are schemes to encourage people to exchange goods and services within their local communities (Williams, 2002). Each LETS is a non-profit-making network of local residents who trade goods and services with each other, using a local currency. The attraction of LETS for Greens is that local currencies encourage local trading and therefore place less pressure upon national and international infrastructures (J. Barry, 1999: 163–4). As with BI, then, the proposal that government facilitates much wider systems of informal exchange has one foot in present realities, since the informal 'economy' is considerably large already, and one foot in a future where work is no longer confused with employment.

This is also true of the third proposal consistent with ecological radicalisation: for systematic reductions in working time. The post-industrial Left are attracted to working-time reductions since, with more people in employment, the power of labour is enhanced (Gorz, 1989; Little, 1998). For Greens, the attraction lies in taking the emphasis away from paid work (although there is an additional requirement to ensure that the jobs which remain are made more ecologically friendly) and so in freeing up time for the wider range of activities which, as we noted in chapter 5, they regard as important for social and environmental well-being.

The final recommendation is for a greater reliance upon ecotaxation (Robertson, 2002). Although the principle of ecotaxes is now widely accepted, so long as their economic and social benefits can be demonstrated, Greens tend to go further than the current orthodoxy allows. This may or may not involve support for much higher levels of ecotaxation than presently exist but, perhaps more importantly, it involves a radical change in the *source* of taxation. Land is of key importance here. In a globalised era, many worry that the levels of taxation needed to maintain high levels of social expenditure are not going to be sustainable. One possible solution is to shift the burden of taxation towards land, with those who occupy the most and/or the wealthiest land having the heaviest liability; and because land does not move – although its value certainly alters – then tax avoidance becomes less of a problem, though some form of global agreement and coordination is still required.

To conclude, moderate sustainability goes beyond the weak sustainability that governments, with varying degrees of enthusiasm and success, have been trying to implement in recent years, but it falls short of the strong sustainability that many within the Green movement argue for. My assumption is that moderate sustainability is the best we can aim for in the near future. This does not foreclose the possibility of moving towards strong sustainability in the longer term, but is to insist that it is more realistic to slow down the rate of unsustainability, rather than to attempt a premature leap into an ecological ideal that may divert us from more immediate and threatening problems. Moderate sustainability then criticises existing welfare systems in terms of their dependency upon growth, employment and centralisation and recommends what I have called 'ecological radicalisation'. Essentially, ecological radicalisation involves the refusal to treat 'reformism' and 'radicalism' as irreconcilable and involves the search for present-day trends that bear a post-productivist potential that may go unrecognised by the productivist orthodoxy.

The ecowelfare triangle

We have now outlined the three components of ecosocial welfare and Figure 6.1 offers a simple model relating these together. I have made distributive justice, attention and sustainability the main nodes of this model, though a more elaborate one would give greater prominence to the various sub-nodes (equality of powers, etc.), multiplying the number of relations and directional flows accordingly. However, there is a reason, other than convenience, why I have plumped for simplicity.

One way to look at ecowelfare is from a considerable distance and do nothing more than recognise its main features: egalitarianism, multicultural liberalism, feminism and environmentalism. This bird's-eye view is helpful as a means of identifying the schools of thought that many have long considered necessary to the renewal of a radical politics, but it does skip over the details of debates with which I think we need to engage.

Figure 6.1 A model of ecosocial welfare

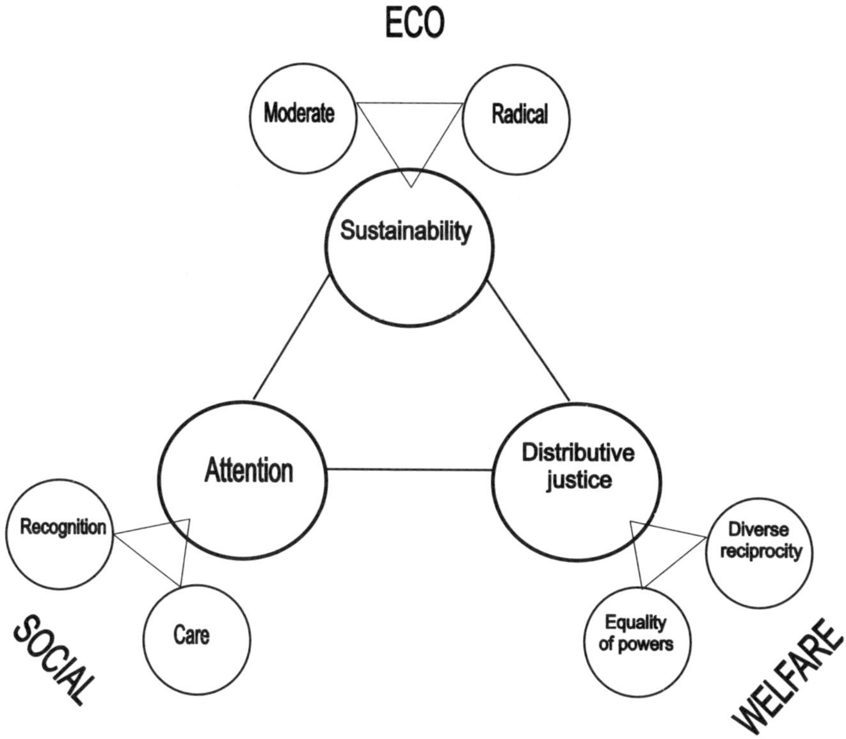

Alternatively, the arguments that have been presented in Chapters 2, 5 and 6 could be regarded as a take-it-or-leave-it proposal, as if disagreement with my account of recognition, or whatever, means that the whole structure is fatally flawed. This is to focus rather too much upon the details, though. Therefore, I want to offer a model that incorporates the specifics of my argument without alienating those who may disagree with certain of its features. Hopefully, Figure 6.1 does this, in that the relevance of the main nodes can be acknowledged even if some readers will prefer alternative accounts and descriptions of the sub-nodes. Obviously, those who stray too far from my position will either consider it to be too radical or else not radical enough (this being a common reaction to my conference papers!), but for others it will illustrate the broad church within which egalitarians, multiculturalists, liberals, feminists and environmentalists are congregating.

The analyses of the next three chapters therefore represent a means of applying this model to some of the key social questions we currently face, a way of working through where you and I may agree and disagree, rather than a comprehensive overview that could be interpreted as the last word, take it or leave it. Before we can proceed, though, I do need to flesh out the main connections of Figure 6.1 to set the scene for the following chapters.

Sustainability and attention

To what extent do the principles of sustainability and attention orbit around the same set of priorities and objectives? On one level the answer is simple. Unless we can guarantee levels of well-being similar to those we currently enjoy (and preferably higher) stretching into the foreseeable future, then recognition and care lose their force. This is not to claim that they become futile: just as there is value in caring for those who are terminally ill, so environmental catastrophe does not erase the force of moral obligations. However, such care work operates according to implicit assumptions of intergenerational continuity, where caring derives its value from the expectation that it stretches beyond the lifetimes of those who care and those who are cared for. But if the future is one of decline, then the moral injunction to attend to others is foreshortened and so less persuasive. This point is obviously simplistic as attention may well be a means of engendering the very sustainability upon which it depends for its moral suasion. As Chapter 5 sought to establish, care is a form of emotional labour that seeks to reproduce that which the productive economy cannot reproduce for itself and so may be thought of as a source of sustainability. Recognition, too, is a means of social preservation which is precisely why Barry (2001: 65) is opposed to the politics of recognition, arguing that either cultures will be preserved by those who identify with them or, if this is not the case, there is no point in maintaining them artificially – an argument that assumes what it seeks to prove, that cultures do not depend upon recognition.

In short, attention requires a timeline that reaches far beyond our lives and sustainability requires that we attend to each other more effectively than at present.

But this does not imply that these principles dovetail neatly. As the next chapter will make clear, there are temporal conflicts involved in any environmental ethic such that hard decisions have to be made about the allocation of resources. Recognition and care are not costless exercises, even if post-productivism revises our notions of what costs and benefits imply, and so there may be occasions when we need to sacrifice one principle in favour of another. I will spell out in Chapter 7 the rules that I think ought to govern us when such occasions arise and then in Chapter 8 we will address a specific aspect of the sustainability/attention debate. The point to be remembered here is that even were sustainability and attention to cohere 99 per cent of the time, there is still a residue that involves trade-offs and the kind of context-sensitive judgements that we discussed earlier in this chapter.

Sustainability and distributive justice

The same is true when we relate these two principles together, only more so. In fact, Chapter 7 will concern itself primarily with the vexed question of relating sustainability (or intergenerational justice) to distributive (or intragenerational) justice. Although I do not want to anticipate the specific arguments that are pursued there, the general conclusion is similar to that above: sustainability and distributive justice are consistent with one another to some extent – and to a greater extent than is normally recognised, in fact – but although this minimises the trade-offs that need to be made; those are not eliminated entirely.

Attention and distributive justice

As already indicated above, Fraser (1997, 2000) has established the extent to which these principles overlap without either being reducible to the other (though she discusses recognition rather than care in this context). Misrecognition will accompany maldistribution more often than not, since denying needed resources to others is a means of lowering their self-esteem and so of raising your comparative status. Similarly, the unfair distribution of resources is based upon the view that some possess less moral worth than others.[8] Recognition therefore requires fair distribution as it is counter-productive, and possibly hypocritical, to valorise a cultural identity without ensuring that the members of that group have a fair access to the very resources without which the group may be unable to maintain its character. It makes no sense to celebrate ethnic difference while denying jobs and decent incomes to the members of ethnic groups. Conversely, distributive justice requires a fair distribution of cultural resources. The black household that is middle class and relatively affluent is materially better off than the black household which is on the breadline, but may still be subject to racism and discrimination. That the poorer household will be subject to the double burden of material *and* cultural deprivation does not mean that its oppression is only one of material injustice; cultural injustice also matters.

Nevertheless, these principles are not going to conjoin perfectly on each and every occasion. In a society of infinite resources and resourcefulness, we might be able to solve each and every aspect of misrecognition and maldistribution, but this is not our society. Therefore, there are times when we may have to prefer recognition to distribution. For instance, when the prosperous black household is being racially abused by its poorer, white neighbour, then justice might demand resources being allocated to the black household, as its need is more immediate. Poverty may be a source of the white household's hostility, but because racism is not only an economic category, then it cannot be resolved with purely economic measures, e.g. by giving more money to the white household. Equally, there are times when we may prefer distribution to recognition. For instance, where white children from poor backgrounds are performing less well at school than Asian children from more affluent ones, then more resources should be targeted at correcting for those socioeconomic circumstances than at issues of cultural recognition, even if there is an additional need for the latter.

Fraser's point, then, is that although recognition and distributive justice will overlap more often than not, such that addressing the one means addressing the other, this will not always be the case. Where I part company with Fraser is in believing that the turn to *Sittlichkeit* must be made earlier than she imagines (see above). But this turn does not leave us in a moral darkness, as there are still ways in which we can negotiate a way through the various dilemmas carefully and systematically: namely, by bringing the relevant groups together in a political community of discourse and dialogue. In Chapter 9, then, I will say something about deliberative democracy and why it offers a means of dealing with the kind of complex issues that cannot be automatically read off from political principles.

Conclusion

Ecowelfare involves reference to the principles of distributive justice, attention and sustainability. In this chapter and in Chapter 2, I have outlined various theories which I think are needed to make sense of those principles, but hopefully without closing down any room for manoeuvre on the part of those who may disagree with various aspects of the relevant arguments. I have also suggested that while these principles push towards one another, there will be occasions where this is not so. But remember that there is nothing unusual about ecowelfare in this respect. Any liberally minded ideology is a broad church where, as in any church, members of the congregation often sing in different keys, a discordant harmony of those who nevertheless share similar visions and hopes.

Notes

1 Charles Taylor (1994) makes overtures in this direction but has not, to my knowledge, dealt with distributive justice at any length.

2 Honneth (1995: 165–6) does acknowledge that an ethic of recognition should not replace a theory of justice, but it is not yet clear how he is to reconcile the two without diluting his strong attachment to Hegelianism.

3 Which is not to claim that Kymlicka's account is unproblematic, merely that it is far more of a liberal account than Barry permits.

4 Note that although 'care' and 'caregiving' are obviously related the latter has been, and will continue to be, used in a more gender-specific sense than the former, i.e. to convey the (currently unfair) distribution of men and women across the public/private spheres.

5 Unfortunately, love also involves asking the loved one to share the damage that has been inflicted upon you by others and then unloving them when they do so. Love must damage itself to survive and just sometimes, by doing so, the self survives as well. We care for the damage we inflict on ourselves through others and so also for the damage we inflict on others by caring. If we did not care for each other, then we would have nothing and no-one to forgive.

6 For a longer account see Fitzpatrick and Cahill (2002a).

7 What follows will be fairly sketchy, as we have already anticipated many of these arguments in Chapter 5.

8 This is an argument similar to that made by Honneth (see above), but remember that our objection to Honneth was to his general neglect of the distributive paradigm.

7

The welfare of future generations

In Chapter 7 we examine one of the many possible links between sustainability and distributive justice (B. Barry, 1999). For instance, we could look at issues of international justice, i.e. between developed and developing worlds, or we could explore the extent to which the concept of justice is applicable to the non-human world. However, despite the relevance of those debates, the issues of sustainability and justice are thrown into sharper relief by addressing the following question: what does it mean to act with justice towards future generations and what might this imply for social policy?

The debate concerning future generations has generated a considerable literature in recent years, but by no means everyone is convinced that justice towards future generations makes sense. Of the sceptics, the most cogent recent defence has been provided by Beckerman and Pasek (2001: 14) who reduce their argument to a syllogism:

1   Future generations – of unborn people – cannot be said to have any rights,
2   any coherent theory of justice implies conferring rights on people, therefore
3   the interests of future generations cannot be protected or promoted within the framework of any theory of justice.

Beckerman and Pasek are not arguing that future generations should be ignored, merely that when we act with their interests in mind, we can only do so out of benevolence and not as a matter of justice and obligation. The problem with this view is that benevolence is a weak peg upon which to hang the interests of anybody, because it is easier than justice to rationalise away. Although it is certainly virtuous to act with charity, it may be equally virtuous to act without it on those occasions when we convince ourselves that charity would do more harm than good. A theory of justice is therefore needed to reveal such instances, and so to ground the virtues of character in more solid foundations than a virtue ethic can provide for itself, to distinguish between in/actions that do and those that do not truly promote the interests of others.

That at least is the premise of the following sections within which I offer the outline of a theory of intergenerational justice and explain what this theory might imply for welfare reform (Fitzpatrick, 2001b, 2001c). In the concluding section I then return to the arguments of Beckerman and Pasek to see whether we can successfully address their main points.

Future philosophies

A theory of intergenerational justice could be constructed from within a number of philosophical schools. Since the *laissez-faire* approach of libertarianism is alien to this book's stance, I will leave it to one side and concentrate upon utilitarian, contractualist and communitarian perspectives. Which of these is the most convincing?

Utilitarianism

The utilitarian approach has been sketched most brilliantly by Derek Parfit (1984: 377) who begins with what he calls the Non-Identity Problem (N-IP): 'If a choice between two social policies will affect the standard of living or the quality of life for about a century, it will affect the details of all the lives that, in our community, are later lived. As a result, some of those who later live will owe their existence to our choice of one of these two policies. After one or two centuries, this will be true of everyone in our community'. In other words, it is impossible for us to harm future generations. Imagine two policy options: policy R will give rise to Red people, while policy B will give rise to Blue people. If we choose policy R, will we be hurting anybody? According to the N-IP we will not. We cannot harm any Blue people, since they will now never exist, and we cannot harm our Red descendents because their existence is axiomatically preferable to the non-existence that would have resulted had we chosen policy B. Now think of a parallel scenario. Policy D leads to the depletion of natural resources and so to future generations whose lives are barely worth living; policy C leads to the conservation of resources and so to future generations whose well-being is comparable to our own. If the N-IP is correct, then we may as well choose policy D (because C requires undesirable short-term sacrifices) without worrying about the consequences. In short, if we cannot harm future generations, then we cannot act with injustice towards them and so cannot act with *justice* towards them either. No theory of intergenerational justice is therefore possible.

Parfit himself suspects that the N-IP can be overcome with reference to some objective standard of assessment. However, in searching for this standard Parfit (1984: 388) encounters the Repugnant Conclusion: 'For any possible population of at least ten billion people, all with a very high quality of life, there must be some much larger imaginable population whose existence, if other things are equal, would be better, even though its members have lives that are barely worth living.' Imagine two societies. In society *A*, ten billion people each possess 100 utility units each (or 1000 billion units in total); in society *Z*, 2000 billion people each possess 1 utility unit each (or 2000 billion units in total). On strictly utilitarian grounds we ought to prefer society *Z*, because 2000 billion units is larger than 1000 billion units, even though its inhabitants live lives of unimaginable suffering. Therefore, utilitarianism seems to demand the indefinite growth of future populations so long as total utility increases also. Few would regard this as desirable and yet Parfit insists that attempts to avoid the Repugnant Conclusion are inadequate (e.g. Boonin-Vail, 1996).

Let us consider two such attempts. First, perhaps we could adopt a principle of *average* rather than total utility. This would imply that we should only permit the human population to increase to the point where mean utility begins to peak, i.e. a point significantly less populated than society *Z*. Yet Parfit dismisses this escape route, as it would prevent us from adding to the population those individuals who, although they would have lives worth living, would reduce the overall average. Second, perhaps we could place a ceiling on the population's expansion on the grounds that, beyond a certain point, the value of additional utility diminishes at an ever-accelerating rate. Yet Parfit closes off this escape route also, by observing that if we devalue additional utility then we are logically compelled to devalue additional *disutility*, i.e. the equivalent of being increasingly untroubled at a society where there was more and more pain and suffering.

However, there is a third argument for avoiding the Repugnant Conclusion, one that questions the N-IP upon which it is based, but which Parfit himself cannot attack because of his utilitarian frame of reference. Carter (2001: 442–8) points out that the N-IP only applies at a holistic level that ignores more specific actions: '. . . even if I were able to affect the identity of every person in the distant future, it would not follow that I could not harm any of them. I could still harm a future person whose identity I determined as long as one of my actions made him or her worse off than he or she would otherwise have been – in other words, as long as that action was not one which determined his or her identity'. In short, acts of identity creation are not necessarily identical to acts of harm and so it *is* possible to harm those who we have brought into being, even if there is another possible world in which they would never have existed at all. What exists in the gap between acts of identity creation and acts of harm? Autonomy. And so how would we harm future generations? By reducing their capacity or willingness to act with autonomy and independence.

But by collapsing 'welfare' into 'utility' and, like all utilitarians, by downplaying the concept of autonomy, Parfit does not have recourse to this solution, suggesting that a utilitarian approach does not offer a convincing approach to the problem of future generations. If we take the objective of harm avoidance seriously, then our task cannot be measured by a utility index and we do not have to decide between an infinite range of future identities. For a utilitarian like Parfit, an infinite range of future identities is possible and therefore we cannot harm future generations. But if we recognise instead that we harm future generations by reducing their autonomy to levels that we ourselves would not accept, then the range of possible identities is not infinite, but is limited to those that *imply* self-determination. Therefore, environmentalists are right to suspect that we harm future generations by bequeathing to them an unsustainable environment that would reduce their powers of self-determination by diverting resources and energies away from autonomy-enhancing pursuits. Of course, future generations may use their autonomy to wreck the environment that we will (hopefully) bequeath. But this is a perpetual risk best overcome by principles of justice that it would be irrational and so unjust of future generations to ignore (see below).

If utilitarianism fails, then is there a better approach?

Contractualism

Rawls (1972: 284–93; 1999: 145–7; B. Barry, 1989: 197–201; Hooft, 1999; Langhelle, 2000) introduces into the original position an ignorance as to where the participants are in history, meaning that they have to determine a savings rate that every actual generation would find to be just. In effect, all future generations are represented in the original position and all can expect to gain through the 'just savings principle', with the exception of the first generation who shoulder the initial burden, but receive nothing in return. However, because each generation is assumed to care for its immediate descendants, the first generation, too, can be expected to accept the just savings principle. This means that the task of each generation is to realise the demands of liberal justice while contributing to an inter-generational process of accumulation that enables closer and closer approximations to the just society which is contracted to in the original position.

The notion of 'immediate descent' is crucial in actually determining the appropriate rate. Those in the original position must ask themselves how much it is reasonable to save for the next generation, based upon what they feel entitled to claim from the preceding generation. This parent/child model not only enables a fair rate of saving to be determined, but ensures that no generation can envy the stock of resources possessed by either its ancestors or its descendants. Consequently, although the members of the original position do not know where they are in time, they do know that they are contemporaries who have sentimental ties to successive generations. Basically, then, a contractualist theory of justice must take into account the least advantaged of every generation: 'Whereas the first principle of justice and the principle of fair opportunity limit the application of the difference principle within generations, the savings principle limits its scope between them. . . . Saving is achieved by accepting as a political judgement those policies designed to improve the standard of life of later generations of the least advantaged, thereby abstaining from the immediate gains which are available' (Rawls, 1972: 292–3). It means that duties are inter- as well as intragenerational and that we harm future generations if we bequeath to them conditions that we ourselves would not consent to in an original position.

By giving priority to liberty and rational determination, this approach takes harm avoidance seriously and so seems to overcome the problems inherent within Utilitarianism. There are two main problems with Rawls's account, however. First, it is arguably too ambitious in its stipulation that the participants in the original position may be located *anywhere* in time. To totally exclude the particulars of our temporal situations from considerations of justice would seem too abstract and formal an approach. Of course, Rawls then inserts a discount rate, but one which is far too stringent, extending across no more than two future generations. So the second problem is that the just savings principle is not ambitious enough, having the quality of a personal inheritance made through ties of sentiment rather than a true cross-generational scheme of accumulation. Therefore, Rawls's theory of intergenerational justice is both too abstract *and* too sentimental. Let us begin with the second problem.

Can we resolve this difficulty by (a) including all generations within the original position (so that the participants are not contemporaries), and (b) eliminating the sentimental motivation? The problem with (a) is that it runs up against a version of the N-IP. Do we include everyone who *will* ever live? Yet this presupposes an advanced knowledge of the policies and principles that we are to adopt when it is precisely those policies and principles that we are trying to formulate. But perhaps we can include in the original position everyone who *could* ever live. Yet how would it be meaningful to include in the original position anyone who is being called upon to possibly legislate themselves out of existence (Carter, 2001: 440)? Such participants may well prefer something resembling the Repugnant Conclusion as a necessary price of their continued existence. Therefore, critics have demanded that we fall back on (b). Brian Barry (1989) argues that Rawls's Humean influences must be discarded, as justice cannot be founded upon the sentimental ties that we have for our successors and Rawls (1993: 274) himself came to accept this. For Barry then, Rawls is formulating principles to which all generations should rationally agree, what we might call a theory of 'meta-generational justice'.

However, this still leaves the objection that Rawls is being too ambitious. I think we can address this problem by acknowledging that although it might be the case that justice cannot be founded *upon* sentiment, this does not mean passion and sentiment are irrelevant to considerations of justice (see Chapter 6). In short, we have yet to consider communitarian critiques of intergenerational justice.

Communitarianism

Avner de-Shalit (1995) has offered a communitarian account, one that essentially depends upon hypothesising the existence of a transgenerational community. If communities are spatial entities, then it seems absurd to deny that they are also temporal entities; and if communities are the most important source of identity and obligation, then the future must be an important source of identity and so a referent to which I bear obligations. As Dobson (1998: 105) points out, de-Shalit is here echoing O'Neill's (1993: 28–38) depiction of the transgenerational self. For although I, the being now in existence, cannot be harmed 50 years after my death, my reputation and my legacy *can* be damaged. Similarly, then, not only can the present generation harm future ones, but *future generations can harm us and we can harm long-dead generations*! Therefore, there may well be a loose reciprocity between generations that grounds the notion of intergenerational justice after all.

The problem here, though, lies in determining the criteria by which harm can be assessed. When past generations burned witches or initiated pogroms they no doubt genuinely believed that their legacy would benefit their descendants. Are we harming past generations by dissenting from such beliefs, therefore? To believe so is equivalent to believing that our ethical standards should be equivalent to theirs, which is nonsensical. Instead, it seems that although past generations can harm us (intentionally or otherwise), we cannot harm the past by choosing to betray their legacy. Therefore, although there is a transgenerational community that points into the future, there is none that points into the past; we can form a community with our descendants but they cannot form one with us, nor can we with our ancestors. We can harm the future, but the future cannot harm us.

It is at this point that the critics of intergenerational justice step in and say something like the following. Justice implies reciprocity and reciprocity is, of its very nature, a two-way process: if the future cannot harm us then we cannot harm it. Can this objection be met? I believe so. The essential question concerns who is being harmed. I have already argued that we harm the future if we do not bequeath to them an environment that is consistent with levels of autonomy that we ourselves would accept. But imagine that we do bequeath that environment and future generations use their autonomy to wreck it. Are we harmed by this? No, because we are no longer around to feel harm. But this does not mean that harm is not occurring. For if the future does wreck that environment, then they will be harming *their* descendants by undermining *their* autonomy by betraying not us but the principles of inter- or meta-generational justice that we are formulating. Similarly, if we suddenly decided to abolish free societies we would not be harming Immanuel Kant *et al.*, but we would be harming a future that would have to struggle to regain the autonomy that we chose to waste.

What this indicates is that although reciprocity is a two-way process, this process is not erased by time's arrow (B. Barry, 1999). We often help others without an expectation of either direct or indirect return, not as an act of benevolence (because we are nice people) but because it is the right thing to do (because we recognise the demands of justice, whatever the implications for ourselves). To claim (a) that *we* cannot harm the future implies (b) that we cannot have *been* harmed by the past and furthermore (c) that we have not been benefited by the past. It is to claim that justice cannot exist unless we can experience the reciprocal consequences of acting justly. But if (b) and (c) are patently false then (a) must be false also. Therefore, across the temporal dimension reciprocity may resemble what Ball (2001: 103–4) calls serial or 'punctuated reciprocity', where each generation recognises an obligation to act with justice towards its descendants according to the demands of inter- or meta-generational justice that it would be irrational to ignore.

This is one of the reasons why in Chapter 2, I was so concerned to challenge the simplistic 'rights imply responsibilities' chant of new social democrats. For, when applied to this debate, that insistence might imply that we have no obligations towards the future because they have no rights at the present time. This is the position of Beckerman and Pasek. But if what we are doing is formulating a theory of meta-generational justice, then this simplistic equation does not hold: rights may imply responsibilities, *but not necessarily on each and every occasion.* So, even though future generations are not around to make claims on our energy and resources, we might still have obligations towards them based upon a theory of justice to which all generations should rationally assent. Therefore, punctuated reciprocity is one facet of the kind of diverse reciprocity that I spend the latter part of Chapter 2 defending.

For Goodin (1985: 177–8) those obligations derive from the unilateral power that we hold over our descendants, their vulnerability in relation to ourselves. Unlike de-Shalit, however, Goodin allows sentimental ties to supplement rather than replace the contractarian approach. Once we remember that, for Rawls (1972: 50; 1993: 3–46), the original position is a site of 'reflective equilibrium', and political rather than metaphysical, then our concern for the vulnerable is permitted to creep beneath the veil of ignorance. So we find a middle way between the over- and underambitious sides of Rawls's just savings principle. The original position should not be located *anywhere* in time since, as I argued in Chapter 6, rational universalism must be context-sensitive (see below); but nor are its inhabitants concerned only with their offspring since although justice may make room for sentiment, it cannot be based *upon* sentiment.

In short, a convincing theory of intergenerational justice has to balance partiality and impartiality with reference to the particular (the established and imagined needs of the present and future, respectively) and the universal (the just savings principle). It is a contractualist theory tempered by elements of communitarianism and so derives from the kind of deontological reasoning that I defended in Chapter 6, a reasoning that makes room for a pragmatic turn towards context-sensitivity. And since, given the ecological constraints we now face, sustainability must now be placed at the heart of all such policies, then it follows that sustainability is the principal means of effecting justice across the generations.

Discount rates

However, if we are to have a clearer idea of what intergenerational justice means and implies, then we have to possess some idea of the relevant timescale, i.e. the temporal context to which our theory is sensitive.

Technically, discounting refers to the means by which we gradually devalue future costs and benefits against, respectively, present benefits and costs (Lind, 1982; Portney and Weyant, 1999). At one extreme, we can imagine a refusal to discount at all, so that the interests of people, say, a million years from now would mean as much to us as our interests – we will call this a discount rate of 0 per cent; at the other, we have a refusal to value the interests of any generation but our own–we will call this a discount rate of 10 per cent.[1] How are we to determine a discount rate which, lying between these extremes, is both practical and desirable? By and large, two answers have been given to this question.

First, there are those who favour a market discount rate. A benefit–cost analysis focuses upon the real rate of return on investment over a particular time horizon. What this implies is the use of real interest rates in calculating the discount rate and a 'private time preference' in which the time horizon is relatively short. The problem with this method is that the medium- to long-term future is discounted fairly heavily (Amsberg, 1995). For instance, let us imagine that an asteroid is passing close by which, during its next orbit in 200 years time, will hit Florida (Nordhaus, 1999: 148). If the damage is estimated at $2 trillion at today' prices, and if we apply a 7 per cent per year discount rate (a rate sanctioned by the US Government), then it is not worth us currently spending anything more than $3 million in trying to save Florida 200 years from now!

Therefore, a second method defines a social discount rate where equity and fairness are as important as efficiency. This 'social time preference' looks farther than the lifespan of individuals and so favours a lower discount rate. For example, public sector projects tend to apply a social rate because governments can borrow at lower interest rates than those offered to private sector investors and because the risks attached to the investment are lower. The problem with this method is that the calculation of the actual rate becomes more a matter of prescriptive guesswork regarding the desirable distribution of costs and benefits across different generations (Cowen and Parfit, 1992).

The debate over discounting returned with the growth of environmental economics in the 1990s. If we set a discount rate that is too high (profligacy), then we might not be able to create and maintain a sustainable ecosystem; if we set a rate that is too low (asceticism), then the present generation may be called upon to make sacrifices that are politically and culturally unrealistic. Is there an alternative? A complication in finding an alternative involves what we might call the 'savings paradox'. Since material well-being has improved throughout recorded history, it seems reasonable to assume that the future will be materially better off than the present. Therefore, saving for the future by reducing present expenditure will only increase the gross wealth of the future, at a cost to the present, and so undermines the rationale for saving; however, if we do not save for future sustainability by reducing present consumption, then although the future may be materially better off, it will have to spend a far higher proportion of its wealth on environmental protection, thus increasing the rationale for saving. Is there a way around the savings paradox that allows us to determine an appropriate discount rate?

Sustainable justice

The real problem with the paradox may be it operates with too narrow a conception of savings, investment and consumption. If these are conceived in terms of resource *depletion* then, because resources are ultimately finite, we are certainly left with a conflictual model of intergenerational relations: more burdens today means more benefits tomorrow, and vice versa (Schelling, 1995). Even if we assume a positive sum game, where the wealth of both the present and future can be simultaneously enhanced, any economy based upon resource depletion must make trade-offs between present and future needs; technological fixes and the like can postpone the trade-offs, but cannot avoid the conflictual model itself. In short, resource depletion gives rise to intergenerational conflict. But what if we base our environmental economics less upon depletion and more upon resource *transformation*? If what we consume are finite resources, then higher savings may well imply lower consumption, and vice versa; but if what we consume, i.e. enjoy as essential to our well-being, is the preservation of resources and the flourishing of the non-human then higher *savings* might well be a condition of higher *consumption*. So, the savings paradox is avoided by replacing a material with non-material conception of well-being (Tacconi and Bennett, 1995: 218), i.e. one that respects reproductive values (see Chapters 4 and 5). To see what this means let us return to our ascetics and profligates.

Ascetics favour a high–low approach, i.e. high savings plus a low discount rate; profligates favour a low–high approach, i.e. low savings plus a high discount rate (cf. Dahle, 1998; Neumayer, 1999). Since asceticism seems to be far closer to the non-material ideal, should we choose a high–low approach as our principle of sustainable justice? If we could instantly transport ourselves into an economy based upon resource preservation, that answer might well be yes. The problem is that it would be inconsistent to ignore the hows and whys of transition from one type of economy to another. To put it simply, pragmatics and political expediency might require a more *moderate* principle of sustainable justice, tying in with the arguments sketched in Chapter 6.

So an alternative is a low–low approach where the discount rate is low but so, in the short-term at least, is the savings rate. The rationale here is to apply a low discount rate in order to effect the ethical revaluation, which in the course of time would alter collective notions of savings and consumption (along the lines suggested above) and permit the economic transition which is crucial; in the interim, we have to work within an economy of resource depletion which may well mean not asking people to make burdensome sacrifices. If social and environmental sustainability become associated with grim austerity (as anti-environmentalists hope they will), then the case for social and environmental (or sustainable) justice will be defeated. If, however, sustainable justice can be established as meaning not less investment, consumption and spending but *different ways* of investing, consuming and spending, then the Green argument can become a new orthodoxy. This means that we have to both count the future (low discount rate) and discount it (low savings rate) at the same time.

Before misunderstanding sets in, though, let me add an important qualification. While I am advocating a low savings rate, the rate I have in mind would still be higher than the one which currently prevails. So although it is wrong to assume that the road to sustainability is paved with the ruins of a consumer society, it *is* the case that Green consumption implies less overall consumption than current levels.

Does a low–low approach satisfy the contractualist theory defended above? Rawls was criticised because he (a) locates the original position anywhere in history, and (b) specifies that participants all belong to a single generation. By contrast, sustainable justice allows the participants to know approximately where they are in history, i.e. their decision is context-sensitive, while including within the original position all representatives from within that time horizon, i.e. they hold weak ties of sentiment to their near contemporaries rather than strong familial ties to their children. Let us assume a horizon of 200 years stretching from 2000 to 2200. The participants know this, and are therefore aware of what is at stake environmentally, though none of the individuals know where they themselves belong. Individuals are unlikely to advocate profligacy, in case they should find themselves in an environmental wasteland of later generations; though nor is asceticism likely to be popular as this imposes draconian sacrifices on earlier generations. So, a low–low approach seems like a reasonable compromise, in that all generations are valued (low discount rate), but earlier generations are permitted to use and transform the world's resources so long as, in doing so, they improve both the condition of the ecosystem and humans' ability to appreciate reproductive values.

If these assumptions are correct, then we are left with principles of sustainable justice that include:

1   intragenerational equity (see Chapter 2);
2   intergenerational equity (just savings, autonomy and diverse reciprocity);
3   the question of transition;
4   the ethic of reproductive values.

So although (1) and (2) do not necessarily lead to a conflictual model, (3) suggests that some conflict cannot be avoided though it can be smoothed out over time with reference to (4). If welfare means GDP growth then, given finite resources, there are trade-off decisions to be made regarding the distribution of sacrifices, i.e. between (1) and (2). But if, as Chapter 5 argued, even Green versions of GDP are stages towards an ISEW, then the issue of trade-offs become less urgent, e.g. the future's enjoyment of the natural environment is not reduced by our enjoyment of the same, and vice versa. We make all generations wealthy by placing environmental public goods at the heart of what we mean by wealth. Nevertheless, the problem of transition means that the question of trade-offs cannot be avoided entirely and for any theory of justice this means taking account of the poor. Can we square the circle of assisting both the present and future poor?

Two rules

The problem is this. Poverty, inequality and injustice currently exist at levels that few regard as desirable. Poverty bears an environmental dimension, since the poorest are those most likely to suffer from ecological degradation. However, although many anti-poverty policies will be environmentally benign, and many pro-environment policies will reduce poverty, the conjunction between social justice and environmental sustainability is by no means total. Some anti-poverty policies may need to be environmentally damaging, e.g. a dash for GDP growth, and some pro-environment policies may be detrimental to the poor, e.g. price rises on scarce resources. The question is, when are such trade-offs acceptable?

In this respect, therefore, I am agreeing with Dobson's (1998) thesis that justice and sustainability are contingently rather than necessarily related (cf. Langhelle, 2000). Dobson's seminal treatment of the subject, *Justice and the Environment*, will therefore be a key source for what follows. Dobson, though, neglects the policy aspects of this subject. Although the relationship between justice and sustainability may always remain contingent in a philosophical sense, it is also true that if we manage to design policies which strengthen that relationship, then the non-conjunction of anti-poverty and pro-environment strategies may eventually fade to insignificance. However, in order to design such policies, we first need to understand when poverty reduction might be allowed to trump sustainability and vice versa. Of course, much will ultimately depend upon the particular circumstances within which such judgements are made, yet Dobson is wrong to believe that this is always a matter of empirical determination.

In other words, we can devise general rules which allow such determinations to be made with greater assurance than otherwise. Let me state what I consider these to be.

The Non-Futility Rule

Principle x should not be allowed to trump principle y when, under particular circumstances, doing so would be self-defeating.

Let us imagine ourselves making poverty reduction the priority. We might, for instance, make efforts to vastly increase global GDP in such a way that the developing world has access to the consumerist living standards that are still largely confined to developed nations. The problem is that the environmental costs of an extra 2–3 billion cars, refrigerators, computers, etc., would be so great that the advantages of that strategy would be confined to several decades at best. Of course, we can also envisage technological innovations and some sustainability measures lengthening such a time horizon, yet only an economic/technological determinist could imagine ecological crises being forestalled forever. According to the Environmental Kuznets Curve (EKC) economic growth only produces environmental deterioration in its early stages, this being superseded by improvements in environmental quality later on (Panayotou, 1995). However, even if the EKC applies to some pollutants in some geographical localities (Perrings and Ansuategi, 2000), it is dangerous to generalise this hypothesis, as it takes no account of the exponential deterioration of environmental quality on a global scale that can be expected to occur *before* the zenith of the EKC, e.g. the greenhouse effect. Of course, it is possible to envisage developed countries on the right side of the curve assisting those on the wrong side (Panayotou, 1997), but developed nations have so far demonstrated little inclination to do so. This may be because they are not yet on the right side, obviously, but this only returns us to the dilemma of exponential degradation. In short, those who treat GDP growth as a panacea (e.g. Neumayer, 1999) tend to assume that future environmental deterioration will not differ significantly from present deterioration.

Let us now imagine making sustainability the priority. The problem is that global inequality has doubled over the last 40 years (UNDP, 1996) to a level that is damaging to sustainability (Stymne and Jackson, 2000). This is first because those at the bottom overconsume resources as a means of trying to catch the affluent and perform environmentally damaging practices as a side effect of coping with their deprivation. Of course, many environmental-benign practices are carried out by those with scarce resources, but it is clear that developing countries do not appreciate being told to develop sustainable economies by affluent nations who seem unwilling to take more than modest steps in the same direction. Second, therefore, inequality encourages those at the top to overconsume resources as a means of maintaining their relative position and so to pollute in greater proportions also. Consequently, sustainability that does not attend to the injustice of global inequalities will not be effective, remaining at the level of carbon sinks and tradable permits that, for the US Government in particular, are an excuse to maintain its environmentally damaging activities.

However, the Non-Futility Rule does not disallow all attempts to permit one principle to trump the other:

The Deferred Enhancement Rule

Principle x is temporally allowed to trump principle y when, under particular circumstances, doing so allows the objectives of principle y to be met more effectively in the medium-term than would otherwise be the case.

There are two circumstances to which this rule might apply. First, when inequality is at levels so extreme that priority *must* be given to justice-enhancing policies. This is obviously so when we are faced with examples of severe deprivation, e.g. famine, but it also follows in cases falling short of such examples, e.g. when income inequality is so great that no moral consensus regarding sustainability can be expected to emerge (or, to put it bluntly, why should the poorest change their activities in order to save a planet ruined by the affluent?). Second, when environmental degradation is so acute that the ecological necessities of life are placed in jeopardy. We can think of these two circumstances in terms of a Titanic metaphor. If the ship is at risk of sinking because the steerage passengers are rebelling, then this has to be the priority – no matter how many icebergs are around! If the ship is about to hit an iceberg, then we had better manoeuvre out of the way and worry about the passengers later on.

However, in both instances we are not defending a principle (either equality or sustainability) for the sake of it, but in order to augment and strengthen the other principle in the longer term. Where injustice is the problem, then egalitarianism and justice enhancement are appropriate responses only until the point where the Non-Futility Rule begins to apply, i.e. the point at which further equality and justice without sustainability would be self-defeating. Under these circumstances, it is an initial equal weighting of justice and sustainability which would be ineffective, so that the latter is better served in the long run by being temporarily deferred. Where the problem is ecological crises, then strategies to enhance sustainability are the appropriate response only until the point where such strategies would be self-defeating without greater equality. Here again, an initial equal weighting would be ineffective, so that justice and equality are better served by being temporarily deferred. Therefore, the Deferred Enhancement Rule is the means by which we create circumstances in which the Non-Futility Rule begins to apply; or, to put it more simply, justice can only trump sustainability, or vice versa, if the objective is to allow the two principles to eventually converge. So, we can see that although there is no necessary relation between justice/equality and sustainability, such that we cannot realise one just by realising the other, the contingent relationship is very close nevertheless.

However, we are still left with the problem mentioned earlier: should we prioritise the needs of the present poor above those of the future poor? Are we any nearer to answering this question? Well, yes and no. The Non-Futility and Deferred Enhancement rules both suggest that we cannot ulti-mately have greater justice/equality without greater sustainability and vice versa. If so, then the policies which are most suitable for the present poor will closely resemble those most suitable for the future poor, i.e. poli-cies that come under the heading of sustainable justice. As such, the real conflict may not be between present and future but as always between Left and Right. If we decide that we want a Leftist approach, then deci-sions over the temporal distribution of benefits and burdens, while impor-tant, are of secondary consideration. In short, to characterise the debate in terms of irreconcilable interests between present and future is to reify it and overlook the fact that the main division remains ideological, what-ever the precise time horizon involved. Indeed, to neglect the idea that the present and future poor are part of the same moral community might only hand the theoretical initiative to the Right by encouraging the Left to ignore the temporal dimension of social justice. By contrast, the Left must recognise that the road to intergenerational equity is through intra-generational equality.

Ecosocial property

Having brought ourselves to this point then, we are obliged to say some-thing about what the most appropriate policies might be and how present and future can be woven into a non-zero sum game. What kind of welfare policies synergistically serve the interests of both present and future poor? A useful entrance into this debate is provided by Dobson (1998, 1999). According to Dobson, we can identify three main concep-tions of environmental sustainability, each of which engenders its own unique account of social justice and the relationship between justice and sustainability.

Conception *A* (Dobson, 1998: 41–7) is concerned with sustaining the most critical aspects of natural capital, i.e. those aspects which are essen-tial for the perpetuation of human life – the ecosystem, for instance (cf. Benton, 1999). Conception *A* incorporates an anthropocentric rationale, in that 'critical natural capital' is to be preserved for the instrumentalist reasons of protecting human welfare. How might such preservation occur? First, through processes of renewal, e.g. reforestation; second, through the substitution of non-renewable critical natural capital, e.g. substitutes for oil; third, through the conservation of critical natural capital that is non-renewable and non-substitutable. Conception A states that the *needs* of future generations must override the *wants* of the present generation, a prioritisation which allows the interests of the non-human to be accounted for also.

Conception B (Dobson, 1998: 47–50) is concerned with sustaining those aspects of the natural world whose loss would be irreversible. In short, while conception B acknowledges the importance of human welfare, it also wants to preserve those elements of non-human nature which risk disappearing forever, even when this loss might not impact upon human welfare at all. Therefore, conception B states that renewability is far less important than substitutability and conservation, since once a species is extinct it cannot, by definition, be renewed. However, there are also limits to the extent to which human-made capital can substitute for natural capital, e.g. an extinct species cannot be artificially recreated. Consequently, this conception gives priority to the needs of present generations of non-humans over the needs of future generations of humans, on the grounds that the loss of a non-human species cannot be justified in terms of the potential benefits of that loss to future generations.

Conception C (Dobson, 1998: 50–4) identifies an intrinsic value to nature, the sustainability of which cannot therefore be measured in terms of human welfare. Of course, the former may enhance the latter, but enhancing the latter cannot be the motivation for the former. Conception C abandons renewability and substitutability, since intrinsic natural value is lost in both instances, and concentrates upon conservation as the main instrument of sustainability. So although conception C does not necessarily want to abandon the prioritisation of human needs, it does want the profile of non-human needs to be raised within the calculus of policy-making.

Each of these conceptions corresponds to a broad 'menu' of ideas relating to social justice. These correspondences are too complex to summarise here, but we can outline the main features. Conception A (Dobson, 1998: 87–164) seems to require the just distribution of critical natural capital, i.e. distribution according to universal needs. This means that critical natural capital cannot be sustained simply by attending to just social relations, as such justice might require the depletion of critical natural capital. Therefore, both the existing pattern of ownership and our ideas about property rights need to alter, perhaps around some notion of environmental space, the distribution of which would have to be global and egalitarian. Con-

ception B (Dobson, 1998: 165–215) points in the direction of a Green communitarianism, such that justice must involve a broader interpretation of
the moral community than that permitted by anthropocentrism and one
moreover which is concerned with a single definition of the good (the
sustainability of irreversible nature) rather than procedural neutrality
between competing definitions. Conception B though is less clear than A
regarding the just distribution of natural resources since distribution is
functional for sustainability. With conception C (Dobson, 1998: 216–39),
however, the link between environmental sustainability and social justice
possibly breaks down altogether. At best, sustainability demands whatever pattern of distribution is most likely to produce benign consequences
for the environment, and if this ever required social injustice, then so be
it. Intrinsic natural value cannot be interpreted as a distributive resource
precisely because it is intrinsic. Dobson (1998: 242–67) concludes with a
discussion of whether there can be a theory of social justice that incorporates notions of environmental sustainability from across the three
conceptions. He accepts the argument of Norton (1991) that a 'future generationalism' might be the means of producing consensus across the
Green movement and between Greens and those non-Greens who are concerned with justice to others.

I am not convinced of the merits of this approach however, due to a
possible criticism that Dobson himself raises. The problem with future
generationalism is that it focuses upon generalisable human interests and
neglects distributional conflicts between rich and poor. Unless we operate
some kind of discount rate, then we may leave present generations vulnerable and unless we have some notion of distributional justice, then we
leave the present poor especially vulnerable. For Dobson then, future gen-
erationism must give precedence to those generations closest to us in time.
While agreeing with this prioritisation, it seems to me that it fatally
weakens future generationalism as conceived by Norton and revised by
Dobson. For if we must possess some principle of social justice in order
to resolve both intra- and intergenerational distributional conflicts over
resources, then conception C must be omitted, due to its biocentric emphasis upon intrinsic value, since this emphasis seems to rule out a close link
between justice and sustainability. We are therefore returned to the point
made earlier (that the future generations debate is a debate between Left
and Right long before it is one about present and future), contradicting
the idea that focusing upon future horizons enables ideological conflicts
to be resolved.

Sustainable justice as I have outlined it therefore maps onto conceptions A and B of Dobson's framework, but that framework does not currently offer a way forward due to its neglect of political ideology. Can we
therefore find a way of proceeding which is more profitable than future

generationalism, i.e. one that enables us to answer the earlier question about serving the needs of both the present and future poor?

Neither conception *A* nor *B* seem to be entirely satisfactory (cf. Rogers, 2000). The problem with conception *A* is its exclusive focus upon *critical natural capital*, for although this may cover a large part of the natural world, it instrumentalises the relationship between human and non-human. Now, to some extent an instrumentalism is appropriate, e.g. we need to repair the ozone layer for our benefit first and foremost, yet it would not seem appropriate to regard the natural world purely in such terms. Since the future well-being of humanity is in no way dependent upon the survival of the blue whale, then the latter cannot be regarded as critical. Of course, it might be that we would lose the pleasure of co-inhabiting the earth with such a creature if it became extinct, but this too would hardly be a *critical* loss and so points beyond an instrumentalist ethic toward conception *B*.

On the other hand, the irreversibility thesis of conception *B* is too stringent. Although 3–30 species are made extinct every day (Beckerman and Pasek, 2001: 185–6), the disappearance of most of them probably does not affect our survival or sense of well-being at all. Obviously, there comes a point at which the loss of biodiversity is crucial, but biodiversity does not require us to maintain the existence of each and every species, even if this were possible! Therefore, we need to develop guidelines helping us to distinguish between those species whose irreversible loss would and would not be acceptable. This sends us back in the direction of conception *A*.

I am therefore going to leave open the question as to whether we should prefer *A* or *B*, or whether there is another theory of sustainability and justice which we could develop incorporating elements of both. For our purposes, it seems clear that for policies to be consistent with sustainable justice, the principle of substitutability (which both *A* and *B* embody) is crucial.

Neither renewability nor conservation imply any major, direct impacts upon social redistribution, though they obviously bear implications for the environmental conditions of future generations. Substitutables are different, however. Take fossil fuels. There is a very good case for using up the earth's supply of fossil fuels, albeit at a lower and less damaging rate than at present. First, because doing so helps to improve social welfare, at least as measured in a material sense. Second, because despite the aeons it took to create them, fossil fuels have no intrinsic or aesthetic value: there is little point in just having them lie in the ground. Of course, pollution is an undesirable side effect of using fossil fuels, but their conservation would have no value in itself. In short, a substitutable is a good whose utilisation is acceptable, because the sum total of human welfare is raised as a result, but only if an environmentally benign replacement can be eventually found that does not reduce those levels of welfare. As noted in Chapter 5, substitution is potentially valuable, though only as a medium-term measure.

However, the process of substitution is not only a technological question, it is also a question of who benefits, i.e. the distributive pattern of the welfare thereby created. Fossil fuels are subject to private ownership across a relatively limited range of countries. This means that the direct benefits of their depletion flow into the bank accounts of a lucky few. I would like to add the following principle to the above definition, therefore:

> Goods should only be substituted if the welfare thereby created is subject to an egalitarian distribution.

The logic is simple: the depletion of a substitutable has implications for everyone, therefore everyone should be able to benefit from it on a scale that current property rights do not permit (Sathiendrakumar, 1996: 159). This means initiating as wide a system of ownership as possible, but does this imply egalitarian private ownership or egalitarian collective ownership?

There are those who abhor any suggestion that nature can be commodified (Naess, 1989), i.e. subject to either private or public ownership. For others, commodifying nature, e.g. through a cost–benefit analysis, is the only way of ensuring that scarce resources are preserved (see O'Neill, 1993: 44–82; Sagoff, 1988) and a pricing mechanism is the best means for signalling when and where a resource is undersupplied. But, as argued in Chapters 5 and 6, the ultimate decision is less between commodification and decommodification and more about whether these imply productivist or post-productivist values. So if collective ownership facilitates post-productivism, then it is desirable, whether or not this represents the commodification of nature. More accurately, the commodification of nature through collective ownership is permissible if this is part of a long-term strategy to transform our values away from the productive towards the reproductive and, we might add, any such strategy succeeds or fails depending upon its implications for poverty.

Therefore, the question of deciding between private and collective ownership also becomes less relevant. Think of the property regimes envisaged by John Roemer (1993) and Roberto Unger (1987), i.e. a system of rights where a certain good is held in common, but each individual possess a right to that dividend which is yielded by the utilisation of the good. In what I shall call an 'ecosocial' property regime, individuals are therefore not able to trade or sell the good itself, but they are entitled to a 'rent', i.e. an equitable share of the value produced by the good translated into a monetary income, a share that reverts back to the commons on the death of the individual. This then is a social dividend system of which BI would be an initial version (see Chapter 6), a property regime based upon the socialisation of substitutable goods. What this would require is a sophisticated taxation system where destructive utilisation is taxed at a higher rate than those activities which raise the level of sustainable welfare, as measured on an appropriate index. Such taxes (as we argued in Chapter 6) would need to be based upon an ethic of stewardship, for if natural resources are collectively owned, then policies must recognise our role as being that of trustees who have a duty to bequeath to the future a level of critical natural capital that we ourselves would be willing to live with. In effect, this means internalising that which is currently externalised, so whereas GDP growth takes no account of hidden environmental costs, a sustainable welfare index would ensure that these are made fully visible. Green taxes and an ecosocial property regime are therefore dependent upon one another: without the latter, the former simply encourage taxpayer revolts; without the former, the latter would not necessarily be any more conducive to sustainability than the current system of capital accumulation.

To illustrate this second point, we might identify similarities between an ecosocial regime and what Blackburn (1999, 2002) calls the 'new collectivism' (Aglietta, 1998; Self, 2000). Blackburn, like Druker (1994, 1996) before him, spies a radical potential in the shift to pension-fund capitalism, with pension funds now totalling some $13,000 billion. If such funds were democratically controlled by the policyholders themselves and invested in equities and bonds, then substantial portions of the economy could be brought under some form of social control. What this represents, of course, is an alternative version of the Meidner plan for wage-earner funds, against which the Swedish bourgeois parties mobilised so effectively in the late 1970s. However, pension-fund reform is a necessary but not sufficient condition of socialisation and a new fiscal and legal framework for the political economy, e.g. global capital controls, would also be required in order to prevent financial globalisation from undermining the trend towards socialised accumulation. Similarly, all citizens would need to be covered by such funds, requiring pension reforms much more far reaching than those introduced by New Labour, for instance (Ward, 2000).[2] If this were to occur, of course, then 'pension fund' might become a misnomer with 'endowment fund' being a preferable alternative (cf. Unger, 1998: 205). Nevertheless, with such reorganisations in place, Blackburn envisages that a proper system of stakeholder welfare would emerge, one less vulnerable than the welfare state to capital flight and taxpayer revolts. Blackburn (1999: 63) represents this as a synthesis of private and collective property rights.

So, in answer to the obvious and legitimate question 'How do we wrestle control of substitutables from private hands?', the most obvious

solution is through the investment and gradual takeover of the companies and trusts who presently control such assets by democratically-
controlled endowment funds. However, unless the new political economy
that Blackburn mentions also incorporates Green taxes, then there is no
incentive for the fundholders to be any more environmental then existing
pension-fund managers. The ideal to work towards would be something
like the following. Field X has been earmarked for the development of a
Conservation Park that would charge for research into natural habitats;
field Y has been earmarked for the construction of a car park. In the
absence of Green taxes, the investment decision will flow in the direction
of whichever plan promises the greatest returns. But with Green taxes,
globally regulated, that take full account of all externalities, then the taxes
on field Y's development will have to be high enough to subsidise the
lower taxes on field X's development, making the former less attractive
to investors. So, an ecosocial regime (i.e. the shift towards socialised
capital through pension-fund reform) requires Green taxes if it is to be
sustainable, and Green taxes require an ecosocial regime in order to secure
their legitimacy and ensure that they are not interpreted as statist intru-
sions into the sphere of private accumulation.

Of course, the system of taxation is likely to alter depending upon
the nature of the sustitutable in question. In the case of fossil fuels,
for instance, taxation could fall most heavily on those activities which,
while being dependent upon fossil fuels, are in no way concerned
with their eventual substitution. This is what would distinguish an
ecosocial property regime from, say, the dividend scheme operating in
Alaska where oil from Prudhoe Bay is distributed to all Alaskan residents
on an annual and egalitarian basis (Fitzpatrick, 1999a: 147–9). Although
the Alaskan scheme combines some of the benefits of both collective
and private ownership, it is not based upon a sustainable welfare index
and so has few ecological credentials. Nevertheless, the same principle
could be made to serve more sustainable objectives if the political will
were in place.

In conclusion, the essential point of this long argument can be stated
as follows. Helping the present poor requires something much more
ambitious then the tax-and-spend redistribution usually favoured by
social democrats. It requires a property regime based upon the socialisation of substitutable goods and Green taxation that yields a social dividend representing the private return on the collective ownership of the
environment. This regime would assist in the transformation towards a
post-productivist ethic of reproductive values that helps to create higher
levels of sustainability than at present and so to reduce (and hopefully
to eventually eliminate) the numbers of the future poor. Therefore the
problem of transition is less between the present and future and more

between those who do and do not support the current concentration of wealth in relatively few hands.

Conclusion

We began by arguing that a theory of intergenerational justice should be based upon contractualism, though with some reference to the notion of an intergenerational community. This yielded a low–low approach that treats future generations seriously, but which permits the utilisation of resources if the long-term aim is the transformation of our sources of value. Four principles of what I called sustainable justice were outlined and two rules (the Non-Futility and Deferred Enhancement Rules) were introduced as means of guiding the convergence of sustainability and distributive justice over the course of time. I concluded by suggesting that the ultimate conflict is less between the present and future than between those who do and those who do not recognise the claims of social justice, whether intra- or intergenerationally. To this end, I argued that the problem of present and future poverty can be addressed by exploring the prospects for an alternative property regime based upon the socialisation of substitutable goods, the ISEW, Green taxes, global regulation and the democratic control of endowment funds. BI and pension-fund reform might be regarded as more short-term policies conducive to these ends.

So, have we countered the arguments of Beckerman and Pasek? Let us revisit their syllogism, mentioned at the start of the chapter.

1   It is probably true that future generations cannot be said to have any rights with respect to ourselves, since they do not yet exist to claim such rights. We could imagine ourselves making claims on their behalf, but if we did so by applying a discount rate of 0 per cent, then this requires us to a weight to their rights equal to ours; a discount rate of less than 0 per cent implies that their rights count for less than ours, which seems to contradict the meaning of a 'right'.

2   However, although a theory of justice implies rights, rights do not have to inhabit each and every aspect of that theory. Justice also implies obligations and obligations can derive from the power we hold vis-à-vis the vulnerable. Future generations are vulnerable with respect to ourselves because we can harm them by bequeathing levels of autonomy to which we ourselves would not assent. To argue that we cannot harm (or benefit) the future is like arguing that we have not been harmed (or benefited) by the past. Certainly, it is difficult to determine the criteria of harm, but we can say with some confidence

that harm is performed when demonstrable principles of justice, to which all rational and autonomous beings should agree, are ignored. Nor is it impossible that we would harm future generations by leaving them a pollution-free and resource-plenty environment – our equivalent of burning witches with good intentions – but the current evidence (on ecological degradation and its implications for human well-being) suggests otherwise.

Beckerman and Pasek therefore object not so much to future generations lacking rights, but to their inability to reciprocate any benefits that we bequeath. Yet this is a narrow view of reciprocity that neglects deontological conceptions of justice where we ought to perform certain acts because it is right, irrespective of whether those who receive the consequences of those acts can pay us back or not. Justice is concerned with the distribution of benefits and burdens but, as argued in Chapter 2, this does not mean that benefits and burdens have to balance exactly on each and every occasion. The present generation cannot be expected to carry all the burdens (since the discount rate ought not to be 0 per cent), merely those that facilitate a future level of autonomy to which all generations, across a given timescale would contract in the original position.

3   Therefore, the second premise fails and so the interests of future generations *can* be protected or promoted within the framework of a theory of justice.

This by no means exhausts the full range of Beckerman and Pasek's arguments, but it is enough to suggest that sustainability and distributive justice possess far stronger implications for one another than they and many others seem to imagine.

Notes

1 For simplicity's sake I am using a 0–10 scale and I am assuming no overlap between generations. Nor am I going to discuss whether the discount rate is constant or non-constant.
2 Though Blackburn is certainly not suggesting that these could ever substitute for an adequately financed basic state pension.

8

The new genetics

The next link in the ecowelfare triangle concerns attention and sustainability. Again, there are many ways in which these two principles might connect. Of particular importance is the debate concerning genetically-modified organisms (GMOs) and biodiversity. Does sustainability require the acceptance of the GMOs or their rejection in favour of organic production? How can we recognise and ensure the maintenance of biodiversity without losing the potential benefits of genetic technology? These are all worthwhile questions that others have begun to address over the last few years (Shiva, 2000a, 2000b) but, having concentrated upon 'external' nature in the preceding two chapters, I now want to concentrate upon 'internal' nature, since it is here that the implications for social policy are perhaps most pronounced. This chapter therefore refers back to Chapter 3, where I argued that, in keeping with the advent of a security state, New Labour conceives of information as asocial, as commodified and as a source of surveillance. This chapter will discuss genetic information rather than information *per se*, but the aim is to construct an approach that resists these kind of priorities.

Some expect biotechnology to supplant the petrochemical and nuclear industries as *the* industry of the twenty-first century (Rifkin, 1998). If so, then before we can begin to yield the benefits of this technology we must prepare to avoid the accompanying dangers. Yet what are those dangers? For welfare egalitarians, the key danger is that the biological reductionism which often seems to be driving the technology shifts attention away from social explanations of human behaviour. In the present ideological climate, this means that biotechnology might help to consolidate the moral and market fundamentalisms of the Right (Knapp *et al.*, 1996; Nelkin, 1999).

As such, this chapter takes issue with two recent interventions by prominent authors of the Right, Charles Murray and Francis Fukayama.

The next section critiques Murray's position and the chapter then proceeds to argue that in order to prevent the emergence of '*laissez-faire* eugenics', we must implement policies based upon a 'regulated eugenics', defending the contentious use of the term 'eugenics' along the way. The chapter then proceeds to examine the principles upon which a theory of regulated eugenics may be said to depend. We conclude by distinguishing regulated eugenics from the position taken by Fukayama.

The new sociobiology

Taking his cue from the sociobiology of Wilson (1998), Murray (2000; cf. Fukuyama, 1999: 97–101, 160–7, 227–30) contends that the new genetics is beginning to prove that the Right's view of human nature (as self-interested, competitive, status-seeking, gendered and rule-governed) is the correct one. Consequently, the Right's prescriptions for social policy will also be shown to be accurate because, '. . . debates over social policy within the democratic west have also been underlain by conflicting understandings of human nature . . . The positions we adopt are based on assumptions about innate differences between men and women. The welfare state makes sense – or doesn't – depending upon underlying beliefs about how human beings achieve satisfaction in life' (Murray, 2000: 29). Since it will be demonstrated that men are innate hunter–gatherers and women are innate carers, one of the casualties of the new genetics will be the egalitarianism of the Left. In addition: '. . . when we know the complete genetic story, it will become evident that the population below the poverty line in the US has a configuration of the relevant genetic makeup significantly different from the configuration of the population above the poverty line' (Murray, 2000: 30). If humans are genetically different and unequal, then the case for social equality and distributive justice is fatally undermined. However, although the *egalitarian* Left will vanish, Murray anticipates a revival of the *eugenic* Left (cf. Singer, 1998). Invoking the legacy of Shaw, Goldman, Wells and the Webbs, Murray fears that *dirigiste* genetic engineering will offer the greatest threat to personal liberty in the twenty-first century, driven (once their interpretation of human nature has been disproved) by little more than the Left's propensity to interfere in the natural order.

Murray can be criticised on any number of grounds (cf. Kohn, 2000). It could be argued that the new genetics will not prove or disprove human nature to be one thing or another. Murray's faith in the innateness of femininity and masculinity is based upon a conceptual confusion: he talks of the *interaction* of biology and environment, but also of how human nature *produces* social and political institutions. Yet if biology and environment interact, then institutions must also be said to produce human nature to some degree. There is an even more invidious confusion. Murray proposes that the revelation of genetic differences between groups (men/women, white/black, English/French) is relatively insignificant: 'so what?', he proclaims, and 'vive la différence'. Yet how does this square with Murray's declaration that the poor are genetically different from the non-poor, especially in the light of his previous observations that the large parts of the poor constitute a semi-criminal underclass (Murray, 1984, 1990)? Either those genetic differences are innate, in which case Murray's 'vive la différence' attitude contradicts his infamous condemnations of welfare dependency, or they are the product of the welfare state gradually undermining the work ethic of the poor, in which case (whether you agree with that view or not) human nature must be an historical and environmental construct, according to Murray's own logic. And if a large proportion of the 'undeserving poor' are black, then Murray's confusion quickly shades into academic racism (Herrnstein and Murray, 1994).

As such, egalitarian and social explanations of human behaviour are not disproved by the new genetics *per se* (although there is a risk of their being drowned out by an alliance of biotechnology and biological reductionism) and Murray's distinction between market individualism and Leftist state eugenics (with the former defending us from the latter) is revealed as being a crude distortion. Indeed, Murray himself states that, 'The popular voluntary uses of gene manipulation are likely to be ones which avoid birth defects and ones that lead to improved overall physical and mental abilities. I find it hard to get upset about that prospect' (Murray, 2000: 31). But Murray does not seem to realise that there are two prospects here: avoiding birth 'defects' (and who is to decide what a defect is?) may improve abilities, but what if the improvement of abilities is the direct aim of affluent parents and profit-driven biotechnology companies? Presumably, if the wealthiest can afford the genetic enhancements and medicines that will be unavailable to those on low incomes, then social and genetic inequalities may feed into each other in a vicious downward spiral, a new race to the bottom. If, like Murray, the Right are generally unmoved by this possibility, then we have reason to believe that the main danger comes not from any statist eugenics of the Left, but from a '*laissez-faire* eugenics' (Kitcher, 1996; Duster, 1990) of the Right.

Murray's analysis is therefore potentially useful in at least two senses. First, he is correct to note the importance of human nature, although it might be more accurate to claim that human nature and social policy *underpin one another*; for if biology and environment really do interact, then human nature is as much a product of social policy as the latter is a product of the former. Identifying a single causal flow from one to the other may be an impossible exercise to perform. Second, Murray's distorted analysis nevertheless opens up a conceptual space that needs to be filled. If *laissez-faire* biotech commercialism and statist eugenics lie at the extremes of the genetic spectrum, rather than, as Murray would have it, at adjacent points on the compass, then there is a middle ground that we urgently need to debate and define.

Eugenics

How then might welfare egalitarians resist *laissez-faire* eugenics? The premise of the following argument is as follows. If genetics deals with heritable characteristics, then eugenics denotes the attempt to determine what should and should not be heritable from one generation to the next. The eugenics which flourished in the first four decades of the twentieth century was the misguided attempt to impose order upon what was perceived as genetic chaos and contingency. In a world of Empires, scientific materialism and aristocracy, the idea that 'chance' prevailed over 'choice' was unbearable to many on both Left and Right. Far easier to distinguish between the degenerate and the non-degenerate and to recommend the sterilisation of the former and the selective breeding of both groups. Although hardly anyone now wishes to revive these kinds of assumptions and policies, it is also the case that, due to the advent of biotechnological innovations, we cannot avoid making difficult choices about the genetic characteristics of future populations. Even if we today erased our knowledge of genetics for all time, we would still be making a choice, i.e. that the genetic characteristics of future populations should be shaped through complete non-intervention. Therefore the real decision we have to face is not between eugenics and non-eugenics, because we cannot choose not to choose, but between a eugenics of the free market (where it is the unintended outcomes of voluntary exchanges that shape future populations) and a eugenics that is set within regulatory frameworks. In short, a regressive eugenics (whether based upon the centralised state or the free market) is one that elevates choice over chance, whereas a progressive, regulated eugenics makes room for both choice and chance in its values and criteria.

Before defending my use of the word eugenics, let me illustrate this point with what is at the time of writing a recent example. In April 2002 it was revealed that a couple in America were planning to conceive a baby who like them would be born deaf. They did so on the grounds that the deaf community had formed a distinct cultural identity and that any child they had would therefore be impoverished unless it too shared that identity. To those who objected, they countered that just as it would be racist to condemn a black couple for conceiving a black baby so it was disablist to condemn a deaf couple for conceiving a deaf baby. I do not want to discuss the rights or wrongs of this case (though I personally believe such decisions to be immoral), but to observe that such bioethical dilemmas are likely to become more and more frequent and that, whatever solution we prefer, we cannot avoid the eugenic implications. If we allow such couples a free choice, then we are effectively permitting a *laissez-faire* eugenics along the lines that Murray seems to countenance. If we ban them, then we either have to rule out *all* forms of genetic manipulation (including those that may improve well-being) or we have to distinguish between moral and immoral uses, which means making some difficult decisions about future generations. If we prefer leaving it to nature, then we are in effect disinventing the technology and so making a decision under the cover of a non-decision. In short, whichever way we turn we cannot avoid the necessity of making a choice. And when 'choice' joins 'chance' in determining future generations' characteristics, then we are dealing with eugenics.

Now, while acknowledging the dilemmas, we will increasingly face, many will understandably quail at this use of the term. Surely it is far easier and safer to associate eugenics with the fascistic attempt to purge the human population of 'biological impurities'. Those with whom I have debated these issues often prefer a term such as 'genetic justice'. Unfortunately, in occupying the moral high ground in this way, we do not thereby avoid the difficult decisions that need to be made. Tom Shakespeare (1998: 668), for instance, defines eugenics as 'the science of improving the population by control of inherited qualities' and goes on to argue that, 'In those rare cases where impairment causes inevitable neo-natal death or permanent lack of awareness, it might be more appropriate to screen out such conditions prenatally. Absolutist positions – abort all impaired foetuses, or ban all termination on the basis of impairment – are equally unhelpful to women and men making very difficult decisions about reproductive choices' (Shakespeare, 1998: 670). This is certainly true and seems to invite policies based upon 'weak eugenics' as opposed to the 'strong eugenics' of state coercion (cf. Glover, 1999: 104). And although they would permit far more genetic engineering than Shakespeare, Buchanan *et al.* (2000) come to a similar conclusion: '. . . just as the state is the principal agent acting in the interests of future generations in such fields as land and resource management, so too does a eugenic role for the state, if needed, fit into the standard categories of legitimate areas of concern for government' (Buchanan *et al.*, 2000: 337). All of which is both to agree and disagree with Diane Paul (1998: 94–111) when she insists that the distinction between eugenic and non-eugenic policies is fading. For Paul, this means that those who embrace and those who reject the concept are *both* missing the point as to how we can now learn from the past. If it were possible to apply a substitute concept that (1) confronted the moral dilemmas of biotechnology and (2) avoided the negative connotations of 'eugenics', then I believe we should do so. To my mind, 'genetic justice' satisfies (2) but not (1), since it allows us to keep our moral hands clean in an area where, like Lady Macbeth, our hands promise to be both very clean and very dirty indeed (Kitcher, 1996; Glannon, 1998).

So if the avoidance of extreme impairment leads by definition to the improvement of social welfare, then although we can run away from the word 'eugenics', we cannot run away from the responsibility of deciding which reproductive choices are and are not acceptable. Indeed, if we run away from the word, then our genetic practices may be *more* likely to replicate the abuses of the past – as happened with the Scandinavian sterilisation programmes of the 1930s–1970s (Broberg and Roll-Hansen, 1996). This means that, whatever our decision, we can now intervene in that biology–environment interaction more directly than ever before (Dickens, 2000: 116). Social policy is no longer just about fulfilling needs from cradle to grave, it is also about deciding which needs are to exist in the first place by either intervening or deciding not to intervene *before the cradle*. It is no longer a question of simply fitting social policies to human nature, but of using social policies as a way of determining what human nature will be (Engelhardt, 1996). In the biotech age, we must peer deeper into history's hall of mirrors and recognise the eugenic reflections that are staring back.

Therefore, the essential choice is not between eugenics and non-eugenics, nor between free markets and statist eugenics (as Murray believes), but between a *laissez-faire* eugenics and the 'regulated eugenics' supported by Kitcher (1996; Glannon, 1998: 204–6). Regulated eugenics allows the elimination of those genetic conditions the experience of which does not allow the bearer to enjoy a minimal quality of life and formulate a sense of him or herself. This means that there are some conditions that should be eliminated, e.g. Hurler syndrome and Tay-Sachs, but others which should not, e.g. Down syndrome limits but does not eliminate self-development. Of course knowing where to draw the line is the dilemma. Can regulated eugenics guide us through this dilemma? This chapter now argues that regulated eugenics rests upon three 'supports': a multidimensional conception of human nature, a principle of differential egalitarianism and the precautionary principle.

Social policy and human nature

If a regulated eugenics is to shape those many social policies that will relate to biotechnology and the new genetics (hereafter known as 'biopolicies'), it stands to reason that we must elaborate an appropriate view of human nature. To date, the subject of social policy has worked with four main conceptions of human nature.

The 'unidimensional' conception proposes that human nature is largely defined by a single characteristic, i.e. altruism or self-interest. Social democrats have often believed individuals to possess a fundamental altruism that is suppressed by market capitalism, but which would flourish once appropriate social and economic reforms were in place (Titmuss, 1970: 209–24; cf. Baldwin, 1990). In the post-classic era by contrast, we have been exposed to new versions of those doctrines that stress individualistic self-interest in the form of a strange blend of market libertarianism and moral conservatism.

Second, there have been constructivist conceptions which challenge the belief that there is any pre-social human nature. For post-structuralists (Foucault, 1984), the relevant question is not 'What is human nature', but 'Why do some groups believe human nature to be x, others y and others z, and how do the prevailing conceptions change over time?' This genealogical approach looks beyond the liberal humanist self to the discourses and practices that constitute the field of the self's construction.

Lying between these two conceptions is a 'multidimensional' conception which identifies human nature as to some degree an extra-historical condition that is founded upon a plurality of subject positions and which can take any one of a series of forms depending upon the social properties of the historical context. For instance, Hewitt (2000) argues that four models of human nature are identifiable from the social policy literature – the atomistic, the organic, the basic needs and the mutualist models – and that these have been 'sutured' together in a variety of ways depending upon the institutional principles and practices that prevail.

The final conception is agnostic, recommending that we bracket the debate and take a practical approach to social reform that addresses specific objectives without reference to the metaphysical foundations of social policy. Le Grand (1997, 2000) has recently argued in favour of a creative ignorance regarding human motivation as a means of leap frogging the sterilities of the selfishness/altruism debate. Such creative ignorance can then give rise to robust welfare strategies that can appeal to a host of human motivations and ideological prescriptions.

Which of the above should we prefer? If *laissez-faire* eugenics is what we ought to avoid, and if Murray's biological reductionism (where human nature 'produces' institutions) opens the door to such eugenics, then perhaps the regressive consequences of biotechnology can be best resisted by a conception of human nature that challenges biological reductionism.

Biological reductionism is an umbrella term for a series of similar disciplines – sociobiology, evolutionary biology, behavioural genetics, evolutionary psychology – that share some basic premises and methodologies (cf. Rose, 1997: 280–95). First, self-replication and reproduction are regarded as the goal to which all lifeforms are driven. For Dawkins (1989), organisms or phenotypes are vehicles and survival machines through which genes copy themselves into the next generation. Second, therefore, not only are genes treated as biological atoms, distinct entities that can be abstracted from the genome, but they are programmed to be self-interested: the function of a gene is to give birth to other genes that will outlive it.[1] Finally, organic processes consist of endless adaptation to the environment as natural selection carves away those features of the phenotype that are biologically redundant.

The attraction of biological reductionism is that it offers a simple explanation of life that nevertheless takes account of life's complexity: the environment is treated as an important dimension of species evolution. However, those such as Gould (1978: 231–67), Rose *et al.* (1984), Rose (1997) and Lewontin (1993) warn us against the reductionism of those such as Wilson (1975, 1998), Dawkins (1982, 1989), Pinker (1995), Dennett (1996) and Ridley (1996, 1999) in what has become known as the Darwin wars (Brown, 1999).

For 'Critical Darwinians' such as Gould, biological reductionism represents an undesirable shift away from environmental explanations of life, all the more so because it comes at a time when politics and economics have been blowing in the same direction, towards pathological explanations that neglect interactionist processes and invite biotechnological fixes to social problems. They argue that we cannot assign explanatory priority to either genes or the environment, as they are inseparable both physically and conceptually. Biological reductionism invites either a passivity in the face of social injustice, e.g. patriarchy is often attributed to innate biological differences, or simplistic approaches to genetic engineering, and often both at the same time (Ridley, 1999: 217–18, 253). The Critical Darwinians therefore draw our attention to the superficial ways in which reductionism deals with environmental factors; genes, in Wilson's (1978: 172) famous phrase, 'hold culture on a leash' and Dawkins (1989: 189–201) went as far as proposing that there is a cultural equivalent of the gene, the 'meme' (Blackmore, 1999). Reductionists also treat altruism as equivalent to nothing more than reciprocity, i.e. a product of enlightened self-interest (Axelrod, 1984).

This takes us to the central problem (Rose, 1997: 213–14): biological reductionists usually want to have it both ways. They want to identify self-interested genes as the determining foundations of human behaviour (Watson, 1998); yet, in order to avoid the charge that reductionism legitimates the selfish status quo, they also propose that we can rebel against our genes if we desire (Pinker, 1995). But how is this possible? If genes really are that important, then how can we rebel against them? On the other hand, if we can rebel against them, then this means either that it is the genes themselves that permit such rebellion, implying that they are not purely self-interested, or that they are not so important after all and that some other factor is at work. In short, if genes are (1) self-interested and (2) the key determinants of human behaviour, then we cannot rebel against them, whereas if we can rebel then either (1) or (2) must collapse.

If biological reductionism is caught on the horns of a contradiction, then what might this 'other factor' be? According to Critical Darwinians it has to be culture (cf. O'Hear, 1997). The reductionists tend to interpret culture in terms of its biological origins and so neglect the specificity of cultural history: the reflexive learning processes of civilisation; but for Gould and other Critical Darwinians culture cannot be reduced to its biological origins because it is a space of cooperative interdependency through which humans transcend their genetic endowments and construct themselves as free beings who determine the conditions of their own future development. Humans have created their own freedom as cultural cooperativists, meaning that the structure of human freedom has long since floated free of its biological base. This brings us neatly back to social policy and human nature.

In what ways can social policy help to resist the siren voices of biological reductionism? What might a criticalist perspective suggest? It is unlikely that the unidimensional conception can do so. Indeed, those who subscribe to the view that humans are inherently selfish might well welcome biological reductionism; and although an appeal to inherent altruism is laudable (Page, 1996), 'pure' altruism is undoubtedly less frequent than the 'reciprocal altruism' that the reductionists profess to explain with constant reference to genetic self-interest. The constructionist conception is of little help either, as this rejects the notion of a pre-social human nature altogether and offends against the commonsense view that there must be something over and above the social constructions out of which the particular self is woven. The robust strategy is also redundant. To suggest that policies can be detached from their metaphysical foundations is at best wishful thinking and at worst a surrender of the academic subject's traditional task of combating injustice.

Therefore the multidimensional conception which is perhaps of most assistance in resisting biological determinism. Its strength is that it interprets human nature and motivation as unsettled, as hovering in an indeterminate 'liminal' space between a number of plausible narratives. So although both self-interest and altruism may be invoked, this conception adopts an overdetermined reading of these and other coherent narratives so that human nature is an 'emergent property' that constantly evolves beyond the sum of its immediate parts (Schwartz, 1997). The multidimensional theory acknowledges that there *is* a pre-social metaphysical ground to human nature, but argues that because we understand this ground through a constructivist kaleidoscope of interpretivist narrations, then we can only ever possess an indistinct grasp of what that pre-social nature might actually be. Therefore we can recognise the importance of our genetic endowments without assigning the excessive weight to them that is promoted by the reductionists.

The first 'support' is therefore in place. If *laissez-faire* eugenics is based upon a biological reductionism, where the social environment matters little, then any viable alternative must derive from an epistemology which is *both* realist *and* constructivist. Yet if regulated eugenics is based upon a multidimensional conception of human nature, then how does it begin to translate into actual social policies? This is a question that we can only answer fully once we have addressed the following: what is the relationship between eugenics and the welfare state?

Eugenics and the welfare state

The final two supports depend substantially upon the kind of values that have long motivated the most progressive and humane aspects of social policy, e.g. equality, liberty, welfare. However, these values are not, in themselves, sufficient and at least two additions must be made: difference and precaution. To illustrate why this is the case, we need to briefly review the relationship between eugenics and the welfare state.

While it would be facile to regard state welfare as an essentially eugenic institution, eugenic beliefs formed the background to the early years of modern social policies to such an extent that it seems equally facile to downgrade their importance in influencing reform (Thane, 1996: 60; cf. King, 1999: 51–96), though eugenics undoubtedly had fewer direct affects upon British legislation than upon that of other countries (Drouard, 1998). So what influence did eugenics have upon the early formation of British state welfare? There are two axes in Figure 8.1. The horizontal line is the descriptive axis that refers to the possible strength of the eugenic influence upon the welfare state; the vertical line is the normative axis which articulates the fact that eugenics was supported by both egalitarians and inegalitarians. This leaves us with four quadrants into which we can fit six theoretical interpretations. (Note that this taxonomy is not intended to distil the history of early modern social policy; it is merely establishing that a case can be made for identifying a eugenic influence upon that history.)

Interpretation (1) articulates the view that eugenics exerted only a weak influence because its doctrine of social inequality contradicted the egali-

Figure 8.1   Eugenic influences on the early welfare state

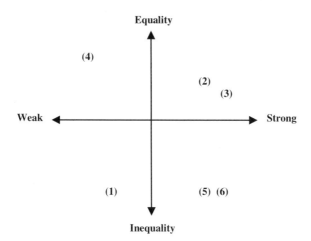

tarian commitments of state welfare (Kevles, 1985: 99; Thomson, 1998: 29–35). This interpretation corresponds to the theory of social Darwinism, where the welfare state represents a successful but regrettable counter-reaction to eugenics that was to make 'biological degeneracy' appear normal and acceptable. Therefore the welfare state's regulation of the economy and deregulation of sexual mores reverses the social Darwinist's commitment to *laissez-faire* economics and the state control of reproduction.

Interpretation (2) states that the influence was strong because both eugenics and the welfare state promote social *equality*. The most appropriate theory here is a 'reform eugenicism' that favourably identifies a convergence of welfare state and eugenic principles. The recruitment experience of the Boer War (Searle, 1976: 22–4, 34–44) inspired some to believe that a combination of state welfare and eugenic assumptions was required to avoid national deterioration (Kevles, 1985: 91–2). Of relevance in this respect is the rarely-cited analysis of Marshall (1953: 85; cf. Oakley, 1991) that the egalitarian citizenship of the welfare state would underpin the social inequalities that reflected the natural inequalities which eugenic science had successfully identified.

Interpretation (3) substantially agrees with (2), but is more a theory of 'population eugenicism'. Restrictive Victorian morality, it was argued, meant that many spouses were mismatched, so that the children they produced were genetically less fit than they might otherwise have been (Kevles, 1985: 65–6). Therefore eugenic improvement required the sexual liberation of women and/or an army of stay-at-home mothers who would ensure their children's genetic fitness (Searle, 1976: 86–90). From here, it is a short leap to the view that systems of birth control, family planning and family allowances are needed to encourage low-income women not to breed excessively (Thomson, 1998: 64–6).[2]

Interpretation (4), however, regards the eugenic influence upon the welfare state as weak, because the former is more egalitarian than the latter. Here we find theories of 'statist eugenicism' which argue that, although distinctions should be made between the genetically inferior and superior, these do not correspond to that between the lower and the upper classes (Kevles, 1985: 86–7): biological inferiority appears at all levels of the social scale. For many early socialists, state welfare was only the first step towards the classless, egalitarian society that was needed if human evolution was to proceed without the burden of the undeserving rich (Thomson, 1998: 200–1). This second step has never been taken however, so that the eugenic influence has ultimately been negligible.

Interpretation (5) expresses the view that the eugenic influence *has* been strong because both it and the welfare state are based upon a fundamental social *inequality*. The theory of 'statistical eugenics' states that mental tests can distinguish between the genetically superior and inferior (Gould, 1978), and it is such mental tests that have worked their way into significant quarters of the welfare state (Eysenck, 1998; Mensch and Mensch, 1990; Selden, 1999).

Finally, interpretation (6) concurs about the joint inegalitarianism of eugenics and state welfare and corresponds to the theory of 'penal eugenics'. Some argue that both eugenics and state welfare constituted twin strategies of disciplinary control. Garland (1985: 130–55) insists that we need to identify substantial continuities between the nineteenth-century minimalist state and the post-Victorian 'penal–welfare' state. He underlines the extent to which eugenics inspired the modern system of social security, so that the latter is the institutional embodiment of the genetic endowments we are assumed to possess. According to this interpretation, social policy prods the genetically *unfit* into labour colonies, workfare and social assistance schemes (King, 1999) and designs labour exchanges and social insurance systems for the genetically *fit*.

Taken individually, none of the above interpretations is entirely satisfactory, yet, when taken together, they point to a conclusion that is difficult to dismiss: that eugenics had only a weak influence upon state welfare *directly* but arguably a stronger *indirect* influence that was partly egalitarian and partly inegalitarian. To some extent, then, the welfare state's traditional concern with liberty, equality and welfare may have been based upon reductive conceptions of human nature, e.g. Marshall's view that genetic inequality requires tripartite and selective education. As such, a regulated eugenics must make certain additions which correct that reductive emphasis. We are now in a position to outline the remaining two supports of a regulated eugenics.

Towards progressive biopolicies

According to the multidimensional conception, human nature displays pre-social origins which must be interpreted with social perceptions, meaning that our knowledge of human nature will always be partial and open-ended. Politically, this means supporting the principle of 'differential egalitarianism' which underpins the discussions of recognition and care in Chapter 6 and of deliberative democracy in Chapter 9.

A respect for difference and diversity is required as a reflection of the imperfectability of our knowledge, e.g. we must avoid overprescriptive views of what a meaningful human life involves in order to avoid assumptions regarding normality that invoke homogeneous notions of what it means to be human – with misogynist, disablist and homophobic notions being especially dangerous. Some degree of social equality is also required in order to ensure that that respect for difference is substantive rather than merely formal, i.e. justice requires not only the just distribution of material resources, but also the just distribution of cultural recognition. The principle of differential equality is far from straightforward for, as we saw at the end of Chapter 6, although distribution and recognition/care overlap, neither can be reduced to the other. A progressive biopolicy therefore requires an application of biotechnology which avoids reductionism by allowing difference-respecting discourses and practices to circulate within socially egalitarian environments. Ultimately, *the aim of progressive biopolicies is to maintain the multidimensionality of human nature*; the rationale for, and the objectives of, progressive biopolicies therefore resemble one another: the need to avoid the closure of the human condition around homogeneous norms.

This implies that, in addition to the usual values upon which social policy is based – welfare, equality and liberty – a respect for difference demands the addition of a fourth: precaution, i.e. do not institute change for the sake of change, but only if good enough reasons can be found. However, because change *can* be justified under certain circumstances, the value of precaution is ordered into the following lexical sequence (cf. Suzuki and Knudtson, 1990: 334–5):

Precaution

1   If it isn't broke, don't fix it. In other words, establish that there is a problem deserving of attention. So much technological innovation involves the construction of problems *ex post*, i.e. something is defined

as a problem atavistically in order to justify the time and expense of producing the innovation. We might ask the question recommended by Postman (1993): what is the problem to which this technology is the solution?

2   If it is broke, establish whether the problem is predominantly social or natural.

3   If the problem is social, *fix society*. In short, we must avoid becoming addicted to technological fixes, as this confers power and responsibility in the hands of scientific, economic and political elites, and may malfunction in ways that require more technological fixes *ad infinitum*. If the problem is natural, and if a biotech solution seems feasible, then establish a moratorium.

4   Do not end the moratorium without reference to:
     (a) *Welfare*   Will the biotechnology fulfil basic needs more effectively? Does a risk assessment reveal that both short-term and long-term risks are at an acceptable minimum?
     (b) *Equality*   Will the biotechnology benefit *all* individuals equivalently?
     (c) *Liberty*   Will the biotechnology enhance the liberty of the individual and will it be implemented with the democratic approval of most individuals?

5   If a case is established, then initiate the biotechnology slowly.

6   Initiate more rapid and radical reforms only if (5) is shown not to be working and with additional reference back to (4).

These, then, are the three criticalist supports upon which regulated eugenics rests: multidimensionality, differential egalitarianism and the precautionary principle. Having outlined it in the abstract, and for reasons explained later on, perhaps the best way of understanding regulated eugenics is by contrasting it to the *laissez-faire* approach in the light of three key social policy issues.

Three dilemmas

Genetic screening

The dilemma is simple (Rothstein, 1997; O'Neill, 1998). If people are required either to disclose the results of genetic screening, or to take a test, before receiving health and/or life insurance, then the genetically disadvantaged may be denied cover, or be required to pay excessively high premiums, or deny themselves cover by refusing to take tests that may benefit their health (Rifkin, 1998: 160–9). However, if people are not required to disclose, then insurance companies will suffer from adverse selection and the genetically *advantaged* may have to pay higher premiums than otherwise (Pokorski, 1997).

For the advocates of *laissez-faire* economics there is no dilemma. In a free market, there is no essential difference between genetic information and the other forms of information that those offering and those seeking insurance exchange in order to gain the best deal for themselves. Companies should be free to require the disclosure of relevant genetic information, setting whatever premiums they see fit, and individuals should be free to either disclose that information or to take their business elsewhere. So long as both insurance providers and insurance seekers act voluntarily in full knowledge of the likely consequences of their actions, then it is not for the state to 'buck' that market.

For those on the Centre-Left, however, such *laissez-faire economics* engenders a *laissez-faire eugenics*, where those who are both materially and genetically poor will be doubly disadvantaged. The use of genetic information in a free market will exacerbate inequalities between the most privileged and underprivileged groups that offends against the Centre-Left's conception of social justice, and so it follows that we can longer debate social justice without also debating genetic injustice.

However, genetic screening cannot simply be prohibited, as there are sound medical reasons for its use. Yet we already have an insurance system that permits both adequate, egalitarian cover *and* genetic screening: social insurance. In a social insurance system, the problems of inadequate coverage and adverse selection disappear because these are non-exclusionary schemes where premiums are uniform and returns are on the basis of need. The solution, then, is either to socialise health insurance where it is still in private hands or at least to require private insurers to behave as if they were social insurers – as is the case in Germany (Wiesing, 1999: 54). The medical benefits of genetic screening may then be utilised, so long as insurance-related problems are dealt with socially and we avoid the complete individualisation of health care that the new genetics could otherwise herald (Hubbard and Wald, 1997). Therefore, we are still engaging in eugenics (because we are making *de facto* decisions about future generations), but in a regulatory and socialised framework.

A similar contrast between *laissez-faire* and regulated eugenics can be made in respect of life insurance and employment law.[3] McGleenan and Wiesing (1999: 116) do not regard the socialisation of life insurance as realistic. If so, we might still require private life insurers to behave as if they were social ones. With some measures against fraud in place, the insurance industry can be left to absorb the potential costs of adverse selection, so long as these costs are moderate, since this is a lesser evil than the risk of genetic discrimination and could be thought of as a sumptuary tax paid by insurers as a necessary side effect of allowing a private market in social welfare. Therefore the debate regarding both health and life insurance proceeds no further than principle (3), above (cf. Reilly, 1999). If genetic screening creates problems for the insurance industry, then they are *social* ones requiring *social* solutions and not natural ones requiring a biotechnological fix (McGleenan, 1999).

Similar considerations apply to employment (Nuffield Council on Bioethics, 1999). There is a risk that job applicants may either be required to take a test or disclose the results of past tests as a condition of employment. Employers may therefore be tempted to: deny jobs to those who are vulnerable to a slight occupational hazard; only employ those who are less likely to require sick pay and leave entitlements; de-emphasise healthy and safe working conditions. However, employers can argue that screening helps everyone by avoiding the possibility of placing certain workers in jobs to which they are, or may become, unsuited.

What happens if we avoid the *laissez-faire* approach which in effect means giving employers a free hand? To a large extent, principle (3) is sufficient here also and implies that employers should be required by law to minimise risks that are environmental in origin. However, there may be exceptional cases where the minimisation of environmental risks is still not enough. For the Nuffield Council on Bioethics (1999), this refers to situations where the working environment is inherently dangerous to those with certain genetic conditions, and situations where the welfare of third parties is involved. As such, limited and carefully proscribed forms of screening may be permissible, so long as the values of welfare, equality and liberty are observed. However, screening programmes can only be allowed with substantial reference to principles (4b) and (4c), i.e. those who refuse to be screened and those who, on being screened, are found to possess a potentially dangerous condition, cannot be fired, coerced or refused employment on either of those grounds, unless the interests of third parties are demonstrably at stake. As the BMA (1998: 171) puts it, individuals '. . . should be free to accept certain risks, providing they are informed of the implications and the decision does not put others, who have not consented, at risk'. This also offers protection to the employer whose liability is reduced in those circumstances where genetic screening would have benefited the individual who refused to be screened, or where individuals accepted the risks associated with a revealed genetic condition (Knoppers, 1999: 53).

Gene therapy

By and large, commentators regard somatic cell therapy as acceptable and germ cell therapy as unacceptable (Suzuki and Knudtson, 1990: 183–91), because whereas manipulation of the former bears implications for the individual alone, manipulation of the latter bears implications for the individual's descendants as well. Yet a *laissez-faire* approach questions this distinction. If I am free to influence and even determine my children's future by providing them with a private education and other social advantages, then why should I not be able to influence/determine their future through genetic intervention as well, whether somatic cell or germ line (Harris, 1998: 173)?

Here the challenge posed by *laissez-faire* advocates is more substantial than was the case with genetic screening. It is difficult in practice to distinguish fully and adequately between the social and the biological, and between the needs of present generations and the needs of future ones. At present, the consensus seems to be that somatic cell therapy should be permissible for non-cosmetic reasons, i.e. to relieve suffering. Yet, since the lines between the cosmetic and the non-cosmetic and between somatic cell and germ cell therapy are often blurred, it might be that somatic cell therapy could be used to 'improve upon nature' and that gene cell therapy could be permitted *were the risks to be calculable*. For instance, the BMA (1998: 197–9) supports the consensus view, but allows for the possibility that the terms of the debate may need to alter once genetic technology improves. In short, it recommends the precautionary principle, but allows for the possibility that, once technological advances are in place, the promise of improving individuals' welfare overrides precaution so long as, we might add, the principles of liberty and equality are also closely observed.

However, even if this were to be the case, this does not imply that the relevant decisions should be left to individuals alone. Indeed, it could be said that the engineering of the genetic characteristics of future generations is *only* permissible in the context of international agreements that set the enforceable limits of individual freedom in this respect. In a free market, predominantly affluent individuals would be able to buy whatever was being offered by private biotechnology companies, leading to the ghettoisation of genetic privilege and underprivilege: the biological equivalents of gated communities and interiorised spaces of private surveillance. If the blurring of the line between the social and the biological demands a consistency on the part of policy-makers, then rather than granting a social and genetic free-for-all, within which affluent parents will come out on top, regulated eugenics requires that the virtue of individual freedom be measured in terms of the effects of free acts upon social equality. In a regulated market, the purchase of genetic advantage would be severely curtailed and largely prohibited, with biotechnology companies being prevented from privatising the human genome through 'life patents' and from monopolising the market in genetic pharmacology. In short, principle (4b) suggests that a *laissez-faire* market in gene therapy is undesirable, even if we one day decide that the somatic/gene cell distinction cannot hold.

Reproduction

Reproductive freedoms and social diversity are on a collision course. Biotechnology represents a quantum leap beyond existing technologies in its capacity to enhance our control over the reproductive process. Such control can involve the filtering out of undesirable qualities (certain diseases and syndromes) and possibly the 'filtering in' of qualities that are regarded as socially desirable (height, attractiveness, intelligence) – though this is a much more remote possibility. At the speculative extreme lies a debate about full human cloning. Full cloning would not involve the creation of armies of automatons, but of individuals who would be genetically identical to their 'nuclear mothers'. For some, this is no more objectionable than the existence of identical twins and test-tube babies; for others, it represents a threat to human identity.

The supporters of *laissez-faire* genetics/eugenics (Harris, 1998, 1999; Silver, 1998; Beyleveld and Brownsword, 1998) argue that if people wish to have cloned children then, if and when the technology becomes available, why shouldn't they? There are a number of hypothetical situations where the cloning of children can seem fairly unproblematic: (a) to save the life of a dying child by cloning him or her a genetically identical sibling, (b) to allow a lesbian couple to bear a biological child, (c) to allow a single women to have a child without donor insemination. However critics (Putnam, 1999; Wilmut *et al.*, 2000) allege that even these apparently benign examples suggest intractable problems. In scenario (a), the cloned sibling is being treated as a means rather than as an end; in scenario (b), there may be identity problems, e.g. the child might have two biological mothers (a nuclear mother and an egg/womb mother); in scenario (c), the identity problem may stem from the child being *both* the offspring of the mother *and* her genetically identical twin. Indeed, if we allow cloning under these circumstances, then why not the cloning of designer babies – a possibility that some *laissez-faire* advocates view as desirable and unpreventable (Silver, 1998: 141–5)?

It would be easy to relegate this issue to the future until such a time as the technology is either available or has proved to be unrealistic. Unfortunately, even if cloning technology proves to be an unscientific fiction, history shows that bad science does not prevent the design of bad policies and so the ethical debate cannot be sidelined until such time as scientists agree that there either is or is not something real to worry about. Would full cloning be available to all or would the affluent have greater access to this service? In an egalitarian society, we would be faced with the above ethical dilemmas only, but in an inegalitarian society we are also faced with the prospect of creating a genetic overclass and under-class.[4] As Silver (1998: 264) observes: 'If it is within the rights of parents to spend $100,000 for an exclusive private school education, why is it not also within their rights to spend the same amount of money to make sure that a child inherits a particular set of their genes?' If such rights are absolute and if social equality is not a consideration, then full cloning may be inevitable; however if, as was argued above, regulated eugenics sets limits on market-based liberties, then biotechnology is as much of an issue for redistributive politics as education, etc. In short, a moratorium is called for because there is a question mark over whether full cloning would satisfy principles (4b) and therefore (4a): cloning should either be available to everyone or to no-one.

However, a moratorium may not be appropriate in all circumstances. Since we may soon have the ability to eliminate certain conditions at the genetic level, do we not have a duty to do so? If we can prevent suffering by eliminating syndromes that offer their bearers only a low quality of life, then why hesitate? The problem is, who is to decide what constitutes a 'low quality of life'? If we allow physical and mental disabilities to be wiped from the human genome, then is this vastly different from the 'designer babies' that so many find distasteful?

There are convincing arguments on both sides. Critics like Shakespeare (1995, 1998) invoke the spectre of Nazism and argue that the new genetics may lead to the following. First, a decline in support for all disabled people, as genetic disabilities become rarer. Second, the inference that those who are born bearing such disabilities have lives less worthwhile than the non-disabled. Third, an increase in 'wrongful life' and 'wrongful disability' suits as children sue their parents for the inheritance of conditions that could have been eliminated. Fourth, a reduction in human diversity as 'genetic correctness' becomes the norm. Finally, the possibility that genetic engineering starts with the elimination of medical defects and ends with the elimination of 'social defects' (criminals, homosexuals, etc.). Therefore biotechnology represents a quantum leap beyond existing forms of selective abortion. However, supporters like Buchanan (1993, 1996; Harris, 1998; Buchanan *et al.*, 2000) raise a number of counter-arguments. First, avoidable suffering should be eliminated whenever possible – if we ban genetic engineering then should we not ban non-genetic techniques on the same grounds? Second, parents should have the right to know the genetic characteristics of their children and make appropriate decisions. Third, eliminating genetic disabilities need not lead to the devaluation of disabled people. Finally, if social justice requires the redistribution of undeserved *social advantages*, then does it not also demand the elimination of undeserved *genetic disadvantages*?

How can we decide between these positions, when 'difference' implies a respect for social diversity yet 'equality' requires us to reduce suffering? There would appear to be three basic options. First, we could ban prenatal testing in almost all cases. This means that there should be no intervention into the genetic characteristics of future generations. The problem with this option is that we already interfere with nature in attempting to reduce suffering. If our genetic natures are interdependent with our social environments, then the injunction to 'not interfere' might imply that we are no more allowed to manipulate the latter than the former. In fact, this option is a kind of 'naturalist *laissez-faire*', where the price for our occupying the moral high ground of non-interference will be paid by those experiencing debilitating genetically-related conditions.

Second, we could adopt the other form of *laissez-faire* whereby we allow parents to make whatever commercial decisions they wish based upon whatever information is technologically available at that time. As we have already argued though, this is to ignore the end-states of market exchange and to invoke an anti-social libertarianism that is reminiscent of Nozick (1974). Given the prejudices that too many people hold, this 'anything goes' approach might open the floodgates to the casual holocaust that those such as Shakespeare warn us against.

Finally, we could apply a regulated approach. This attempts to both reduce suffering and respect the diversity of human experience. Achieving both goals involves a balancing act so difficult that we may never get it quite right. In fact, unlike the above options, this approach can only be partly formulated in the abstract, prior to its application in the real world. The principles of regulated eugenics only become meaningful and fully comprehensible through their application. Therefore the establishment of a regulatory framework requires a perpetual, deliberative debate: a reflective, democratic discourse between scientific and policy experts and the lay public. That said, my own suspicion is that we should err on the side of caution (the precautionary principle): just as pleasure does not necessarily denote the presence of a minimal quality of life, so pain does not necessarily denote its absence. This places regulated eugenics far closer to Shakespeare's position than to that of Buchanan and implies that certain limits should be placed on reproductive rights, e.g. *if* it were possible to reveal sexual orientation through prenatal testing, then the continuance of homophobic prejudice suggests that testing should not be used for this purpose (Stein, 1998). Second, reproductive decisions should not be a substitute for social justice. Even the slightest suspicion that biotechnology will be used against the poor and/or against social diversity means that its use should be internationally banned.

Whose posthuman future?

Because his eyes do not swivel half as rapidly as Murray's, there is probably much in the above with which Francis Fukayama would agree. For all of the usual simplicities into which his analysis falls, (Orwell is treated as a soothsayer who 'got it wrong' apparently) Fukayama (2002: 99–100) wishes to resist the libertarian drift towards posthumanism and to defend an international regulation of biotechnology. Nevertheless, Fukayama's position rests upon foundations that are weak in two critical senses.

First, his is a sort of 'reluctant collectivism' in which regulation is treated as the least-worst option: 'The inefficiency of any scheme of regulation is a fact of life' (Fukayama, 2002: 184). But if the default position is assumed to lie always with deregulation and if the burden of proof weighs heavily upon those who would regulate, then Fukayama is effectively undermining the very case that he seeks to make. By introducing premises that emphasise the costs rather than the social benefits of regulation, Fukayama trips over his own feet. From a European perspective, those benefits are much more visible (Hutton, 2002).

Second, and more importantly, Fukayama adopts a form of conservative naturalism that dichotomises the debate while claiming to avoid the extremisms of others:

> There are good prudential reasons to defer to the natural order of things and not to think that human beings can easily improve on it through casual intervention. (Fukayama, 2002: 97)

> ... human nature is the sum of the behaviour and characteristics that are typical of the human species, arising from genetic rather than environmental factors. (Fukayama, 2002: 130)

But even if we accept that for instance IQ is determined by genetics by a factor of 40 to 50 per cent (Fukayama, 2002: 137), then this means that environment would still outweigh it by a factor of 50 to 60 per cent. So even according to the research which Fukayama favours, we have little reason to define human nature in such reductionist terms or to 'defer to the natural order of things'.

Therefore although Fukayama demands the regulation of biotechnology his underestimation of the social and of the benefits of social goods means that his bias is always in favour of the status quo. His is a kind of 'evolutionary communitarianism' where, 'Human beings have been wired by evolution to be social creatures who naturally seek to embed themselves in a host of communal relationships' (Fukayama, 2002: 124). Regulation is needed so that we avoid excessive interference with human nature and so preserve the future for liberal democratic capitalism. This differs from the regulated eugenics defended above for two reasons. First, because if we accept the concept of emergent properties where the later stages of evolution are more than the sum of the earlier ones, then culture cannot be treated merely as an evolutionary effect of nature. This means that 'the social' is more important than Fukayama can admit. Second, we do not have to believe that humans are 'infinitely plastic' to advocate greater intervention than Fukayama (2002: 13–14) allows; nor is it the case that excessive intervention is necessarily due to an anti-naturalistic bias: the communist experiment that Fukayama abhors occurred not because human nature was ignored, but because the commissars believed that they, and only they, truly understood the nature of nature, a conceit remarkably close to that held by the Right.

Therefore, although his support for regulation is welcome, Fukayama misses the Left's central contention: that biotechnology is permissible if and only if it serves the goals of attention, sustainability and (we may as well add) distributive justice. The Left does not have to advocate genetic engineering as a form of redistribution, nor does it have to abandon its preference for explanations that favour the social over the natural (Fukayama, 2002: 159–60); it simply has to challenge the biological reductionism upon which the Right's case is ultimately made as unfortunately is Fukayama's. So although the politics of biotechnology does not fall *neatly* into familiar political categories, those categories are rendered nowhere near as redundant as Fukayama (2002: 211) imagines.

Conclusion

The conclusion then is this: we should only be allowed to improve human well-being through biotechnology if we are also prepared to improve it through the implementation of policies based upon distributive justice and attention (the recognition of and care for diversity). This is the central insight that social policy has to offer the biotechnology debate: just biopolicies require the maintenance of just welfare systems. The recent history of welfare reform therefore gives cause for concern and suggests that biopolicies are currently more likely to follow a regressive path that we have all too often been down before.

Since this path is arguably one down which New Labour have been leading us, as Chapters 2 and 3 argued, then it is necessary to conceive of alternative routes. So whereas they have interpreted information as asocial, commodified and as a source of surveillance, this chapter has sketched a different approach. Here, information is regarded as embedded in the complexities of social relations, as a feature of the mediated interaction between human nature and its environment, as that which cannot be abstracted from its context into commodified forms of exchange without alienating the beings to whom the information belongs, as that which should not be used for the purposes of surveillance (especially in the field of health care) unless the information is itself subject to surveillance and control by social equals through open, accountable institutions and systems of discourse.

Notes

1 'Self-interest' is a more accurate term than 'selfishness' because, as Mary Midgely (1995: 91) observes, the latter attributes motivation to bits of goo. The metaphor though shows no signs of fading and has landed Dawkins in well-deserved trouble on numerous occasions.
2 Note: this is not to claim that such systems have not been also inspired by other motives.
3 Long-term care is also relevant in this context (Lenaghan, 1998: 113–14), but this is here left to one side as the regulatory solution is substantially the same as for health and life insurance.
4 As a means of avoiding this, Steiner (1994, 1999) recommends that the genetically advantaged pay a 'genetic tax' into a global fund for redistributive purposes.

9

Democratising welfare

Finally, we turn our attention to what I call welfare democracy and, in the account that follows, I argue that this is a means of bringing together the principles of attention and distributive justice. In Chapter 6, we saw that the principles overlap without either being reducible to the other and, although these ideas will no doubt continue to be discussed by social theorists in years to come, there is a need to debate the possible policy implications of these principles, a need that is generally being neglected. Our aim in this chapter is not to establish the full range of these implications, since they span a much wider intellectual terrain than we are required to explore in this book. However, I do want to examine one aspect of that terrain: welfare reform. I will suggest that dialogical institutions and systems are the best means of achieving recognition, care and distributive justice while allowing the relevant tensions to be aired and discussed creatively, albeit in a way that never permits a final resolution. This means engaging with ideas of deliberative (or discursive) democracy and relating them to the field of social policy.

We begin with social citizenship and I will argue that conservatives were able to grab the initiative partly because social rights were detached from the need to further advance the democratic project. We then contrast aggregative democracy and deliberative democracy and I observe that a reconciliation of 'procedure' and 'pluralism' is even more crucial for the latter than the former. We then apply these arguments to social policy and I sketch a theoretical outline of a welfare democracy. Essentially, the democratisation of welfare must represent a political alternative to conservatism and we spend much of the chapter analysing the obstacles in the path of that alternative and how they might be surmounted. This leads into a discussion of social movements and why such movements might offer an alternative to conservatism if they can build new constituencies with social democratic parties. We finish by exploring associative democracy and concluding that association and deliberation are invaluable aspects of a new, progressive politics.

The political deficits of social citizenship[1]

Traditional forms of state welfare have been on the defensive since the 1970s, often by those opposed to, or critical of, universalism. The Right are opposed to the practice of state universalism, since they believe that universal services and benefits waste resources by being inefficiently targeted upon low-income households and by encouraging dependency. However, while this requires the transformation of state welfare into a selectivist and punitive system, the *principle* of universalism (to which they are not necessarily opposed) can be embodied in market relations, because markets treat everyone the same. Conversely, some on the Left have been critical of universalism in theory, but not necessarily in practice. They allege that universalism has either neglected or even suppressed a spectrum of social identities, categorical boundaries and cultural boundaries by implicitly treating white, heterosexual, able-bodied men as the normative ideal (Butler, 1990). This does not mean that universal services should be abandoned, merely that universality should be much more sensitive to the particular differences of diverse social groups (Thompson and Hoggett, 1996).

For some this assault adds up to the same thing: the abandonment of class-based social justice (Taylor-Gooby, 1994, 1997). But my view is that such traditionalism is too defensive, too quick to confuse the Right's rejection of state practice with the (cultural) Left's suspicion of crude universalism (Fitzpatrick, 1996). For, whereas suspicion towards materialist and distributive paradigms undoubtedly increased in the 1970s and 1980s, often under cover of postmodernist and post-structuralist critiques, the 1990s brought a greater spirit of *rapprochement* that may yet translate into a new form of radical politics. Therefore there has emerged a 'post-universalism' that may supply the resources capable of rebuilding welfare systems on a ground that is more immune to attacks from the Right than traditional state-centred collectivism. This is because what post-universalism offers is a means of repairing the democratic deficit that assisted the crisis of universalism in the first place.

For post-universalism, the essential problem lies in the tendency to regard liberal democracy as the final stage of modernity, rather than as a key but transitional stage in the democratisation of society. This assumption is latent within Marshall's famous account, where social rights are thought to complete the journey towards full citizenship such that the conjunction of market, democratic and welfarist institutions represents the summit of the modern project (Marshall and Bottomore, 1992). Whatever the specifics of Marshall's theory, he articulates the confidence of post-war social democrats that *laissez-faire* capitalism had been routed once and for all, a confidence that had been shattered by the mid-1980s and from which social democracy is still trying to recover. Of course, the idea that liberal democracy is *not* the end of modernity was widely shared on the Left and tracks back as far as Marx in the 1840s. Unfortunately, with the discrediting of political radicalism (whether your baseline is 1956, 1968, 1979 or 1989) two options have dominated; some have hung on to the dream of modernity by settling for liberal democracy, others have wanted to go beyond liberal democracy by transcending modernity also, hence the fashion for postmodernism and the cultural turn. A third option – of regarding the radicalisation of the democratic project *as* a project of modernity – is still struggling for intellectual space.

But if this third post-universalist option is worth exploring, then what does it imply for democracy and for the greatest achievement of social democracy, the welfare state?

To some extent the Right were correct to identify the failure of state welfare to empower the powerless. For a variety of reasons (not all of them bad) post-war governments settled into a mean of complacency, where a Man-from-the-Ministry-knows-best attitude prevailed and when paternalist collectivism seemed to succeed more often than it failed. Consequently, there was usually an administrative gulf between those who produced and those who used welfare services, with the latter often feeling that they did not really own the welfare state. The enduring ambiguity of the traditional welfare state is that it both empowered *and* disempowered, laying in the social soil only shallow roots that would struggle to replenish the conditions of its own continuation.[2] Unfortunately, the Right were wrong to imagine that disempowerment was due to the association of 'rights' with 'social' as, in truth, social rights carried this ambiguity because they were detached from the category of the political. Social rights were vulnerable, not because they were too radical, but because they were not radical enough and failed to carry forward the democratisation of the economy and society. So, rather than seek to replace welfare clients with welfare citizens, the Right sought to redefine us as welfare *consumers*: the lack of empowerment was interpreted as a lack of market choice (exit) rather than a lack of democratic input (voice).

In short, social democrats like Marshall had taken one version of citizenship – where civil, political and social rights are semi-detached from one another in a 'hyphenated' society – and interpreted it as the final version. In retrospect, it was depressingly easy for conservatives to unpick this conception and adapt welfare institutions to an ethic within which social rights and entitlements play a diminishing role. This ethic of market individualism, authoritarian populism and coercive obligations has in turn infiltrated the social democratic vocabulary, though especially that of the NSD, even as the high-water mark of conservatism has passed. Social citizenship therefore continues to compel, but it currently emptied of a determinate content, whether conservative or anything which is recognisably social democratic.

So we have experienced three stages of post-war social policy.[3] First, the one-size-fits-all assumptions of state collectivism offered some measure of security to individuals defined as worker-clients, but little actual control over welfare institutions. Second, the Right interpreted empowerment in terms of market consumerism and social duties, ignoring democracy altogether. Third, the NSD has not broken away from the Right's hegemony in its expectation that people should be socially active (in employment), but politically passive. We are not condemned to this third stage, though. If the democratic deficit left the social dimensions of citizenship vulnerable to the simplistic analyses of the Right, repairing that deficit may make social rights less vulnerable to any further assaults from the Right in the future. However, this would seem to demand more than the simple recreation of state-centred collectivism, as traditionalists imagine, since it was collectivist paternalism which helped create the deficit in the first place.[4]

Imagining deliberative democracy

For post-universalists, the problem is not democracy *per se*, but *aggregative* democracy. Aggregative democracy treats citizens largely as voters whose preferences are already given and merely need to be aggregated through the mechanisms of electoral representation. The problem with aggregative democracy is that, by treating citizens as little more than voters, it both distances the state from civil society *and* allows the former too great a control over the latter. Aggregative democracy therefore engenders a distorted public sphere: one that is too attenuated to be popularly accountable and yet too congested upon political parties to replicate the transparent agora of ancient democracy. For these and other reasons, many now call for deliberative reforms that stress voice as well as exit and vote (Dryzek, 1990, 1996, 2000; Phillips, 1995; Gutmann and Thompson, 1996; Benhabib, 1996; Elster, 1998; Cooke, 2000; Warren, 2002). Whereas aggregative democracy merely counts preferences, deliberative democracy enables preferences and beliefs to be transformed through discursive interaction with others; whereas the former is instrumentalist, the latter takes account of ends as well as means; and whereas the former is representative, the latter introduces participatory elements that seem more practical and realistic than calls for direct democracy. Of course, the distinction between aggregative and deliberative democracy is not hard and fast and, unless we were to aim at a thoroughgoing participative democracy (an option that seems too remote), the representative mechanisms of aggregation would have to be incorporated within a deliberative context, if for no other reason than that a deliberative democracy cannot emerge *sui generis*. However, many insist that deliberative democracy would represent a considerable advance on aggregative representation, with demands for citizens' juries and parliaments (Smith and Wales, 2000), policy panels, frequent referenda and electronic public spaces (Tsagarousianou *et al.*, 1998) of increasing interest.

But if this is how aggregative and deliberative democracy basically contrast, then why has the latter recently become so popular among social theorists? What is the problem to which deliberative democracy is the potential solution?[5]

We find ourselves in a curious situation. Never in human history has democracy been so popular, and yet never has it so clearly failed to engage and animate the electorates who benefit from it. Apathy has infected the polity across a number of countries (though by no means all), indicated most obviously by low voter turnouts, as government elites manage from distances ever more removed from the spaces that their managerial actions affect. Occasionally something happens to stir this apathy away and for a time the blood of politics flows more rapidly through democracy's veins, yet these have largely been temporary moments that have not yet revived the social body in full. What political energy there is has tended to be re-active, and the re-awakening of the European Far Right in recent years has only compounded this. Whatever its abstract popularity as an idea then, democratic practices and institutions have begun to atrophy.

In this respect, society resembles human psychology in that both subsist upon the sound of different voices. But whenever a consciousness merely talks to itself in different voices, all that emerges are replicated echoes of what is essentially the same sound. What follows is isolation, breakdown and a drift into silence. Contrast this with the situation where genuinely different voices talk to each other in a cacophony of sound, where consciousness becomes another in a conversation of others. Here, consciousness no longer feeds merely on itself, but has a wider world on which to nourish. The job of democracy is to conduct this cacophony, to make sense of the noise which it encourages, to maintain the health of unity and difference. Unity searches for difference because it cannot do anything else; it has nowhere else to go. But the relationship between unity and difference may be either well or ill. Unity may seek a new context or it may set out to blame difference for itself; it may embrace itself within a network of differences or try to uncritically assimilate difference within itself; it may become what is affirmable or simply try to affirm what already is; it may exteriorise itself or else make everything into an interior that has no outside with which to converse. Democracy is therefore an ordered yet chaotic conversation in which sameness comes to consciousness of itself through the voices of difference.

It is here that existing democracies are failing. It is not as if there is not enough sound; indeed, the 'noise from below', from the shadows and corners of civil society, has rarely been louder. Yet this noise is not connecting with the body politic for two reasons. First, because although the noise can sound political, it searches for a new politics that traditional systems and institutions have little desire to hear; second, because the noise is often not being given a political voice at all. The fault is therefore similarly twofold. Those elites who will not listen for the new sounds are equally culpable with those within civil society who reject the political, whether old or new. The future of democracy therefore depends upon repairing this connection, upon transforming the noises from below into institutions capable of hearing them. This is the central rationale for deliberative democracy: to repair the hearing of political institutions by opening them to the discursive sounds of civil society. (And increasing social capital is not enough (Putnam, 2000). Democracy requires social capital, but not a social capital whose purpose is simply to plug the communal gaps of market individualism. For although we must trust those with whom we converse, we must be as busy talking to those we would *not* want to go bowling with as those with whom we would.) Yet here is the dilemma.

Democracy depends upon both procedures and pluralism. By 'procedures' I mean the constitutions, laws, conventions, rules and systems through which democracy runs, the machinery of politics; by 'pluralism' I mean the clamour, spontaneities, reflectiveness and dreams that provide meaning, the messiness of social life, of the lifeworld. If there is too much emphasis upon procedure, then pluralism is stifled, has no air to breathe; if there is too much emphasis upon pluralism, then procedures are potentially destabilised as chaos overwhelms the borders within which it must be contained to be socially valuable. Achieving this balance is the permanent problem of democracy. Yet the problem is particularly acute in the case of deliberative democracy precisely because the purpose of deliberation is to break procedures open to the discursive noise that they have been keeping at bay. How then is this to be done? How can democracy deliberate while still being recognisably democratic?

As Borjeson (2002) pointed out in response to an earlier version of these arguments (Fitzpatrick, 2002b), there is no easy solution, but some cause for optimism. After all, because the trajectory of deliberative democracy is not to replace its aggregative predecessors but to revitalise them, the former has much to learn from the latter, specifically, the ways in which pluralism can itself be an aspect of procedural mechanisms. For the most part, pluralism is written into procedure in the form of elections and written constitutions that allow for their own reformation under particular, carefully controlled circumstances. Moreover, there are examples from the history of aggregative democracy that inspire deliberative reform by anticipating it. Think of the repeal of prohibition in the USA, for instance, when a more mature approach to civil society was forced upon the governing elite by the noisy, ridiculing non-compliance of civil society itself (even if this non-compliance had its darker side in the form of organised crime). Therefore, it is possible to envisage pluralism-sensitive procedures that build upon the systems already available to us. But whereas aggregative democracy treats elections merely as a vote for the take-it-or-leave-it packages of parties, deliberative elections would need to intervene in the agenda-setting process much earlier than our top-heavy political parties currently allow. In short, we need to envisage a much more creative interface between parliamentary and non-parliamentary forms of politics and I will have more to say about this later.

Beforehand, let me say something briefly about one sphere that will be absolutely crucial if this balancing of procedures with pluralism is to be effective and if the deliberative citizen is to emerge.[6]

The links between substantive democracy, active citizenship and effective education have long been noted (e.g. Enslin *et al.*, 2001). To this mixture, Gutmann has added social justice because beyond a certain threshold (Rawlsian perhaps) inequality renders the practices of democracy, citizenship and education increasingly meaningless. Therefore: 'We must rely on our imperfect democratic politics to generate demands for better living and working conditions and more democratic political institutions. What conceivable change in our economic or political institutions is likely to generate these demands more effectively in the future than improving the education of children today?' (Gutmann, 1987: 286). As you will see below, I concur with this analysis, even if I think that Gutmann's prescription is fairly complacent. The problem is that education is itself a site of political contestation, as conservatives have spent over 30 years demonstrating in their repeated assaults on trendy liberal teachers, methods and theories. Therefore, we cannot improve the education of children without understanding the democratic and social objectives that we want an educational system to serve and since those objectives will always be subject to struggle, so will our ideas as to what educational improvement actually involves.

In the UK the introduction of 'Citizenship' into the National Curriculum (as of September 2002) is one potential counter-assault to the Right

(Crick, 2000: Chs 7–9; Pring, 2001; Schuller, 2001) since it makes room for the kind of reflective discussions that chalk-and-talk conservatives dislike. The problem is that the 'light touch' it applies (to avoid accusations that lessons could represent indoctrination into one version of citizenship) may still not do enough to encourage in pupils the kind of critical faculties that are anathema to the capitalist need for energetic, moderately intelligent and skilled workers.

In a sense, what I have in mind here is a version of Macintyre's (1982: 219) statement that, '. . . the good life for man is the life spent in seeking for the good life for man, and the virtues necessary for the seeking are those which will enable us to understand what more and what else the good life for man is'. For what Macintyre envisages here is an 'education in the virtues', i.e. in the ability to recognise, value and enjoy the 'practices', i.e. the internal, non-instrumental qualities of activities. This kind of education therefore pulls away from prevailing conceptions where citizenship implies wage earning and so education shrinks towards the sphere of employment. But Macintyre's is ultimately a strong communitarianism for which the nature of virtue resides within tradition and within the accepted canons. It treats the virtues as given and so its ethics is conservative and hierarchical, out of step with the modern, reflexive self.

Yet Macintyre's injunction to search for the good life is compelling and leads us towards a deliberative idea of welfare. This would be grounded in received notions of well-being (the realisation of socially-relative basic needs), but would also go further. For deliberative welfare is ultimately about a collective, democratic quest whose value resides in the fact that the expedition is endless. At its highest level, well-being arrives through the *search* for well-being, a search that is rooted in a democratic deliberation that does not seek its end. Thus welfare is given an Aristotelian spin that we can call *self-referential well-being*. Well-being is not a thing, a condition, nor even a set of fulfilled needs, but a performative process of becoming. As noted in Chapter 2, we improve the sum of social welfare, not by promoting a single version of the good, but by expanding individuals' capacities to improve the available range of meaningful goods. Therefore, a welfare democracy is that which would give institutional form to this notion of self-referential well-being. A welfare democracy requires the deliberative citizens that only it itself can properly educate. Not 'education for employment' nor 'education in the virtues' but 'education for discourse', for the arts of speaking and listening that are at the heart of democratic interaction. Here we find the deliberative citizen capable of following procedures, without allowing them to ossify into ineluctable authorities, and of playing with plural discourses, without allowing them to overwhelm.

Education for discourse therefore implies that social time (time spent by autonomous citizens in sociable and justice-enhancing activities) can only be fully emancipated by citizens who are capable of sharing it. Freed time loses meaning without self-referential well-being, and self-referential well-being requires the freeing up of social time so that we are no longer squeezed between the reinforcing grips of employment and consumption. And for time to be emancipated as social time, employment activity must not only be reduced, but new civic spaces of discursive interaction opened up. And it is within these spaces that deliberative citizens can most effectively maintain the balance of procedures and pluralism.

So although there are many examples of educational practice along the lines I have suggested, e.g. those that use Socratic methods to nurture the autonomy, creativity and sociability of children, these practices are currently trapped in an economic context where 'education for productivism' is the overwhelming priority. Hopefully, this chapter supplies deliberative citizenship with a new context, one where discourse is at the centre of democracy rather than being subservient to market relations.

A welfare democracy

We therefore have two premises. First, that post-war welfare reforms assumed that the democratic revolution was over, such that social citizenship rights did not need to question the nature and operation of political citizenship. Second, that aggregative democracy has gone as far as it can go, leading to the atrophy of democratic institutions and practices that do not connect with the discursive noise of civil society. If we now put these premises side by side, we begin to suspect that repairing the welfare state's democratic deficit requires far more than the introduction of more democracy into social policies, e.g. elections, consultation exercises, constitutions, welcome as these would be. Instead, a different *type* of democracy is required, one in which the producers and consumers of welfare services move as close together as is feasibly possible, and procedural mechanisms such as elections express the democratic conversation rather than substituting for it. In short, a 'welfare democracy' would be the institutional equivalent of deliberative democracy (Ellison, 1999), an extension of discursiveness to welfare systems without which the deliberative project is likely to stall. I have already given some indication of what this might imply for education. The big question is, how might be begin to engineer a welfare democracy? To answer this question, we have to be aware of the main obstacle that lies in our path.

Essentially, a welfare democracy would need to challenge the hegemony of conservatism. Why? Because a substantive democracy requires a greater degree of social equality than over two decades years of free market capitalism has been able (or willing) to create (Gutmann and Thompson, 1996).[7] Without social equality, some voices are inevitably more powerful than others, able to access and mobilise resources faster and more effectively than the relatively powerless – this does not mean they are the poorest communicators (Dryzek, 2000: 172), merely the most disadvantaged ones. So, although capitalist markets may be able to live with massive inequalities (and, of course, to require them), democracy breaks down beyond a certain point. Indeed, democracy has suffered most in those countries which have applied a free-market logic with the greatest fervour, with knock-on effects for civil liberties and the quality of public life. Therefore, since *laissez-faire* capitalism undermines crucial aspects of democracy (Dahl, 1985; Bowles and Gintis, 1986), and hinders the further democratisation of society, then any attempt to democratise welfare systems that is not based upon social equality would barely empower the disempowered, no matter what constitutional safeguards were in place (Ellison, 1999: 78).[8]

So, the obstacle that lies in the path of a welfare democracy is both political (how to discredit conservatism in a manner that the NSD has failed to achieve) and intellectual (how to ensure that deliberative democracy and social equality conjoin at the theoretical level). Let us take the intellectual component first, for if we can work this out, then we may be able to build the resources needed for a political challenge. Three dimensions of social equality can be identified as essential in this respect.

First, the equalisation of material resources is important, for the reasons just stated. Evidence suggests that some welfare states can redistribute income fairly successfully (Goodin *et al.*, 1999) but that the redistribution of other resources, such as capital, has rarely been on the political agenda. The democratic deficit of state collectivism could be partly attributed to this reluctance to address the property relations that underpin welfare capitalism, for it is in reconfiguring these relations that political control of the economy is ultimately ensured, rather than in applying measures such as Keynesianism and nationalisation, neither of which engenders the required decentralisation of power. Democratisation therefore requires some kind of socialised property system as its condition (Krouse and McPherson, 1988) – see Chapter 7 and again below.

Second, welfare democracy requires the equalisation of care, a gender equality which ensures that the public sphere is dominated neither by men nor by those who represent the interests of employees and employers. This means transcending the distinctions between producers and recipients, independence and dependence (White, 2000: 164). As we have

seen in a number of previous chapters, these distinctions facilitate an institutionalised paternalism that gives priority to wage earning and undermines the status of 'the dependant'. Traditionalists will object that there
are essential needs that some (especially children) will always be unable
to provide for themselves. Yet the objection is not to paternalism, but to
the institutionalisation of paternalism around an axis of needs-experts and
non-experts. This is why, in advocating her universal caregiver model,
Fraser (1989, 1997) demands room for oppositional vocabularies that can
challenge expertise, on the grounds that needs do not exist in themselves,
but are always located in a discursive context. A welfare democracy
would seem to require the equalisation of vocabularies such that many of
the 'cared-for', including children, can enter into the means of their care
as discursive and often as equal participants. Such has been the aim of the
disability movement for many years now.

Finally, and as already indicated, an equalisation of time is also important (Gorz, 1999; Beck, 2000; Fitzpatrick, 2003b). If western societies
(especially conservative ones) currently suffer from 'time poverty', i.e.
overwork and stress, and if this is related to social inequality, where relatively few achieve a desirable balance between employment and non-
employment time, due to the imperatives of a 'free' labour market, then
both the motivation and the goal of deliberative competence are one and
the same: the freeing up of social time (cf. Gershuny, 2000). I have suggested that more time is crucial if time is to be meaningful and that only
deliberative citizens are fully equipped to render such meaning. A welfare
democracy therefore requires much more than those who have only been
trained for earning and shopping, it needs the communicative participation of 'time-rich' discursive actors across a range of deliberative domains.

So the number of social forms that are compatible with a welfare
democracy are not infinite and are biased towards institutional reforms
that correct the imbalance of resources, care and time that presently lie
at the heart of social injustice. This is why a welfare democracy is not
compatible with free-market capitalism.

At this point, critics will allege that there is a contradiction to my
argument. For if democracy implies pluralism (see the discussion above
and in Chapter 1), then how is it possible to exclude from a deliberative
welfare democracy the discourses of conservatism? I should first point out
that the intention is not to *exclude* conservatism from the discursive conversation, partly because aspects of conservatism may be true (even if we
reject the whole), partly because conservatism may be help to 'disclose'
society (see Chapter 1) whenever Left principles ossify into dogma, as
happened in the Soviet Union for instance, and partly because that
conversation is necessary if conservatism is to be challenged and disen-
tangled from the egalitarian politics of social democracy. However, if

a welfare democracy implies egalitarianism, then it would have to both accommodate and marginalise those whose political philosophy is non-egalitarian.[9] Although democracy requires basic procedures upon which all participants can agree, these procedures will always be subject to subtle but important revisions, due to the very contestation over the desired outcome which is the lifeblood of democratic interaction. So although deliberative democracy's emphasis is upon procedure – in contrast to, for instance, epistemic democracy's emphasis upon 'correct answers' (Estlund, 2002) or republicanism's emphasis upon public reason (Pettit, 2001) – there is no such thing as pure proceduralism; procedures are themselves subject to democratic contestation. So I am not advocating that conservative parties and groups be deprived of rights and opportunities, but certainly greater action is needed than hitherto against that which has unduly skewed the influence over social and economic agendas in a conservative direction, e.g. political donations and lobbying, media bias and cross-media ownership, business monopolies, corporate influence, public-sector managerialism. Chapter 1 made the point that, whereas pluralism is valuable, what ultimately drives pluralism is a battle between those wish to steer liberal democracy in the direction of their favoured principles and values.

But if this criticism falls, then have we surmounted the intellectual obstacle mentioned a sort while ago, i.e. the need to show how and why deliberative democracy and social equality conjoin? Not quite. For what we have done is indicate why democratisation requires the equalisation of resources, care and time; what we have not done is to explore the converse: why equality requires democracy. The problem is that social egalitarianism has been under sustained attack since the 1970s, despite occasional victories, despite the examples of the Nordic welfare states and despite what electorates tell pollsters and social scientists. This attack has been driven by conservatism, but may ultimately be attributed to the bureaucratic, rigid and uncreative equality that welfare states created and which still seems deficient compared to the dynamic freedoms market capitalism allegedly creates. We face a paradox, then. If democratisation requires greater social equality, then social equality cannot be created without democratisation. For in order to create social equality, people must first be persuaded of its merits, yet they cannot be persuaded without the kind of deliberation of which social equality is a necessary condition. If we could transport ourselves to an 'original position' then the paradox might not arise. Unfortunately, in the real world we are faced with the problem of transition, and the kind of cooperative activity and interactive reflection envisaged by Rawls has to emerge from within capitalist societies where egalitarian politics continue to lack much support. Therefore, distinguishing between the political and intellectual components of the obstacle in the way of a welfare democracy only gets us to far. In truth, we cannot discuss theory without giving some thought to strategy and so to the actors who are to advance that strategy.

Given the fact that ecowelfare draws upon a variety of egalitarian, feminist and environmental ideas, this suggests that our analysis should centre upon social movements and their ability to counter the conservative hegemony and to radicalise social democracy. Before proceeding, two points need to be made. First, I will not delve into the details of social movement theories, namely how, why and under which circumstances social movements emerge and mobilise. This will divert us too far from our main task, which is to examine whether a welfare democracy could reconcile the principles of attention and distributive justice. Second, I will assume that the distinction between old and new social movements is unhelpful, overemphasising discontinuities and putting in question the relevance of a class analysis. Again, there is no time to go into detail, but I will be assuming that, in the developed societies, social movements operate against the background of societies that have to be described primarily as capitalist (rather than patriarchal, colonialist, homophobic, etc., even if all of these things), albeit societies that crack along a number of discursive fractures. This means – and here we anticipate our conclusion – that we can never create economic equality without addressing forms of discrimination and injustice that are more specific to gender, ethnicity, etc., nor can we create gender equality, ethnic equality etc., without tackling economic inequalities. In other words, a social movement can only be fully understood in its relationship to others within a hegemonic/counter-hegemonic field that is to be understood in terms of the inequalities that free market capitalism can moderate, but either cannot or will not eliminate.

Social movements and the prospects for democracy

The history of ideas is littered with attempts to derive moral norms from ontological foundations that always crumbled when they were examined in retrospect. And with the destruction of those foundations so the moral superstructure topples over, leaving philosophers to salvage whatever they can from the ruins and try again. It was impatience with this endeavour which led many in the twentieth century to design philosophies that could float free of foundations and essences and so remain immune from disintegration. Wittgenstein and Foucault were only ever the godchildren of Nietzsche. This impatience was validated by the final discrediting of Marxism and so began a series of the long marches towards reconciliation with 'the real' (allowing capitalism immunity from the forensic analyses that discredited Marxism), towards a desire to play among the ruins rather than reconstruct them into grand narratives, and towards high theories that do not have to get their political hands dirty. Critical theorists have found themselves pushed and pulled between these three convoys, raiding from each what they might need to restart a new procession of their own. The attempt has been to devise moral (and so political) norms, without loading them with too many ontological assumptions. This has been the project of Habermas, to mention one among many others, in his search for a communicative rationality that could be spoken by the post-metaphysical self.

Why is this story relevant to social movements? Because if social movements do represent an alternative to conservative capitalism, then how we think of them and how they think of themselves makes a difference. A social movement that interprets itself as 'playing among the fragments' offers an alternative potential to that which sees itself as progressive in the traditional sense. As indicated, we are not going to run through each and every aspect of social movement theory, but there is one question we cannot avoid: do social movements carry within them the potential for universal emancipation?

Those who have questioned the aim of universal emancipation have gone under a number of different names but 'radical democrats' seems most appropriate in this context (Laclau and Mouffe, 1985; Laclau, 1996; Mouffe, 2000). For radical democrats, power (as both production and repression) is inescapable and so social movements relate to one another through discordant lines of friend/enemy antagonisms and discursive conflict over meaning and identity. Indeed, social movements are themselves only transitory and conflictual formations. Everything is infused with democratisation, and deliberation always refers back to the context of the deliberators, since we have no recourse to an extra-contextual frame of reference; democracy is always entwined within relations of power. The trick is to ensure that enemies are 'democratic enemies' in that they do battle upon a space that both agree to maintain. This space, though, is not a universal *ground*, for universalism is not a pre-existing source of identity and rationality, but a constructed denominator that surfaces occasionally through a contingent, hegemonic alliance of particularisms (Butler *et al.*, 2000). Because the subject is never complete, closed or identical to itself, then this makes democracy an ineluctable part of identity and association. Democratic consensus, then, is always open-ended and disputable. In short, radical democrats do not reject universalism *per se*, merely those principles that are presented as final, universal truths exempt from contestation. Social movements and democracy are therefore emancipatory but this is not a universal emancipation, if by universalism we mean 'true for all people at all times'.

A longer critique of radical democracy is given in Fitzpatrick (2002b), but here all we need point out is that radical democracy is somewhat parasitic upon the critical theories that it eschews. They represent radical democracy as incommensurable with the kind of universal rationality theorised by Habermas and yet also insist that a democracy cannot survive without a 'plurality of competing forces' (Mouffe, 1999: 51). Does this mean that they are recommending we reject Habermas's ideas or not? If so, then does this not contradict their support for democratic plurality? If not, then what status in a radically democratic society would those ideas possess? Presumably, we cannot say that universal rationality has some persuasiveness after all, since this fundamentally contradicts the philosophy of radical democracy. Or is it that the idea of universal rationality should be considered both objectionable, but also necessary for the maintenance of democratic plurality, the equivalent of stating 'I disagree with what you say, but defend your right to say it'? But whereas this is normally taken to imply that even ideas you believe to be wrong may contain some grain of truth (on the lines established by Mill (1989)) radical democrats cannot make such an appeal, given the contrast they set up between a universalism that is a hegemonic construction (radical democracy) and a universalism that is true for all people at all times (critical theory).

In short, radical democracy speaks the language of pluralism, but without reference to an extra-discursive realm, debates and disagreements about the nature of which is precisely what gives democracy both its plurality and its meaning. By treating everything as contextual, radical democrats leave democracy hollow and without intellectual force. This does not mean that universal rationality determines the content of democracy, because the extra-contextual realm can never be fully transparent to us, but it does imply that some universals, true for all people at all times, can be discovered.

It therefore follows that to spy a potential for universal emancipation within social movements and within democracy properly conceived is not as difficult as those such as radical democrats imagine. What might the basis of that potential be? Let me state bluntly that it consists first and foremost in opposition to oppression, for oppression stifles the ability to articulate claims and so enter into democratic discourse in the first place. The exact nature and circumstances of oppression (and therefore of anti-oppressive strategies) are certainly contestable. In South Africa prior to 1990, for example, the anti-Apartheid movement had to articulate the linkages between the economic and racial dimensions of oppression, and then rearticulate as transformation of its own identity once Apartheid fell. But what is not contestable, what is a universal and not merely a hegemonic truth, is that democracy is only ever incomplete in the presence of oppressive relations. Democracy must therefore aim itself towards the creation of non-oppressive social relations, and so the democratic project requires the reconfiguration of actually existing democracies. How? Through social movements committed to non-oppression and therefore to the democratisation and equalisation of power.[10]

But what this universal potential does *not* imply is the idea either that each social movement must universalise its aims, i.e. attend to *all* forms of inequality and oppression, or that social movements should formally unite under one heading, the equivalent of Marx's world historical class. Radical democrats are correct to resist such suggestions. However, what social movements must do is make connections between struggles and carry those connections around with them, i.e. be ready to challenge other forms of oppression when they impact upon their more direct concerns. For example, this means that although trade unions will be mainly concerned with workplace relation, this should not exclude from their purview other relations that affect the workplace, even when these do not appear to be directly connected, e,g, domestic violence. Similarly, women's groups will be mainly concerned with issues of distributive and cultural justice that pertain to women, but will also recognise other matters that relate to reproductive value, e.g. the health implications for their children of an unsustainable environment.

(Before I am accused of stating the obvious, let me acknowledge here that I am fully aware of the extent to which social movements already practice this kind of 'grounded universalism'. They are often much smarter than the social theorists who deign to lecture at them, and Walby (2001) is correct to underline why it is the theorists who must catch up with the practitioners rather than the other way around! Nevertheless, what social theory can do is provide practice with an historical and conceptual context, and I will indicate why this is important in a moment.)

In short, the universal potential of social movements lies in creative yet never complete reconciliations that they achieve between the principles of distributive justice and attention (see Chapter 6). To protest and struggle against oppression is to demand a form of equality that even several hundred years of progress has still not achieved. But struggling against one form of oppression is redundant without the recognition that oppression is a relation, a web of dominative power, requiring the additional recognition of one's position in a network of counter-oppression. It is to care for all forms of oppression, including those that are not one's immediate business, to acknowledge the presence of everyone in the network, even though alliances will bring some closer than others. The first reason why social theory is important is because social movements sometimes get it wrong. Eyes fixed on the proximity, they can forget to take stock of the wider battle; understandably focused upon one form of domination, they sometimes imagine that it can be corrected through a new oppression rather than by dispelling the dominative impulse. Social theory can remind us that domination is not the solution to itself. To put it simply then, oppression is organic and, just as there is little point in healing only one part of an ailing body, so there is little point in resisting one form of domination to the exclusion of others. The potential of social movements is therefore for an organic universalism, a potential that they often realise but sometimes do not.

What this suggests in turn is that we must be able to read the traces of the disease that we are trying to cure. The interplay of distributive and attentive concerns does not occur naturally; it requires the identification of common enemies, the principal obstacles blocking the paths of emancipation. In short, agency is meaningless without a strategy and there can be no strategy without something to resist. Organic universalism implies not only a network of movements, but strategic orientation towards a common goal. So we have another balancing act to perform. Counter-oppression implies the coordination of the non-coordinable: too much coordination and social movements collapse into each other; too little and they fly apart and fail to recognise themselves within each other. The second reason why social theory is justified, therefore, is as a means of balancing forces whose value lies in their tendency to resist balance. What this boils down to is the observation that social movements require deliberative democracy as much as deliberative democracy requires them, for, without the former, the noise of civil society is muted and without the latter, the noise may never fully connect with the democratic process.

And if deliberative democracy refers both to welfare democracy and to social movements, it follows that social movements are also vital to the democratisation of welfare. In other words, the paradox which I sketched earlier (concerning democratisation and social equality and the idea that each is the condition for the other) is potentially resolved through forms of collective action and political mobilisation that aim to reform social policies and welfare systems in such a way that equality is democratised and democracy is made more egalitarian. If the link between democracy and equality was noted two centuries ago by Tocqueville (1990), and if liberal democracy is not necessarily the final stage of the democratic revolution, then a more thorough convergence of the two principles is called for and state welfare may be the most effective instrument currently available to us if this 'democratic equality' (Levine, 1998: Ch 5) is to be achieved. How? By social movements paying more attention to welfare issues and egalitarian parties, policy-makers and political groups taking greater account of social movements. If social movements really do represent the ever-partial reconciliation of distributive justice and attention, then the mutual learning of social movements and social policy can only strengthen these principles and offer a counter-hegemonisation to the inequalities and cultural myopias of conservatism. We therefore have *prima facie* reason to believe that a welfare democracy could reconcile the principles of attention and distributive justice.

But what might this 'democratic welfare equality' actually look like?

The convergence of association and deliberation

As before, I do not want to be accused of reinventing the wheel and I am aware of the extent to which social movements – the labour and women's movements particularly – have successfully influenced the development of social policy. Indeed, it could be said that social democracy has flourished most where it has relied as much upon social movements as upon politicians and bureaucrats (Moschonas, 2002: 156–8). Where this has not been the case (in the UK for instance), where they have been less firmly rooted in the lifeworld, then conservatives have found it easier to detach social democratic institutions from those they were originally designed to assist. What has changed is the context. The free market capitalism of the late twentieth and early twenty-first centuries is a response to this very interaction of social democracy parties and social movements that was itself a reaction to the *laissez-faire* liberalism of nineteenth- and early twentieth-century capitalism.

Therefore, social democracy and social movements have to relearn one another. The former has to hear the new noises that are coming from below, the latter has to speak to those who fight for equality in other forums – rather than condemning all parties and politicians as 'just the same'.[11] As Maschonas (2002: 236) observes, social democrats have been adept at following the trends and formations of social movements but much less skilful at anticipating and shaping them. And although it is true that social movements lack the grounded solidarity of the industrial working class (Moschonas, 2002: 256) – the traditional source of social democracy's strength – this only reinforces the need for social democrats to construct new collective identities, rather than trying to discover solidarities that it can then comfortably 'borrow'. In short, social democracy has to remobilise itself from within the fissures of civil society, to abandon the passivities of its golden age (when it could recline upon working-class support) and the conservatisms of the NSD (an endless adaptation to the existing mainstream), to rediscover the energy of the nineteenth century, when social democracy was as much the labour movement's normative antecedent as its political consequent. Therefore, I am arguing not for the abandonment of class politics, but rather for its renewal within a politics of social movements, not the pursuit of single-issue causes that can be spliced uneasily together, but the articulation of diverse solidarities around key principles (distributive justice, attention, sustainability), not the rejection of middle-class 'insecurities of affluence', but their renarration in terms of an egalitarian ethic.

This is what I meant earlier when I mentioned the need for a more creative interface between parliamentary and non-parliamentary forms of politics. The disconnection (the deafness of formal systems to the discursive conversations taking place around them) from which developed, aggregative democracies currently suffer cannot be set right by cutting the parliamentary and the non-parliamentary sectors adrift. This is the dream of many within both elite and non-elite organisations. For the former, democratic consultation can be limited to focus groups, newspaper letter pages, stage-managed rallies and media events; for the latter, the new politics bears no resemblance to the old and so consists of gesture, symbolism and violence for the sake of violence. Perversely, the spin doctors and the rejectionists both use the very same argument in order to despise the other: government is for insiders only. Fortunately, most citizens have not stopped talking to government just because the governing classes are reluctant to listen.

However, it is not my task to sketch what this more creative interface between the parliamentary and non-parliamentary might resemble as a whole. Instead, I want to say something about it with specific reference to welfare democracy. The point of a welfare democracy would be to empower and so help to reverse the experiences and feelings of powerlessness that are creating the pathologies of contemporary society. For, when people do not feel in control of their lives, they tend to reach for scapegoats and simplistic solutions; extremism and fanaticism *do* empower, if only in a destructive way. Yet the new extremism (ethnic nationalism, religious fundamentalism, xenophobia) represents less the unravelling of the mainstream as its negative image. By being unwilling to carry the democratic revolution forward, by facilitating economic and social forces that wash away the fixed grounds needed for ontological security, by crowding into the Centre and favouring an elitist, gridlocked politics, the new spaces of extremism have been opened by a mainstream betraying its own legacy.

Yet it is not as if the mainstream has been unaware of the dangers that it has engendered. It would not be inaccurate to characterise social democracy during the post-communist era as the search for a reconciliation between deregulated capitalism and a civic rootedness that would re-socialise global forces. This explains why a number of 'big ideas' have proliferated. 'Stakeholding' was a big idea that ultimately foundered on the disagreement between those who saw it as an alternative to deregulated capitalism (Hutton, 1995, 2002) and those for whom it meant limited inclusion against a background of inequality (Blair, 1998). 'Stakeholder welfare' has therefore come to possess little meaning, other than the attempt to lever poor households into the private welfare market. 'Social capital', too, has enthused the policy wonks, tying in nicely with the fashionable emphasis upon employment and community. The very title gives the game away, sadly. For rather than suggest a new form of economics, much of the literature of social capital has been designed to shore up the spaces of stability, the informal networks and the civic trust that post-Keynesian economies can only undermine (Fukayama, 1996): it is a bandage for the wounds of global capitalism. And EU integration holds to the ideal of a social Europe that will accommodate citizens and not just market actors. Yet this ideal is constantly impaired by a confusion of 'citizen' with 'worker' and by the EU's tendency to follow the liberalising agenda of the IMF, World Bank and WTO.

The social democratic mainstream has therefore pinned itself to a contradiction: it has committed itself not to a globally regulated capitalism, but to a reregulation of the social spaces that *laissez-faire* economies constantly destabilise. This contradiction is more in evidence where the NSD has taken hold (see Chapter 3) but could be said to describe the contemporary dilemma of social democracy *per se*. However, this period has also seen new ideas emerge from within the academy that could help to renew social democracy. Take the debate concerning 'associative democracy' for instance (Cohen and Rogers, 1995; Carter, 2002).

The aim of associative democracy would be to create new forms of collective and communal forms of association that would mediate between state and civil society, without allowing either the state to become too big (so *dirigisme* would be avoided) or imposing a unitary identity upon civil society, i.e. the way in which communitarians overcompensate for the fragmentations of market economics. Associative democracy is therefore something of a middle way between state socialism and market capitalism, but one that, unlike the Third Way, does not remain complacent about the social detritus that the market revolution has left in its wake. Its purpose is to re-empower by bringing the spaces of economic and social production and consumption as close together as feasibly possible. It could represent a more creative interface between the parliamentary and the non-parliamentary by not confusing the former with state collectivism or the latter with market individualism; associative democracy would try to democratise each by democratising both.

Although associative democracy therefore bears implications across the economic, political and social spheres, I want to take a particular look at the work of Paul Hirst, since it is Hirst who has come closest to applying these ideas to social policy (Fitzpatrick, 2002a). Hirst (1994, 1997, 1998) argues that large parts of government can and should be devolved to self-governing, voluntary, publicly-funded and publicly-accountable associations, whose members would have varying degrees of control over public systems of provision. An associational welfare system would maintain an emphasis upon distributive justice, but would be less collectivist than the classic welfare state. Self-governing associations would deliver and/or purchase many of the services that are currently provided either by the state or the market, yet play a more systematic role in the welfare of society than the traditional independent sector. Hirst envisages that we would all become members of these associations, with rights to vote and to exit if we choose, and that the associations will have to meet certain criteria if they are to receive public funds via some form of formula-funded voucher system.

The attraction of associational welfare is that it would empower the users of public services more effectively than either state collectivism or a Third Way approach. Those who defend the former (Stears, 1999) tend to overestimate the paternalistic virtues of the welfare state and to underestimate the extent to which any inability that citizens now possess to take greater control of their lives is a regrettable *effect* of paternalism, rather than a justification of yet more paternalism (cf. Hirst, 1999a). Those who defend the latter overemphasise both the importance of globalisation and the declining validity of older versions of social democracy (Hirst and Thompson, 1996; Hirst, 1999b).

However, there are three main problems with Hirst's formulation of associative welfare (cf. Carter, 2002). First, he places too much stress upon exit and not enough upon voice. His associations would be representative democracies in which the main constraint upon associations' leaders would be the withdrawal of their members and the consequent loss of public funds (Hirst, 2000: 289). This fails to break away from today's consumerist ethos, where voice is only ever an individualistic prelude to exit rather than a cooperativist strategy. This is not to argue that a welfare democracy would have to limit the right of exit; instead, it is to recognise that *it is the market system which limits the right of exit* whenever public goods are concerned. Therefore, the point is to regard voice and exit as compatible, if they are both conceived in cooperativist and mutualist terms. It is here that social movements could be particularly relevant, since if they were to embody the organic universalism mentioned above, then social movements would need to disperse themselves across associations (rather than congregate upon particular associations as a form of single-issue politics) in order to promote the aims of democracy and social equality. Social movements would encourage the voices of associative deliberation.

The second problem, then, is that whereas he once regarded it as a means of renewing socialism, Hirst came to present associative democracy as politically neutral. This is similar to Offe's (2000) mistake in imagining that working out the proper civic mix between state, market and community can be done without reference to ideological schemes. What this ignores is the fact that any associational welfare worthy of the name would have to be egalitarian (otherwise the practices of exit and voice would do no more than mirror existing patterns of inequality) and so subject the current meanings of 'state', 'market' and 'community' to challenge, challenges that could not occur without ideological orientations. As I argued above with reference to deliberative democracy, this need not mean that a welfare democracy would exclude non-egalitarians from the conversation, but it would have to directly confront and present alternatives to the conservative hegemony. The classic welfare state shifted the political battleground to the Left and associational welfare would have to possess a similar goal.

The final problem is that Hirst does not pay enough attention to the centralised state, insisting that the methods of governance would flow *from* the state *to* associations. Yet here, again, we are presented with an either/or logic which treats the state and associations in exclusivist terms. Any shifts in the loci of governance must aim to *enhance* the democratisation of the state, rather than merely sublimating democratic governance to the civic sphere. It may be that Hirst confuses collective ownership with state ownership, such that if the latter is no longer credible, then the former has to be abandoned also. What remains underexplored, then, is the extent to which an associative democracy could facilitate economic democracy along the lines sketched in Chapter 7. Some associations could control socialised firms and funds, channelling the investment strategies of their members towards socially and environmentally desirable goals. But if this were to be the case, then some state action would be needed to regulate this system, as well as helping to maintain parity between associations, and a considerable amount of state action would be needed at the regional and global levels to bring about the socialisation of productive assets. This is obviously a daunting and long-term task, but Hirst (among others) does the debate no favours by ignoring it.

In short, although Hirst's associational system approximates to what a welfare democracy might look like, the latter would have to give far greater emphasis to voice, it would need to draw upon egalitarian conceptions of cooperative mutualism and it would need to reconstitute the welfare state around an egalitarian politics (of socialised ownership), rather than merely devolving it to voluntary associations. It is possible to envisage welfare associations (Fitzpatrick, 1999c) – mutuals, cooperatives and not-for-profit social enterprises – acting as the conduits for such reforms. Without these kind of revisions to the basic blueprint, then were it ever translated into the political reality, associative democracy would risk the same fate as befell stakeholding, i.e. of shoring up a conservative system. Unless association and deliberation converge around an egalitarian social democracy then associative democracy may fail to hear the democratic noise and deliberative democracy may lack an institutional form that transcends experiments with citizens' juries and policy panels. Similarly, unless social democracy rediscovers itself at the interface of state and civil society, then its traditional rationale may continue to lose its hold on the social imagination: how to collectively control a market economy without giving too much power to a state that would allow civil society to wither.

Empowerment therefore requires both association, deliberation and equality, and so a welfare democracy would need to be founded upon both new forms of governance (procedure) and discursiveness (pluralism). And ultimately, the creative interface of parliamentary and non-parliamentary politics requires that social democrats and social movements begin to learn from one another more effectively than has been the case during the detour towards the NSD. This leads us back to the problem mentioned earlier, the problem of transition and how to translate these ideas into political reality. With parties traditionally seeking to institutionalise social movements and movements both welcoming and resisting such institutionalisation, then what can be done to encourage the more creative learning processes that I have presented as vital to deliberative democracy? There is no easy answer to this and I return to it in the concluding chapter. For now, let me make the simple point that so far as deliberative democracy is concerned, we do not talk about it and *then* create it, we begin to create it *by talking about it*. The problem of transition is a problem for those who recognise the need for transition; and if both egalitarian social democrats and non-oppressive social movements recognise that need *and* each other's recognition, then the problem of transition may lie as much behind us as before us.

Conclusion

We began with a post-universalist account of social citizenship and the view that social rights had become discredited because they were detached from the need to advance the democratic project further. We then contrasted aggregative democracy and deliberative democracy to see what this advance might resemble and I noted that a reconciliation of 'procedure' and 'pluralism' is of key importance. I then sketched a theoretical outline of a welfare democracy and characterised it as an egalitarian alternative to conservatism. However, this alternative cannot be imagined without reference to questions of actors and strategies, suggesting that the universal potential of non-oppressive social movements should make common cause with social democratic parties, despite the fact that many within those parties have fallen under the conservative sway. We concluded by exploring associative democratic ideas and I suggested that association and deliberation are both essential components of an egalitarian politics.

This brings our analysis of the ecowelfare triangle to a close. In Chapter 6, I observed that its main principles should not be collapsed under a single heading, since it is facile to imagine that they always and everywhere cohere. Instead, ecowelfare ought to be regarded as diverse set of ideas that nevertheless revolve around the same set of objectives: to renew social democracy and turn it away from the NSD. The last three chapters give some illustration of just some of the theoretical debates with which this post-productivist social democracy might engage. And as I stated in Chapter 6, whether you agree with most, some or little of what I have said is not important, what is crucial is that you recognise there is something important to be disagreed with. If that is the case, then alternatives to the NSD have already been sighted.

Notes

1 For a longer account of the following argument, see Fitzpatrick (2002b).
2 Though the 'shallowness' of those roots differs from country to country; see Chapter 4.
3 These stages apply most directly to the UK but could, with some effort, be applied to other developed nations.
4 I should here add that I have also discussed the links between environmentalism and democracy elsewhere (Fitzpatrick, 2002d) and so suspect that democratisation is a means of linking together the ecowelfare triangle's three principles with greater coherence than is being suggested in Part II. However, not having worked out the full implications of this, I do not want to spend time on ill-formed speculations, nor do I wish to suggest that deliberative democracy is a panacea (see below). Therefore, all I can do here is to indicate a direction for future work.
5 I will not be offering a systematic critique of deliberative democracy and believe that it should not be seen as a panacea for the ills of western democracy. In particular, deliberative democracy can be accused of neglecting non-rationalistic forms of voice, of underemphasising the inequalities of voice, of not always specifying the necessary limits to democratic debate and of failing to get to grips with the problem of social scale, i.e. how can small-scale delib-

erative fora provide large, complex societies with the legitimacy they require? These issues are discussed in Dryzek (2000, 2001), Young (2000, 2001), Weeks (2000) and Thompson & Hoggett (2001).

 6 For reasons of limited space, I will leave to one side another important sphere, which is that of the media and ICTs. However, I acknowledge that these are absolutely crucial to future of democracy and are relevant to the discursive education that I am about to defend.

 7 In contrast to her earlier work, Young (2000: 92–9, 105) now makes room for the importance of economic structures and inequalities that are not reducible to the cultural (see Chapter 6). However, she has yet to grapple with the difficult implications this bears for deliberative democracy.

 8 However, I leave open the question of how much equality is required. I will simply be assuming that the post-1970s lurch towards greater inequality must be reversed and so the economic philosophy of conservatism finally overturned. However, I suspect that unless we revisit an issue that I am about to mention (concerning property relations) then any inroads into social inequalities will be modest and short-lived.

 9 And remember that such decisions are inescapable within any liberal and democratic society, including unequal ones; how does a society live with those who would undermine it?

10 Note, then, that I am not claiming that all social movements are non-oppressive. Obviously, this is not the case. Instead, I am deploying the universal truth of non-oppressiveness to distinguish between those social movements which are progressive and those which are not. It is the former who might constitute the basis of an deliberative politics.

11 In this respect, the experience of environmentalism is salutary. Green movements and parties have undoubtedly constituted a welcome addition to politics and yet the intellectual gulf between Greens and social democrats remains largely wide and uninspiring, caught in the same old pincer movement between realists and idealists.

Conclusion

Chapter 1 argued that although it is simplistic to equate New Labour with conservatism, both it and the NSD which it represents fail to offer a real alternative to the conservative hegemony. The NSD has inserted itself into a mainstream agenda where being tough on problem individuals is thought to be more moral than being tough on social problems. This has helped to consolidate what I called the 'age of mainstreams', a shrinking of the social imagination around the extremist Centre. However, rather than cause us to abandon social democratic thought, we should detect within it a genuinely radical potential.

This potential can be viewed in contrast to the philosophy of justice preferred by New Labour. For whereas this philosophy is built around a combination of 'weak equality' and 'strong reciprocity', I argued in Chapter 2 for an alternative that favours 'strong equality' and 'diverse reciprocity'. This alternative version of distributive justice constitutes the first principle of ecowelfare as explored in Part II.

Chapter 3 continued the critique of New Labour, arguing that it should be interpreted as both an effect and perpetuation of the security state, a state within which the attempt to realise basic needs for all has been replaced by the attempt to assuage the basic fears of some. But this trans-formation is not merely of theoretical interest and we saw how and why it has influenced New Labour's conception of information and its policies towards ICTs.

Chapter 4 proposed that the 'old' social democracy is not as discred-ited as new social democrats would have us believe. Social democracy undoubtedly faces some very real challenges, but it is far from clear that the NSD is any better equipped to address them than the old. As such, I suggested that social democrats should explore post-productivist values and ideas as a means of reconnecting social democracy to radical roots that the NSD seems to have abandoned.

Ecowelfare was therefore defined as 'post-productivist social democracy' and the meaning of post-productivism was sketched in Chapter 5. Essentially, post-productivism recontextualises growth, productivity and well-being in terms of reproductive values, values that refer to the ecological and social conditions of a productive economy, the very underlying conditions which that economy is increasingly unable to replenish. I contended that economic practice has to be assessed in terms of 'reproductivity', meaning that labour has to refer less to waged work and more to the kind of emotional and ecological labour that economic orthodoxies continue to neglect.

Chapter 6 provided a basic model of ecowelfare as based around three principles: that of distributive justice as defined and defended in Chapter 2; the principle of 'attention', which I theorised in terms of both recognition and care; the principle of sustainability which I discussed in terms of what I called moderate sustainability and ecological radicalisation. Chapter 6 therefore set the scene for the next three chapters, where the links between these principles were further explored.

Chapter 7 outlined a theory of intergenerational justice and concluded that the ultimate conflict is less between present generations and future ones as between those who would and those who would not favour a more equitable distribution of natural and social resources. I tried to show that intergenerational justice engenders a series of implications for social policy that are as radical for ourselves as for the future.

In Chapter 8 we turned our attention to the new genetics and I proposed a multidimensional conception of human nature, where the maintenance of diversity through social (rather than technological) solutions should be the main priority. However, since we are also obliged to prevent harm whenever it is possible and desirable to do so and since we cannot disinvent biotechnology, we have some difficult decisions to make regarding the genetic characteristics of future generations. Chapter 8 therefore argues for a 'regulated eugenics' as an alternative to the '*laissez-faire* eugenics' which free market capitalism might engender.

Finally, Chapter 9 considered the meaning and significance of deliberative democracy and of the welfare democracy which would need to be at its heart. We saw that a welfare democracy could offer an egalitarian alternative to both conservatism and the NSD by encouraging new forms of political association and debate. Yet for a welfare democracy to emerge, we need to start creating a much more democratic conversation between parliamentary and non-parliamentary forms of politics and so between social movements and social democratic parties also. The chapter concluded with an analysis of associative democracy and welfare proposals, finding that a combination of both associative and deliberative approaches is required.

In the year it has taken to plan, research and write this book, the world has never looked so different and yet also so horribly familiar. A new age of innocence and safety was created, the world before our world. Before arms pointed upwards shielding eyes from the morning glare, before the last call home and too many words for those to whom no words need be said, after the calls were silenced and before the noise began. And now innocence may never be available to us ever again. America isolates the rest of the world from itself, bullying those whose grief is any less, attacking that which is other, failing again to hear the sounds to which only empires are deaf, of new enemies born weeping beside the craters of Freedom and Democracy. The Middle East finds ever new circles of hell into which to descend. The Judeo-Christian and Muslim traditions sweep by in confused alarms of struggle and flight, failing to recognise themselves in one another, finding common ground only in the rock-strewn graveyards of bereavement and hate. Civilisations clash not because they must, but because anti-liberal extremists within both worlds desire it; prophets who march their followers to the very wastegrounds of pain and death that they foretold would bury only their enemies. The fundamentalists of power that can only ever stare inward and the fundamentalists of the powerless, those who spent patient decades watching the skies, waiting for two glints of metal to arc out of the cloudless air. The West and the Rest. Each seeking to destroy that which it has exiled from itself.

In Europe too, many are trying to rebuild the walls of suspicion and fear. The days of limitless possibility that followed 1989 have long since darkened. The more the space of Europe has grown, the smaller the shelters of identity have appeared and so the greater the desire for the reassuring interiors of stability, the havens of sameness. White ethnicity risks recoiling upon itself, rejecting the homelessness that it fears may come to it without the soothing arms of nationhood. The symphony of European integration is conducted at a distance from those it affects, populations who are called upon to play their instruments in tune to a music that they have had little opportunity to compose. So in the absence of public spaces that are properly European, the project finds a passive acceptance at best. And as we struggle to find distinctness within commonality, those who would abandon the search altogether and reinvent the familiar have found a new audience. The resurgence of the Right and far Right derives from a common source: the difficulty of imagining a post-national society. So racism wears a suit and becomes respectable again. Is it convenient that the obsession with crime and immigration has coincided with a new mistrust of the diasporic other, whether Jewish or Muslim or both? Or are they both signatures of the same insecurity: the struggle for control on the part of those who feel that they do not really control their lives?

For this is the essential problem and the reason why social democrats have borne the brunt of the new insecurities (Moschonas, 2002: 108–9). It could be argued that there is no real crisis of social democracy, that the electoral victories of 1997–98 and the defeats of 2001–2 are coincidental and have to be read in terms of each nation's particular context. If this is the case, then social democrats need do no more than plan and wait for the next electoral cycle to roll around, for the doors of government to reopen and permit access to the Left's agenda once again. Yet we do not have to talk in messianic terms of a 'crisis of social democracy' to recognise that something has gone wrong. Given the opportunity to vote for the Left in 1997–98, the electorates of Europe took it; and given the opportunity to vote against the Left in 2001–2, the electorates of Europe also took this option. Why? A common response is that while it may successfully create an economic context for egalitarian solidarity, the Left has neglected the cultural aspects. It has failed to demand enough of the socially excluded and it has not addressed the real and very widespread concerns about the social fabric being destabilised from the outside. In short, it has ignored fears about crime and immigration and the cultural insecurities that they bring. The case for the NSD is therefore strengthened rather than weakened, because only the NSD fully recognises the lifestyle politics through which feelings of either security or insecurity are woven (Giddens, 2002b).

Yet if insecurity is the problem, manifested as fears about crime and immigration, then is the Left really to blame for neglecting the moral and cultural aspects of social solidarity? Or is it that what both old and new social democrats have really ignored is a deeper cause of insecurity? For what the above explanation conveniently avoids are other sources of insecurity that the NSD, far from closing off, has actively promoted! In an economy where the shareholder is king, where skills are less about doing something tangible and more about the skill to acquire further skills, where relationships are ephemeral and entitlements become portable, where we are expected to give companies a loyalty that relatively few return, where flexibility is defined largely in terms of the needs of employers, where competition with anyone and everyone around the globe is the highest virtue, where we have portfolios rather than careers, where the retirement age seems to ratchet upwards every few years, where in other words we live to work instead of work to live, then it is little surprise that the sense of self and of belonging begins to splinter. (Apologists for the contemporary labour market assert that it actually provides more security than is often perceived (Reeves, 2001), but this is to ignore the effects that the ideology of flexibility has on workers treated increasingly as disposable commodities.) And once this fragmentation reaches a critical point, is it any surprise that we will reach for scapegoats, those who cause our insecurity and whose punishment will resolve it, or rebuke those who either patronise our fears when they are not ignoring them altogether? This is not to suggest that insecurity is always and everywhere economic in origin (especially since the economics of insecurity are more evident in some countries than others), but it is to suggest that without a substantial rethinking as to what we mean by economic value, then social democracies may simply be at an earlier stage of social disintegration than conservative nations (Hutton, 2002: Ch. 11).

So the old social democracy cannot be absolved either. For whereas it has been very good at nourishing the material aspects of solidarity, it has been less effective at encouraging the democratic ones. Nordic corporatism (the idea of social partnership) is integrative, but only at a very high level, the level of representative democracy. What it has been less effective at doing is decentralising control of both society and economy, perhaps out of concern that this will cause the consensus upon which its high levels of social equality are built to crumble. But if fear and insecurity, from which the Left is currently suffering a political backlash, is produced when people do not possess and know that they do not possess enough control over their lives, then although social equality is much *it is still not enough*. Without the democratisation of institutions, systems and practices, then equality may simply represent the European equivalent of American consumerism; a bread-and-circuses compensation for the infantilisation of the populace. Therefore, the Left has to ask itself anew some apparently simple questions. How do we maximise the control that people have over their lives? How do we increase levels of self-determination? How do we empower people to empower themselves?

In order to answer this question and translate it into a new politics, we do not have recourse to the answers that conservatives, communitarians and new social democrats have given in recent decades. For conservatives, self-determination is delivered through the permanent revolution of market forces, for communitarians it implies status and familism, for new social democrats it implies wage earning, aspiration and duty. For reasons that this book should have made clear, each of these answers offends against the egalitarianism that is, and should be, at the heart of the social democratic tradition. Social democrats therefore need to stress not inequality nor even equality *per se*, but the kind of participative equality that we began to explore in the last chapter and which, as Note 8 of Chapter 9 indicated, may be crucial to the future prospects of the Left. Democratic equality means that freedom cannot be expressed, as conservatives would wish, simply as mobility and choice within a market since both democracy and equality are principles that markets may assist, but can never replicate. It means that freedom cannot be expressed, as communitarians would wish, in terms of hierarchy and obedience to received

norms since democracy's aim is to question those social forms by facilitating participation between social equals.[1] And it means that freedom
cannot simply be expressed, as new social democrats wish, as inclusion
within an employment society, since wage earning is only one form of
valuable social activity and democracy requires a temporal and spatial
politics that is squeezed out when people have to spend most of their
waking lives 'labouring for another' (Fitzpatrick, 2003b).

Participative equality therefore implies a new form of civic engagement
and public space, one which subjects public issues, debates and decisions
to the kind of democratic gaze that is presently threaded through a limited
range of pressure groups, protest groups and lobbying organisations, all
of which specialise in one area of concern. Philosophers from Arendt to
Habermas have claimed that this kind of public participation was, at least
for a segment of the population, more current in the past than in the
present, before the public sphere became a remote territory into which
most of us fail to venture most of the time. The politics of representation
breaks that public sphere open from time to time and often quite effectively, yet also confirms its remoteness and impenetrability, a citadel that
like Kafka's castle shimmers and fades away from us the closer to it we
seem to get. There is therefore an urgent need for 'counterpublics' that
will not only break the public sphere open more effectively, but also allow
it to be reconfigured as a network of spheres within the associative rooms
and dwellings of civil society, transforming civil society in the process. In
short, public space needs a greater degree of civicness and civil society a
greater degree of politicisation.

In itself, there is nothing stunningly new about these ideas as they have
been discussed and exchanged for many years now, a means of counter-
ing a newly resurgent Right, while seeking to reconstruct the Left. But
what has been lacking is a convincing means of translating them into a
new politics, one that avoids the statism of the old Left while rejecting the
expediencies of the NSD. The aim of this book has been to apply the language of social philosophy to this problem of translation and has outlined
various principles around which a new constituency could be built. One
that regards material equality as essential to any serious conception of
reciprocity and responsibility, one which recognises the value of care
and cares for those whom we recognise, one that regards sustainability as
crucial to human well-being (now as much as in the future), one that
relocates the desire for productivity, affluence and growth on the site of
reproductivity and the values of emotional and ecological labour.

What kind of constituency would this resemble? Not simply a 'rainbow
coalition' as this idea, given its American origins, implies the kind of
cultural separatism that liberal egalitarianism eschews; nor a class war,
as any class-based politics has to acknowledge the lines of social fracture

along which classes run; nor simply a middle-class politics where we chase the elusive few in the electoral middle ground, because while we should not ignore popular misconceptions ('the courts are too soft', 'we're a soft touch for asylum seekers'), and one aim of counter-public spaces is to confront them, we must not repeat the NSD mistake of pandering to them either. As noted in the last chapter, this is to call not for a politics of class or of non-class, but a politics of social movements that comprehends both the generality and specificities of oppression. And if oppression is only ever universal *and* particular, then anti-oppressive mobilisations have to follow suit. Therefore the point of this book has not been to group the members of the constituency under a single heading, but to reiterate the simple but incredibly important point that the usual suspects (socialists, egalitarians, feminists, social liberals, environmentalists) may talk to the favoured principles and priorities of others in the course of talking to their own.

And are perhaps doing so. For although the major events of the last year offer many reasons for pessimism, we have to be optimists despite ourselves. The Global Social Justice movement (the loose affiliation of those who have gone under a number of names since the mid-1990s) is one such source of optimism in a pessimistic world. By challenging the hegemony of corporate capitalism, by arguing for fair trade rather than free trade, by opening the closed doors of international negotiations, by intervening in a variety of social and military conflicts, the movement has given flesh to the idea of a global civil society and has allowed counter-public spaces to flicker here and there into life. Yes, as many smug journalists have observed, it often lacks intellectual rigour and political coherence, but that is as much a potential strength as a weakness, a sign of creativity and plasticity that can recreate itself in any number of social settings. And if the movement lacked real force and direction, then the Right would not have spent so much time since 11 September 2001 trying to establish a link (guilt by association) between 'anti-capitalists' and anti-Western terrorism, the kind of political capital that makes the Right what it is, an organised hypocrisy.

If social democrats therefore accept my arguments that we need new alliances as a means of bridging the gap between the parliamentary and non-parliamentary, then here is one opportunity for the creative learning process that I mentioned in Chapter 9. If there is a pressing need for a global regulatory system that embraces criteria and objectives different to that of the IMF, etc., then both the International movement and social democrats have a mutual interest in trying to construct that system. If there is a democratic vacuum within the EU, then here also they have a mutual interest in trying to strengthen forms of democratic governance. In 10 or 20 years the opportunity may be different in character, though in

10 or 20 years there may *be* no opportunity if we fail here and now. Social movements have to learn how to institutionalise themselves (as many movement organisations have already learned to do) without disappearing into the hollows of formal politics; social democratic parties and trade unions have to learn to become less respectable, less deferential to the mores of established politics, more receptive to the messy sounds of civil life. And both sides have to learn how to be both inside and outside the established order, contributing to the maintenance of that order, while also engaging in new forms of civic experimentation and discursive challenge that subject the order to a constant critical review.

But there is no manual that can teach this; the students *are* the teachers. And the ultimate destination is no less important than the aim: to topple the economics of insecurity and the culture of fear and blame, to remember that each individual controls their life only in so far as they enable others to control theirs, to evoke the common project upon which we are all engaged whether we like it or not. We are individuals only in so far as we belong to one another. We are free only if we can democratically and collectively begin to reverse the tides of conservative dogma and shift the political Centre back towards a progressive agenda. We live fully only in those parts of our lives to which we refuse entry to quantitative criteria and statistical indicators.

There is a world to change. What else is there to do and how else but together can we do it?

Note

1 This is at least true of those communitarians who swing towards the conservative end of the spectrum.

References

Aglietta, M. (1998) 'Capitalism at the Turn of the Century: Regulation Theory and the Challenge of Social Change', *New Left Review*, 232: 41–90.

Allender, P. (2001) 'What's New About New Labour?', *Politics*, 21(1): 56–62.

Amsberg, J. (1995) 'Excessive Environmental Risks: An Intergenerational Market Failure', *European Economic Review*, 39: 1447–64.

Andersen, M. and Liefferink, J. (eds) (1997) *European Environmental Policy*, Manchester: Manchester University Press.

Andrews, L. and Nelkin, D. (2001) *Body Bazaar*, New York: Crown Publishers.

Arneson, R. (1989) 'Equality and Equal Opportunity for Welfare', *Philosophical Studies*, 56: 77–93.

Arneson, R. (1995) 'Against "Complex" Equality', in Miller, D. and Walzer, M. (eds) *Pluralism, Justice and Equality*, Oxford: Oxford University Press.

Arneson, R. (2000) 'Welfare Should be the Currency of Justice', *Canadian Journal of Philosophy*, 30(4): 497–524.

Axelrod, R. (1984) *The Evolution of Cooperation*, New York: Basic Books.

Baldwin, P. (1990) *The Politics of Social Solidarity*, Cambridge: Cambridge University Press.

Ball, T. (2001) 'New Ethics for Old? Or How (Not) to Think About Future Generations', *Environmental Politics*, 10(1): 89–110.

Ball, T. and Dagger, R. (1991) *Political Ideologies and the Democratic Ideal*, New York: HarperCollins.

Bara, J. and Budge, I. (2001) 'Party Policy and Ideology: Still New Labour?', *Parliamentary Affairs*, 54: 590–606.

Barlow, A. and Duncan, S. (2000a) 'Supporting Families? New Labour's Communitarianism and the "Rationality Mistake": Part 1', *Journal of Social Welfare and Family Law*, 22(1): 23–42.

Barlow, A. and Duncan, S. (2000b) 'Supporting Families? New Labour's Communitarianism and the "Rationality Mistake": Part 2', *Journal of Social Welfare and Family Law*, 22(2): 129–43.

Barry, B. (1989) *Theories of Justice*, Berkeley and Los Angeles: University of California Press.

Barry, B. (1995) *Justice as Impartiality*, Oxford: Oxford University Press.

Barry, B. (1999) 'Sustainability and Intergenerational Justice', in Dobson, A. (ed.) *Fairness and Futurity*, Oxford: Oxford University Press.

Barry, B. (2001) *Culture and Equality*, Cambridge: Polity.

Barry, J. (1999) *Rethinking Green Politics: Nature, Virtue and Progress*, London: Sage.

Barry, J. and Proops, J. (2000) *Citizenship, Sustainability and Environmental Research*, Aldershot: Edward Elgar.

Bauman, Z. (1998a) *Globalization*, Cambridge: Polity.

Bauman, Z. (1998b) *Work, Consumerism and the New Poor*, Milton Keynes: Open University Press.

Bauman, Z. (2001) *Community*, Cambridge: Polity.

Baumol, W. (1967) 'The Macroeconomics of Unbalanced Growth', *American Economic Review*, 52(3): 415–26.

Beck, U. (1992) *Risk Society*, London: Sage.

Beck, U. (2000) *The Brave New World of Work*, Cambridge: Polity.

Beck, U., Giddens, T. and Lash, S. (1994) *Reflexive Modernisation*, Cambridge: Polity.

Beckerman, W. and Pasek, J. (2001) *Justice, Posterity and the Environment*, Oxford: Oxford University Press.

Beer, S. (2001) 'New Labour, Old Liberalism', in White, S. (ed.) *New Labour*, London: Palgrave.

Benello, C., Swann, R. and Turnball, S. (1997) *Building Sustainable Communities*, 2nd edition, New York: Bootstrap Press.

Benhabib, S. (ed.) (1996) *Democracy and Difference*, Princeton: University of Princeton Press.

Benton, T. (1999) 'Sustainable Development and Accumulation of Capital: Reconciling the Irreconcilable?', in Dobson, A. (ed.) *Fairness and Futurity*, Oxford: Oxford University Press.

Beyleveld, D. and Brownsword, R. (1998) 'Human Dignity, Human Rights and Human Genetics', in Brownsword, R., Cornish, R. W. and Llewelyn, M. (eds) *Law and Human Genetics*, Oxford: Hart Publishing.

Blackburn, R. (1999) 'The New Collectivism: Pension Reform, Grey Capitalism and Complex Socialism', *New Left Review*, 233: 3–65.

Blackburn, R. (2002) *Pension Power*, London: Verso.

Blackmore, S. (1999) *The Meme Machine*, Oxford: Oxford University Press.

Blair, T. (1998) *The Third Way*, London: Fabian Society.

Blair, T. and Schroder, G. (1999) *Europe: The Third Way*, London: The Labour Party.

Blume, P. (2000) 'Data Protection of Law Offenders', in Thomas, D. & Loader, B. (eds) *Cybercrime*, London: Routledge.

BMA (1998) *Human Genetics*, Oxford: Oxford University Press.

Body-Gendrot, S. (2000) *The Social Control of Cities?*, Oxford: Blackwell.

Bonoli, G., George, V. and Taylor-Gooby, P. (2000) *European Welfare Futures*, Cambridge: Polity Press.

Boonin-Vail, D. (1996) 'Don't Stop Thinking About Tomorrow: Two Paradoxes About Duties to Future Generations', *Philosophy and Public Affairs*, 25(4): 267–307.

Borjeson, M. (2002) '. . . and Why There is No Simple Solution, but Reasons for Optimism', *International Journal of Social Welfare*, 11: 170–1.

Bourdieu, P. (1998) *Acts of Resistance*, Cambridge: Polity.

Bowles, S. and Gintis, H. (1986) *Democracy and Capitalism*, New York: Basic Books.

Bowles, S. and Gintis, II. (1998) *Recasting Egalitarianism*, ed. by E. O. Wright, London: Verso.

Braithwaite, J. (2000) 'The New Regulatory State and the Transformation of Criminology', *British Journal of Criminology*, 40: 222–38.

Brennan, T. (2000) *Exhausting Modernity*, London: Routledge.

Brennan, T. (2001) 'Which Third Way?', *Thesis Eleven*, 64: 39–64.

Broberg, G. and Roll-Hansen, N. (1996) *Eugenics and the Welfare State*, East Lansing, Michigan: Michigan State University Press.

Brown, A. (1999) *The Darwin Wars*, London: Simon & Schuster.

Brown, P. (2000) 'The Globalisation of Positional Competition', *Sociology*, 34(4): 633–53.

Brundtland Commission (1987) *Our Common Future*, Oxford: Oxford University Press.

Buchanan, A. (1993) 'The Morality of Inclusion', *Social Philosophy and Policy*, 10(2): 233–57.

Buchanan, A. (1996) 'Choosing Who Will be Disabled: Genetic Intervention and the Morality of Inclusion', *Social Philosophy and Policy*, 13(2): 18–46.

Buchanan, A., Brock, D., Daniels, N. and Wikler, D. (2000) *From Chance to Choice*, Cambridge: Cambridge University Press.

Buckler, S. (2000) 'Theorising the Third Way: New Labour and Social Justice', *Journal of Political Ideologies*, 5(3): 301–20.

Butler, J. (1990) *Gender Trouble*, London: Routledge.

Butler, J., Laclau, E. and Zizek, S. (2000) *Contingency Hegemony Universality*, London: Verso.

Callaghan, M. (2000) *The Retreat of Social Democracy*, Manchester: Manchester University Press.

Calleja, R. (2000) 'The Regulation of Investigatory Powers Act 2000', *Computer Law and Security Report*, 16(6): 400–1.

Callinicos, A. (2001) *Against the Third Way*, Cambridge: Polity.

Carter, A. (2001) 'Can We Harm Future People?', *Environmental Values*, 10: 429–54.

Carter, A. (2002) 'Associative Democracy', in Carter, A. and Stokes, G. (eds) *Democratic Theory Today*, Cambridge: Polity.

Castells, M. (1996) *The Rise of the Network Society*, Oxford: Blackwell.

Castells, M. (1997) *The Power of Identity*, Oxford: Blackwell.

Castells, M. (1998) *The End of Millennium*, Oxford: Blackwell.

Choi, Y-Y. (1994) 'A Green GNP Model and Sustainable Growth', *Journal of Economic Studies*, 21(6): 37–45.

Christie, N. (1994) *Crime Control as Industry*, 2nd edition, London: Routledge.

Christoff, P. (1996) 'Ecological Modernisation, Ecological Modernities', *Environmental Politics*, 5(3): 476–500.

Clarke, J., Gewirtz, S. and McLaughlin, E. (eds) (2000) *New Managerialism, New Welfare?*, Milton Keynes: Open University Press.

Clift, B. (2000) 'Is There a French "Third Way"?', *New Political Economy*, 5(1): 135–40.

Clift, B. (2001) 'Social Democracy in the 21st Century: Still a Class Act? The Place of Class in Jospinism and Blairism', *Journal of European Area Studies*, 9(2): 191–215.

Coates, D. (2000) *Models of Capitalism*, Cambridge: Polity.

Coates, D. (2001) 'Capitalist Models and Social Democracy: The Case of New Labour', *British Journal of Politics and International Relations*, 3(3): 284–307.

Cohen, G. A. (1989) 'On the Currency of Egalitarian Justice', *Ethics*, 99: 906–44.

Cohen, G. A. (1995) *Self-Ownership, Freedom and Equality*, Cambridge: Cambridge University Press.

Cohen, J. and Rogers, J. (1995) *Associations and Democracy*, London: Verso.

Cohen, R. and Rai, S. (eds) (2000) *Global Social Movements*, London: Athlone.

Cohen, S. (1994) 'Social Control and the Politics of Reconstruction', in Nelken, D. (ed.) *The Futures of Criminology*, London: Sage.

Coleman, R. and Sim, J. (2000) ' "You'll Never Walk Alone": CCTV Surveillance, Order and Neo-Liberal Rule in Liverpool City Centre', *British Journal of Sociology*, 51(4): 623–40.

Commission on Social Justice (1994) *Social Justice*, London: Vintage.

Cook, D. (1997) *Poverty, Crime and Punishment*, London: CPAG.

Cooke, M. (2000) 'Five Arguments for Deliberative Democracy', *Political Studies* 48: 947–69.

Cowen, T. and Parfit, D. (1992) 'Against the Social Discount Rate', in Laslett, P. and Fishkin, J. (eds) *Justice Between Age Groups and Generations*, New Haven and London: Yale University Press.

Crick, B. (2000) *Essays on Citizenship*, London and New York: Continuum.

Culpitt, I. (1999) *Social Policy and Risk*, London: Sage.

Dahl, E., Dropping, J. A. and Lodemel, I. (2001) 'Norway: Relevance of the Social Development Model for Post-War Welfare Policy', *International Journal of Social Welfare*, 10: 300–8.

Dahl, R. (1985) *A Preface to Economic Democracy*, Cambridge: Polity.

Dahle, K. (1998) 'Toward Governance for Future Generations', *Futures*, 30(4): 277–92.

Dahrendorf, R. (1995) *Report of Wealth Creation and Social Cohesion in a Free Society*, London: Commission on Wealth Creation and Social Cohesion.

Daly, H. (1997a) 'Georgescu-Roegen versus Solow/Stiglitz', *Ecological Economics*, 22: 261–6.

Daly, H. (1997b) 'Reply to Solow/Stiglitz', *Ecological Economics*, 22: 271–3.

Daly, M. (2002) 'Care as a Good for Social Policy', *Journal of Social Policy*, 31(2): 251–70.

Dawkins, R. (1982) *The Extended Phenotype*, Oxford: W. H. Freeman.

Dawkins, R. (1989) *The Selfish Gene*, 2nd edition, Oxford: Oxford University Press.

Deacon, A. (2000) 'Learning from the USA? The Influence of American Ideas upon New Labour Thinking on Welfare Reform', *Policy and Politics*, 28(1): 5–18.

Dean, H. (2002) 'Business versus Families: Whose Side is New Labour On?', *Social Policy and Society*, 1(1): 3–10.

Dean, M. (1999) *Governmentality*, London: Sage.

Dell, E. (2000) *A Strange Eventful History*, London: HarperCollins.

Dennett, D. (1996) *Darwin's Dangerous Idea*, Middlesex: Penguin.

De-Shalit, A. (1995) *Why Posterity Matters*, London: Routledge.

Dickens, P. (2000) *Social Darwinism*, Milton Keynes: Open University Press.

Dobson, A. (1998) *Justice and the Environment*, Oxford: Oxford University Press.

Dobson, A. (ed.) (1999) *Fairness and Futurity*, Oxford: Oxford University Press.

Doherty, B. and de Geus, M. (eds) (1996) *Democracy and Green Political Thought*, London: Routledge.

Douthwaite, R. (1996) *Short Circuit*: Dublin: Lilliput Press.

Douthwaite, R. (1999) *The Growth Illusion*, 2nd edition, Totnes: Green Books.

Downes, D. and Morgan, R. (2002) 'The British General Election, 2001', *Punishment and Society*, 4(1): 81–96.

Driver, S. and Martell, L. (1997) 'New Labour's Communitarianism', *Critical Social Policy*, 17(3): 27–46.

Driver, S. and Martell, L. (1998) *New Labour*, Cambridge: Polity.

Driver, S. and Martell, L. (2000) 'Left, Right and Third Way', *Policy and Politics*, 28(2): 147–61.

Driver, S. and Martell, L. (2001) 'From Old Labour to New Labour: A Comment on Rubenstein', *Politics*, 21(1): 47–50.

Drouard, A. (1998) 'On Eugenicism in Scandinavia: A Review of Recent Research', *Population*, 53(3): 633–42.

Drucker, P. (1994) *Post-Capitalist Society*, Oxford: Butterworth-Heinemann.

Drucker, P. (1996) *The Pension Fund Revolution*, Transaction Books.

Dryzek, J. (1990) *Discursive Democracy*, Cambridge: Cambridge University Press.

Dryzek, J. (1996) *Democracy in Capitalist Times*, Oxford: Oxford University Press.

Dryzek, J. (1997) *The Politics of the Earth*, Oxford: Oxford University Press.

Dryzek, J. (2000) *Deliberative Democracy and Beyond*, Oxford: Oxford University Press.

Dryzek, J. (2001) 'Legitimacy and Economy in Deliberative Democracy', *Political Theory*, 29(5): 651–69.

Duster, T. (1990) *Backdoor to Eugenics*, London: Routledge.

Dworkin, R. (2000) *Sovereign Virtue*, Cambridge, MA: Harvard University Press.

Dyer-Witheford, N. (1999) *Cyber-Marx*, Urbana and Chicago: University of Illinois Press.

Eckerberg, K. (2000) 'Sweden: Progression Despite Recession', in Lafferty, W. and Meadowcroft, J. (eds) *Implementing Sustainable Development*, Oxford: Oxford University Press.

Eckerberg, K. (2001) 'Sweden: Problems and Prospects at the Leading Edge of LA21 Implementation', in Lafferty, W. (ed.) *Sustainable Communities in Europe*, London: Earthscan.

Ellison, N. (1999) 'Beyond Universalism and Particularism: Rethinking Contemporary Welfare Theory', *Critical Social Policy*, 19(1): 57–85.

Ellison, N. (2000) 'Proactive and Defensive Engagement: Social Citizenship in a Changing Public Sphere', *Sociological Research Online*, 5(3).

Elshtain, J. (1981) *Public Man, Private Women*, Princeton: Princeton University Press.

Elster, J. (ed.) (1998) *Deliberative Democracy*, Cambridge: Cambridge University Press.

Engelhardt, H. T. (1996) 'Germ-Line Engineering and Moral Diversity: Moral Controversies in a Post-Christian World', *Social Philosophy and Policy*, 13(2): 47–62.

Enslin, P., Pendlebury, S. and Tjiattas, M. (2001) 'Deliberative Democracy, Diversity and the Challenges of Citizenship Education', *Journal of the Philosophy of Education*, 35(1): 115–30.

Esping-Andersen, G. (1990) *The Three Worlds of Welfare Capitalism*, London: Sage.

Esping-Andersen, G. (1999) *Social Foundations of Post-Industrial Economies*, Cambridge: Cambridge University Press.

Estlund, D. (2002) 'Political Quality', in Estlund, D. (ed.) *Democracy*, Oxford: Blackwell.

Etzioni, A. (1994) *The Politics of Community*, London: Fontana.

Eysenck, H. (1998) *Intelligence: A New Look*, Somerset, NJ, Transaction Publishers.

Fairclough, N. (1999) *New Labour, New Language*, London: Routledge.

Feld, R. (2000) 'Sweden: From the Third Way of the Eighties to the "Globalised Social Democracy" of the 21st Century?', *Prokla*, 30(2): 301–28.

Fisher, J. (1997) 'The Postmodern Paradiso: Dante, Cyberpunk and the Technology of Cyberspace', in Porter, D. (ed.) *Internet Culture*, London: Routledge.

Fitzpatrick, T. (1996) 'Postmodernism, Welfare and Radical Politics', *Journal of Social Policy*, 25(3): 303–20.

Fitzpatrick, T. (1998a) 'The Rise of Market Collectivism', in Brundson, E., Dean, H. and Woods, R. (eds) *Social Policy Review 10*, London: SPA.

Fitzpatrick, T. (1998b) 'The Implications of Ecological Thought for Social Welfare', *Critical Social Policy*, 18(1): 5–26.

Fitzpatrick, T. (1999a) *Freedom and Security: An Introduction to the Basic Income Debate*, London: Macmillan.

Fitzpatrick, T. (1999b) 'Social Policy for Cyborgs', *Body and Society*, 5(1): 93–116.

Fitzpatrick, T. (1999c) 'New Welfare Associations: An Alternative Model of Well-Being', in Jordan, T. and Lent, A. (eds) *Storming the Millenium: A New Politics of Change*, London: Lawrence & Wishart.

Fitzpatrick, T. (2000) 'Critical Cyber Policy: Network Technologies, Massless Citizens, Virtual Rights', *Critical Social Policy*, 20(3): 375–407.

Fitzpatrick, T. (2001a) *Welfare Theory: An Introduction*, London: Palgrave.

Fitzpatrick, T. (2001b) 'Dis/Counting the Future', in Sykes, R., Ellison, N. and Bochel, C. (eds) *Social Policy Review 13*, Bristol: Policy Press.

Fitzpatrick, T. (2001c) 'Making Welfare for Future Generations', in Cahill, M. and Fitzpatrick, T. (eds) *Environmental Issues and Social Welfare*, Oxford: Blackwell.

Fitzpatrick, T. (2001d) 'A New Agenda for Criminology and Social Policy: Globalisation and the Post-Social Security State', *Social Policy and Administration*, 35(2): 212–29.

Fitzpatrick, T. (2002a) 'In Search of a Welfare Democracy', *Social Policy and Society*, 1(1): 11–20.

Fitzpatrick, T. (2002b) 'The Two Paradoxes of Welfare Democracy', *International Journal of Social Welfare*, 11(2): 159–69.

Fitzpatrick, T. (2002c) 'Critical Theory, Information Society and Surveillance Technologies', *Information, Communication and Society*, 5(3): 357–78.

Fitzpatrick, T. (2002d) 'Green Democracy and Ecosocial Welfare', in Fitzpatrick, T. and Cahill, M. (eds) *Environment and Welfare*, London: Palgrave.

Fitzpatrick, T. (ed.) (2003a) *New Technologies and Welfare*, special edition of *Critical Social Policy*, London: Sage.

Fitzpatrick, T. (2003b) 'Temporal Justice and Social Policy', *Time and Society*, forthcoming.

Fitzpatrick, T. (2003c) 'Environmentalism and Welfare', in Ellison, N. and Pierson, C. (eds) *New Directions in British Social Policy*, London: Palgrave.

Fitzpatrick, T. and Cahill, M. (2002) 'Introduction', in Fitzpatrick, T. and Cahill, M. (eds) *Environment and Welfare*, London: Palgrave.

Fitzpatrick, T. with Caldwell, C. (2001) 'Towards a Theory of Ecosocial Welfare: Radical Reformism and Local Currency Schemes', *Environmental Politics*, 10(2): 43–67.

Foucault, M. (1984) *The Foucault Reader*, ed. by Paul Rabinow, Middlesex: Penguin.

Franklin, J. (2000) 'What's Wrong with New Labour?', *Feminist Review*, 66: 138–42.

Fraser, N. and Honneth, A. (2001) *Redistribution or Recognition*, London: Verso.

Fraser, N. (1989) *Unruly Practices*, Cambridge: Polity.

Fraser, N. (1997) *Justice Interruptus*, London: Routledge.

Fraser, N. (2000) 'Rethinking Reconition', *New Left Review*, 2nd series, 3: 107–20.

Fraser, N. (2001) 'Recognition Without Ethics?', *Theory, Culture and Society*, 18(2–3): 21–42.

Freeden, M. (1996) *Ideologies and Political Theory*, Oxford: Oxford University Press.

Freeden, M. (1999) 'The Ideology of New Labour', *Political Quarterly*, 70(1): 42–51.

Frissen, P. (1997) 'The Virtual State: Postmodernisation, Informatisation and Public Administration', in Loader, B. (ed.) *The Governance of Cyberspace*, London: Routledge.

Fukayama, F. (1996) *Trust*, New York: Free Press.

Fukuyama, F. (1999) *The Great Disruption*, London: Profile Books.

Fukuyama, F. (2002) *Our Posthuman Future*, London: Profile Books.

Garland, D. (1985) *Punishment and Welfare*, Aldershot: Gower.

Garland, D. (2001) *The Culture of Control*, Oxford: Oxford University Press.

Garrett, G. (1998) *Partisan Politics in the Global Age*, Cambridge: Cambridge University Press.

Gauthier, D. (1986) *Morals by Agreement*, Oxford: Oxford University Press.

Gershuny, J. (2000) *Changing Times*, Oxford: Oxford University Press.

Gibbard, A. (1991) 'Constructing Justice', *Philosophy and Public Affairs*, 20: 264–79.

Giddens, T. (1991) *Modernity and Self-Identity*, Cambridge: Polity.

Giddens, T. (1994) *Beyond Left and Right*, Cambridge: Polity.

Giddens, T. (1998) *The Third Way*, Cambridge: Polity.

Giddens, T. (1999) *Runaway World*, London: Profile Books.

Giddens, T. (2000) *The Third Way and Its Critics*, Cambridge: Polity.

Giddens, T. (ed.) (2001) *The Global Third Way Debate*, Cambridge: Polity.

Giddens, T. (2002a) *Where Now for New Labour?*, Cambridge: Polity.

Giddens, T. (2002b) 'The Third Way can Beat the Far Right', *Guardian*, 3 May.

Giddens, T. and Hutton, W. (2000) 'In Conversation', in Hutton, W. and Giddens, T. (eds) *On the Edge*, London: Jonathan Cape.

Gilligan, C. (1982) *In A Different Voice*, Cambridge, MA: Harvard University Press.

Glannon, W. (1998) 'Genes, Embryos, and Future People', *Bioethics*, 12(3): 187–211.

Gledhill, J. (2001) ' "Disappearing the Poor?" A Critique of the New Wisdoms of Social Democracy in an Age of Globalization', *Urban Anthropology*, 30(2–3): 123–56.

Glennerster, H. (1999) 'A Third Way?', in Dean, H. and Woods, R. (eds) *Social Policy Review 11*, London: SPA.

Glover, J. (1999) 'Eugenics and Human Rights', in Burley, J. (ed.) *The Genetic Revolution and Human Rights*, Oxford: Oxford University Press.

Glyn, A. (1998) 'The Assessment: Economic Policy and Social Democracy', *Oxford Review of Economic Policy*, 14(1): 1–18.

Goodin, R. (1985) *Protecting the Vulnerable*, Chicago: University of Chicago Press.

Goodin, R. (2001) 'Towards a Post-Productivist Welfare State', *British Journal of Political Science*, 31: 13–40.

Goodin, R., Headey, B., Muffels, R. and Dervin, H-J. (1999) *The Real Worlds of Welfare Capitalism*, Cambridge: Cambridge University Press.

Gorz, A. (1989) *Critique of Economic Reason*, London: Verso.

Gorz, A. (1999) *Reclaiming Work*, Cambridge: Polity.

Gough, I. (2000) *Global Capital, Human Needs and Social Policies*, London: Palgrave.

Gould, S. (1978) *Ever Since Darwin*, Middlesex, Penguin.

Graham, S. and Wood, D. (2003) 'Digitising Surveillance: Categorisation, Space, Inequality', in Fitzpatrick, T. (ed.) *New Technologies and Social Welfare*, London: Sage.

Gramsci, A. (1971) *Selections from Prison Notebooks*, London: Lawrence & Wishart.

Grant, W., Mathews, D. and Newell, P. (2000) *The Effectiveness of European Union Environmental Policy*, London: Palgrave.

Gray, J. (1996) *After Social Democracy*, London: Demos.

Gray, J. (1998) *False Dawn*, Granta: London.

Green, D. (1993) *Reinventing Civil Society*, London: IEA.

Green-Pedersen, C., van Kersbergen, K. and Hemerijck, A. (2001) 'Neo-liberalism, the "Third Way" or What? Recent Social Democratic Welfare Policies in Denmark and the Netherlands', *Journal of European Public Policy*, 8(2): 307–25.

Gutmann, A. (1987) *Democratic Education*, Princeton: Princeton University Press.

Gutmann, A. and Thompson, D. (1996) *Democracy and Disagreement*, Cambridge, MA: Harvard University Press.

Habermas, J. (1975) *Legitimation Crisis*, London: Hutchison.

Haraway, D. (1991) *Simians, Cyborgs and Women*, London: Routledge.

Harris, J. (1998) *Clones, Genes and Immortality*, Oxford: Oxford University Press.

Harris, J. (1999) 'Clones, Genes, and Human Rights', in Burley, J. (ed.) *The Genetic Revolution and Human Rights*, Oxford: Oxford University Press.

Harvey, D. (1996) *Justice, Nature and the Geography of Difference*, Oxford: Blackwell.

Hay, C. (2001) 'Globalisation, Economic Change and the Welfare State: The "Vexatious Inquisition of Taxation"?', in Sykes, R., Palier, B. and Prior, P. (eds) *Globalisation and European Welfare States*, London: Palgrave.

Hayek, F. A. (1982) *Law, Legislation and Liberty*, London: Routledge and Kegan Paul.

Heffernan, R. (2000) *New Labour and Thatcherism*, London: Palgrave.

Held, D., McGrew, A., Goldblatt, D. and Perraton, J. (1999) *Global Transformations*, Cambridge: Polity Press.

Hellawell, S. (2001) *Beyond Access*, London: Fabian Society.

Hemerijck, A. and Visser, J. (2001) 'The Dutch Model: An Obvious Candidate for the "Third Way"?', *European Journal of Sociology*, 40(1): 221–39.

Henderson, H. (1981) *The Politics of the Solar Age*, New York: Doubleday.

Heron, E. (2001) 'Etzioni's Spirit of Communitarianism: Community Values and Welfare Realities in Blair's Britain', in Sykes, R., Ellison, N. and Bochel, C. (eds) *Social Policy Review 13*, Bristol: Policy Press.

Herrnstein, R. and Murray, C. (1994) *The Bell Curve*, New York, Free Press.

Hewitt, M. (2000) *Welfare and Human Nature*, London: Macmillan.

Hirsch, F. (1977) *The Social Limits to Growth*, London: Routledge.

Hirst, P. and Thompson, G. (1996) *Globalisation in Question*, Cambridge: Polity.

Hirst, P. (1994) *Associative Democracy*, Cambridge: Polity.

Hirst, P. (1997) *From Statism to Pluralism*, London: UCL Press.

Hirst, P. (1998) 'Social welfare and Associative Democracy', in Ellison, N. and Pierson, C. (eds) *New Developments in Social Policy*, London: Macmillan.

Hirst, P. (1999a) 'Associationalist Welfare: A Reply to Marc Stears', *Economy and Society*, 28(4): 590–97.

Hirst, P. (1999b) 'Has Globalisation killed Social Democracy?', *Political Quarterly*, 70(1): 84–96.

Hirst, P. (2000) 'Statism, Pluralism and Social Control', *British Journal of Criminology*, 40: 279–95.

HMSO (1999) *Modernising Government*, Cm 4310, London: HMSO.

Hobsbawm, E. (1994) *Age of Extremes*, London: Abacus.

Holliday, I. (2000) 'Productivist Welfare Capitalism: Social Policy in East Asia', *Political Studies*, 48: 706–23.

Hollis, M. (1994) *The Philosophy of Social Science*, Cambridge: Cambridge University Press.

Hombach, B. (2000) *The Politics of the New Centre*, Cambridge: Polity.

Honneth, A. (1995) *The Struggle for Recognition*, Cambridge: Polity.

Honneth, A. (2001) 'Recognition of Redistribution? Changing Perspectives on the Moral Order of Society', *Theory, Culture and Society*, 18(2–3): 43–55.

Hooft, H. (1999) *Justice to Future Generations and the Environment*, Dordrecht: Kluwer Academic Publishers.

Houtart, F. and Polet, F. (eds) (2001) *The Other Davos*, London: Zed Books.

Hubbard, R. and Wald, E. (1997) *Exploding the Gene Myth*, Boston: Beacon Press.

Huber, E. and Stephens, J. (2001) *Development and Crisis of the Welfare State*, Chicago: University of Chicago Press.

Hudson, J. (2003) 'E-galitarianism? The Information Society and New Labour's Repositioning of Welfare', in Fitzpatrick, T. (ed.) *New Technologies and Social Welfare*, London: Sage.

Hughes, G. (1996) 'Communitarianism and Law and Order', *Critical Social Policy*, 16(4): 17–41.

Humphries, P. (2002) 'Caught up in the Net', *Guardian*, 8 February.

Huntington, N. and Bale, T. (2002) 'New Labour: New Christian Democracy?', *Political Quarterly*, 73(1): 44–50.

Huther, J. (2000) 'Relating Labor Productivity to Ages in Service Sectors: A Long-Run Approach', *Economic Inquiry*, 38(1): 110–22.

Hutton, W. (1995) *The State We're In*, London: Vintage.

Hutton, W. (2002) *The World We're In*, London: Little, Brown.

Hutton, W. and Giddens, T. (eds) (2000) *On the Edge*, London: Jonathan Cape.

IMF (1991) *Determinants and Consequences of International Capital Flows*, Washington DC: IMF.

IPPR (2001) *Building Better Partnerships*, London: IPPR.

Iversen, T. (2001) 'The Dynamics of Welfare State Expansion: Trade Openness, De-Industrialisation and Partisan Politics, in Pierson, P. (ed.) *The New Politics of the Welfare State*, Oxford: Oxford University Press.

Iversen, T. and Wren, A. (1998) 'Equality, Employment and Budgetary Restraint: The Trilemma of the Service Economy', *World Politics*, 50(4): 507–46.

Jackson, T. (2002) 'Quality of Life, Sustainability and Economic Growth', in Fitzpatrick, T. and Cahill, M. (eds) *Environment and Welfare*, London: Palgrave.

Jaggar, A. (1983) *Feminist Politics and Human Nature*, Totowa, NJ: Rowman & Allanheld.

Jamison, A. and Baark, E. (1999) 'National Shades of Green: Comparing the Swedish and Danish Styles in Ecological Modernisation', *Environmental Values*, 8: 199–218.

Jayasuriya, K. (2000) 'Capability, Freedom and the New Social Democracy', *Political Quarterly*, 71: 282–99.

Jessop, B. (1994) 'The Transition to Post-Fordism and Schumpeterian Workfare State', in Burrows, R. and Loader, B. (eds) *Towards a Post-Fordist Welfare State?*, London: Routledge.

Jessop, B. (1999) 'The Changing Governance of Welfare: Recent Trends in its Primary Functions, Scale and Modes of Coordination', *Social Policy and Administration*, 33(4): 348–59.

Jessop, B. (2002) *The Future of the Welfare State*, Cambridge: Polity.

Jordan, B. (1998) *The New Politics of Welfare*, London: Sage.

Jordan, B. (2001) 'Tough Love: Social Work, Social Exclusion and the Third Way', *British Journal of Social Work*, 31: 527–46.

Jordan, B. with Jordan, C. (2000) *Tough Love as Social Policy*, London: Sage.

Jordan, B., Agulnik, P., Burbidge, D. and Duffin, S. (2000), 'Stumbling Towards a Basic Income – Direction for Tax and Benefit Reform', Citizen's Income Study Centre, London.

Jordan, B. and Arnold, J. (1995) 'Democracy and Criminal Justice', *Critical Social Policy*, 15(2–3): 170–82.

Jordan, B. and Travers, A. (1998) 'The Informal Economy: A Case Study in Unrestrained Competition', *Social Policy and Administration*, 32(3): 292–306.

Keen, J., Ferguson, B. and Mason, J. (1998) 'The Internet, Other "Nets" and Healthcare', in Loader, B. (ed.) *Cyberspace Divide*, London: Routledge.

Kemshall, H. (2002) *Risk, Social Policy and Welfare*, Buckingham: Open University Press.

Kevles, D. (1985) *In the Name of Eugenics*, Cambridge, MA: Harvard University Press.

King, D. (1995) *Actively Seeking Work?*, Chicago: Chicago University Press.

King, D. (1999) *In the Name of Liberalism*, Oxford: Oxford University Press.

Kitcher, P. (1996) *The Lives to Come*, New York: Touchstone.

Klein, M. (2000) *No Logo*, London: Flamingo.

Knapp, P., Kronick, J., Marks, R. W. and Vosburgh, M. (1996) *The Assault on Equality*, Westport, CT: Praeger Publishers.

Knoppers, B. M. (1999) 'Who Should Have Access to Genetic Information?', in Burley, J. (ed.) *The Genetic Revolution and Human Rights*, Oxford: Oxford University Press.

Kohn, M. (2000) 'Market Eugenics', *Prospect* (May edition): 25–9.

Korpi, W. and Palme, J. (1998) 'The Strategy of Equality and the Paradox of Redistribution', *American Sociological Review*, 63(5): 661–87.

Kosonen, P. (2001) 'Globalisation and the Nordic Welfare States', in Sykes, R., Palier, B. and Prior, P. (eds) *Globalisation and European Welfare States*, London: Palgrave.

Krawczak, M. and Schmidtke, J. (1998) *DNA Fingerprinting*, 2nd edition, Oxford: BIOS Scientific.

Krieger, J. (1999) *British Politics in a Global Age*, Cambridge: Polity.

Krouse, R. and McPherson, M. (1988) 'Capitalism, "Property-Owning Democracy" and the Welfare State', in Gutmann, A. (ed.) *Democracy and the Welfare State*, Princeton NJ: Princeton University Press.

Kymlicka, W. (1995) *The Rights of Minority Cultures*, Oxford: Clarendon.

Kymlicka, W. (2002) *Contemporary Political Philosophy*, 2nd edition, Oxford: Oxford University Press.

Laclau, E. (1996) *Emancipation(s)*, London: Verso.

Laclau, E. and Mouffe, C. (1985) *Hegemony and Socialist Strategy*, London: Verso.

Lacy, D. (1996) *From Grunts to Gigabytes*, Urbana and Chicago: University of Illinois Press.

Lafferty, W. (ed.) (2001) *Sustainable Communities in Europe*, London: Earthscan.

Land, H. (2002) 'Spheres of Care in the UK: Separate and Unequal', *Critical Social Policy*, 22(1): 13–32.

Langhelle, O. (2000) 'Norway: Reluctantly Carrying the Torch', in Lafferty, W. and Meadowcroft, J. (eds) *Implementing Sustainable Development*, Oxford: Oxford University Press.

Larkin, P. (2001) 'New Labour in Perspective: A Comment on Rubenstein', *Politics*, 21(1): 51–5.

Le Grand, J. (1997) 'Knights, Knaves or Pawns? Human Behaviour and Social Policy', *Journal of Social Policy*, 26(2): 149–69.

Le Grand, J. (2000) 'From Knight to Knave? Public Policy and Market Incentives', in Taylor-Gooby, P. (ed.) *Risk, Trust and Welfare*, London: Macmillan.

Leadbetter, C. (1999) *Living on Thin Air*, London: Viking.

Leibfried, S. (ed.) (2001) *Welfare State Futures*, Cambridge: Cambridge University Press.

Leisering, L. and Leibfried, S. (1999) *Time and Poverty in Western Welfare States*, Cambridge: Cambridge University Press.

Lenaghan, J. (1998) *Brave New NHS?*, London: IPPR.

Levine, A. (1998) *Rethinking Liberal Equality*, Ithaca and London: Cornell University Press.

Levine, A. (1999) 'Rewarding Effort', *Journal of Political Philosophy*, 7(4): 404–18.

Levitas, R. (1998) *The Inclusive Society?*, London: Macmillan.

Levitas, R. (2000) 'Community, Utopia and New Labour', *Local Economy*, 15(3): 188–97.

Lewis, J. (1992) 'Gender and the Development of Welfare Regimes', *Journal of European Social Policy*, 2(3): 159–73.

Lewis, J. (2001) 'The Decline of the Male Breadwinner Model: Implications for Work and Care', *Social Politics*, 8(2): 152–69.

Lewontin, R. (1993) *The Doctrine of DNA*, Harmondsworth, Penguin.

Leys, C. (2001) *Market-Driven Politics*, London: Verso.

Lianos, M. and Douglas, M. (2000) 'Dangerization and the End of Deviance: The Institutional Environment', *British Journal of Criminology*, 40: 261–78.

Lind, R. (ed.) (1982) *Discounting for Time and Risk in Energy Policy*, Baltimore: John Hopkins University Press.

Lindbom, A. (2001) 'Dismantling the Social Democratic Welfare Model? Has the Swedish Welfare State Lost its Defining Characteristics?', *Scandinavian Political Studies*, 24(3): 171–93.

Lister, R. (2001a) 'Towards a Citizens' Welfare State: The 3 + 2 "R's" of Welfare Reform', *Theory, Culture and Society*, 18(2–3): 91–111.

Lister, R. (2001b) 'New Labour: A Study in Ambiguity from a Position of Ambivalence', *Critical Social Policy*, 21(4): 425–48.

Little, A. (1998) *Post-Industrial Socialism*, London: Routledge.

Loader, B. (ed.) (1998) *Cyberspace Divide*, London: Routledge.

Lukes, S. (1995) *The Curious Enlightenment of Professor Caritat*, London: Verso.

Lund, B. (1999) ' "Ask Not What Your Community Can do for You": Obligations, New Labour and Welfare Reform', *Critical Social Policy*, 19(4): 447–62.

Lundqvist, L. (2001a) 'Implementation from Above: The Ecology of Power in Sweden's Environmental Governance', *Governance*, 14(3): 319–37.

Lundqvist, L. (2001b) 'A Green Fist in a Velvet Glove: The Ecological State and Sustainable Development', *Environmental Values*, 10: 455–72.

Lyon, D. (1994) *The Electronic Eye*, Cambridge: Polity.

Lyon, D. (2001) *Surveillance Society*, Buckingham: Open University Press.

Macintyre, A. (1982) *After Virtue*, London: Duckworth.

Mahon, R. (2000) 'Swedish Social Democracy: Death of a Model?', *Studies in Political Economy*, 63: 27–59.

Mandelson, P. and Liddle, R. (1996) *The Blair Revolution*, London: Politico's.

Marquand, D. (1991) *The Progressive Dilemma*, London: William Heinemann.

Marquand, D. (1998) 'What Lies at the Heart of the People's Project?', *Guardian*, 20 May.

Marshall, T. H. (1953) 'Social Selection in the Welfare State, *The Eugenics Review*, 45(2): 81–92.

Marshall, T. H. and Bottomore, T. (1992) *Citizenship and Social Class*, London: Pluto.

Marx, G. (1995) 'The Engineering of Social Control: The Search for the Silver Bullet', in Hagan, J. and Patersen, R. (eds) *Crime and Inequality*, Stanford CA: Stanford University Press.

Marx, G. (1999) 'Measuring Everything that Moves: The New Surveillance at Work', *Research in the Sociology of Work*, 8: 165–89.

Marxism Today (1998) 'Wrong' *Marxism Today*, November/December.

McCahill, M. and Norris, C. (1999) 'Watching the Workers: Crime, CCTV and the Workplace', in Davis, P., Jupp, V. and Francis, P. (eds) *Invisible Crimes*, London: Macmillan.

McGleenan, T. and Wiesing, U. (1999) 'Policy Options for Health and Life Insurance in the Era of Genetic Testing', in McGleenan, T., Wiesing, U. and Ewald, F. (eds) *Genetics and Insurance*, Oxford: Bios Scientific Publishers Ltd.

McGleenan, T. (1999) 'Genetic Testing and the Insurance Industry', in McGleenan, T., Wiesing, U. and Ewald, F. (eds) *Genetics and Insurance*, Oxford: Bios Scientific Publishers Ltd.

McRobbie, A. (2000) 'Feminism and the Third Way', *Feminist Review*, 64: 90–112.

Meade, J. (1995) *Full Employment Regained*, Cambridge: Polity.

Mensch, E. and Mensch, H. (1990) *The IQ Mythology*, Illinois: Southern Illinois University Press.

Merkel, W. (1999) *The Third Ways of European Social Democracy at the End of the Twentieth Century*, Heidelberg: University of Heidelberg.

Mertens, S. (1999) 'Nonprofit Organisations and Social Economy: Two Ways of Understanding the Third Sector', *Annals of Comparative and Public Economics*, 70(3): 501–20.

Meyers, P. (1998) 'The "Ethic of Care" and the Problem of Power', *Journal of Political Philosophy*, 6(2): 142–70.

Midgely, J. (1997) *Social Welfare in Global Context*, London: Sage.

Midgely, M. (1995) *Beast and Man*, London: Routledge.

Mill, J. S. (1989) *On Liberty*, Cambridge: Cambridge University Press.

Miller, D. and Walzer, M. (eds) (1995) *Pluralism, Justice and Equality*, Oxford: Oxford University Press.

Miller, D. (1995) 'Complex Equality', in Miller, D. and Walzer, M. (eds) *Pluralism, Justice and Equality*, Oxford: Oxford University Press.

Miller, D. (1999) *Principles of Social Justice*, Cambridge, MA: Harvard University Press.

Miller, S. and Weckert, J. (2000) 'Privacy, the Workplace and the Internet', *Journal of Business Ethics*, 28(3): 255–66.

Mishra, R. (1999) *Globalisation and the Welfare State*, Aldershot: Edward Elgar.

Mol, A. and Sonnenfeld, D. (2000) *Ecological Modernisation Around the World*, London: Frank Cass.

Moore, A. D. (2000) 'Employee Monitoring and Computer Technology: Evaluative Surveillance vs. Privacy', *Business Ethics Quarterly*, 10(3): 697–710.

Moschonas, G. (2002) *In the Name of Social Democracy*, London: Verso.

Mouffe, C. (ed.) (1999) *The Challenge of Carl Schmitt*, London: Verso.

Mouffe, C. (2000) *The Democratic Paradox*, London, Verso.

Mouzelis, N. (2001) 'Reflexive Modernisation and the Third Way: The Impasses of Giddens's Social Democratic Politics', *Sociological Review*, 49(3): 436–56.

Mulgan, G. (1998) *Connexity*, Cambridge, MA: Harvard Business School.

Murray, C. (1984) *Losing Ground*, New York: Basic Books.

Murray, C. (1990) *The Emerging British Underclass*, London: IEA.

Murray, C. (2000) 'Genetics of the Right', *Prospect* (April edition): 28–31.

Myles, J. and Pierson, P. (2001) 'The Comparative Political Economy of Pension Reform', in Pierson, P. (ed.) *The New Politics of the Welfare State*, Oxford: Oxford University Press.

Naess, A. (1989) *Ecology, Community and Lifestyle*, Cambridge: Cambridge University Press.

Nelkin, D. (1999) 'Behavioural Genetics and Dismantling the Welfare State', in Carson, R. and Rothstein, M. (eds) *Behavioural Genetics*, Baltimore: John Hopkins University Press.

Nelkin, D. and Andrews, L. (1999) 'DNA Identification and Surveillance Creep', *Sociology of Health and Illness*, 21(5): 689–706.

Neumayer, E. (1999) 'Global Warming: Discounting Is Not the Issue But Substitutability Is', *Energy Policy*, 27: 33–43.

Niemi-Iilahti, A. (2001) 'Finland: In Search of New Implementation Patterns', Lafferty, W. (ed.) (2001) *Sustainable Communities in Europe*, London: Earthscan.

Nixon, P. and Keeble, L. (2001) 'New Communication Technologies – Connected Welfare: New Media and Social Policy', in Sykes, R., Ellison, N. and Bochel, C. (eds) *Social Policy Review 13*, Bristol: Policy Press.

Noddings, N. (2002) *Starting at Home*, Los Angeles and Berkeley: University of California Press.

Nordhaus, W. and Tobin, J. (1972) 'Is Growth Obsolete?' in *Economic Growth*, Fiftieth Anniversary Colloquium V, National Bureau of Economic Research, New York.

Nordhaus, W. (1999) 'Discounting and Public Policies that Affect the Distant Future', in Portney, P. and Weyant, J. (eds) *Discounting and Intergenerational Equity*, Washington: Resources for the Future.

Norris, C. and Armstrong, G. (1999) *The Maximum Surveillance Society*, Oxford: Berg.

Norton, B. (1991) *Toward Unity Among Environmentalists*, Oxford: Oxford University Press.

Nozick, R. (1974) *Anarchy, State and Utopia*, Oxford: Blackwell.

Nuffield Council on Bioethics (1999) *Genetic Screening*, London: Nuffield Foundation.

O'Malley, P. (1992) 'Risk, Power and Crime Prevention', *Economy and Society*, 21: 252–75.

O'Connor, J. (1973) *The Fiscal Crisis of the State*, New York: St. Martin's Press.

O'Connor, J. (1998) *Natural Causes*, New York: Guilford Press.

O'Hear, A. (1997) *Beyond Evolution*, Oxford: Oxford University Press.

O'Neill, J. (1993) *Ecology, Policy and Politics*, London: Routledge.

O'Neill, O. (1998) 'Insurance and Genetics: The Current State of Play', in Brownsword, R., Cornish, R. W. and Llewelyn, M. (eds) *Law and Human Genetics*, Oxford: Hart Publishing.

Oakley, A. (1991) 'Eugenics, Social Medicine and the Career of Richard Titmuss in Britain, 1935–50', *British Journal of Sociology*, 42(2): 165–94.

OECD (1994) *New Orientations for Social Policy*, Paris: OECD.

OECD (1999) *A Caring World*, Paris: OECD.

Offe, C. (1984) *Contradictions of the Welfare State*, London: Hutchison.

Offe, C. (1993) 'A Non-Productivist Design for Social Policies', in van Parijs, P. (ed.) *Arguing for Social Policy*, London: Verso.

Offe, C. (1996) *Modernity and the State*, Cambridge: Polity.

Offe, C. (2000) 'Civil Society and Social Order: Demarcating and Combining Market, State and Community', *European Journal of Sociology*, 61(1): 71–94.

Offe, C. and Heinze, R. (1992) *Beyond Employment*, Cambridge: Polity Press.

Okin, S. (1989) *Justice, Gender and the Family*, New York: Basic Books.

Oppenheim, C. (ed.) (1998) *An Inclusive Society*, London: IPPR.

Orloff, A. (1993) 'Gender and the Social Rights of Citizenship: The Comparative Analysis of Gender Relations and Welfare States', *American Sociological Review*, 58(3): 303–28.

Page, R. (1996) *Altruism and the British Welfare State*, Aldershot: Avebury.

Palier, B. and Sykes, R. (2001) 'Challenges and Change: Issues and Perspectives in the Analysis of Globalisation and European Welfare States', in Sykes, R., Palier, B. and Prior, P. (eds) *Globalisation and European Welfare States*, London: Palgrave.

Panayotou, T. (1995) 'Environmental Degradation at Different Stages of Economic Development', in Ahmed, I. and Doelman, J. (eds) *Beyond Rio*, London: Macmillan.

Panayotou, T. (1997) 'Demystifying the Environmental Kusnets Curve: Turning a Black Box Into a Policy Tool', *Environmental and Development Economics*, 2(4): 465–84.

Pantazis, C. (2000) ' "Fear of Crime", Vulnerability and Poverty', *British Journal of Criminology*, 40: 414–36.

Parenti, C. (1999) *Lockdown America*, London: Verso.

Parfit, D. (1984) *Reasons and Persons*, Oxford: Oxford University Press.

Paul, D. (1998) *The Politics of Heredity*, Albany: State University of New York Press.

Pavarini, M. (1997), 'Controlling Social Panic: Questions and Answers about Security in Italy at the End of the Millennium', in Bergalli, R. and Sumner, C. (eds) *Social Control and the Political Order*, London: Sage.

Pearce, D. (2000) *Blueprint for a Sustainable Economy*, London: Earthscan.

Pennings, P. (1999) 'European Social Democracy Between Planning and Market: A Comparative Exploration of Trends and Variations', *Journal of European Public Policy*, 6(5): 743–56.

Perelman, M. (1998) *Class Warfare in the Information Age*, London: Macmillan.

Perrings C. (1997) 'Georgescu-Roegen and the "Irreversibility" of Material Processes', *Ecological Economics*, 22(3): 303–4.

Perrings, C. and Ansuategi, A. (2000) 'Sustainability, Growth and Development', *Journal of Economic Studies*, 27(1–2): 19–37.

Pettit, P. (2001) 'Deliberative Democracy and the Discursive Dilemma', *Philosophical Issues*, 11: 268–99.

Phillips, A. (1995) *The Politics of Presence*, Oxford: Oxford University Press.

Phillips, A. (1999) *Which Equalities Matter?*, Cambridge: Polity.

Pierson, C. (2001) *Hard Choices*, Cambridge: Polity.

Pierson, P. (ed.) (2001a) *The New Politics of the Welfare State*, Cambridge: Cambridge University Press.

Pierson, P. (2001b) 'Post-Industrial Pressures on the Mature Welfare States', in Pierson, P. (ed.) *The New Politics of the Welfare State*, Cambridge: Cambridge University Press.

Pinker, S. (1995) *The Language Instinct*, Middlesex: Penguin.

Plant, R. (1993) *Social Justice, Labour and the New Right*, London: Fabian Society.

Plant, R. (1998) 'So You Want to be a Citizen?', *New Statesman*, 6 February.

Plant, R. (2002) 'Social Democracy', in Carter, A. and Stokes, G. (eds) *Democratic Theory Today*, Cambridge: Polity.

Plantenga, J., Schippers, J. and Singers, J. (1999) 'Towards an Equal Division of Paid and Unpaid Work: The Case of the Netherlands', *Journal of European Social Policy*, 9(2): 99–110.

Pokorski, R. (1997) 'Insurance Underwriting in the Genetic Era', *American Journal of Human Genetics*, 60: 205–16.

Popper, K. (1945) *The Open Society and Its Enemies*, 2 vols, London: Routledge & Kegan Paul.

Portney, P. and Weyant, J. (eds) (1999) *Discounting and Intergenerational Equity*, Washington: Resources for the Future.

Postman, N. (1993) *Technopoly*, New York, Knopf.

Powell, M. (2000) 'New Labour the and Third Way in the British Welfare State: A New and Distinctive Approach?', *Critical Social Policy*, 20(1): 39–60.

Prabhakar, R. (2002) 'Capability, Responsibility, Human Capital and the Third Way', *Political Quarterly*, 73(1): 51–8.

Pring, R. (2001) 'Citizenship in Schools', in Crick, B. (ed.) *Citizens: Towards a Citizenship Culture*, Oxford: Blackwell.

Putnam, H. (1999) 'Cloning People', in Burley, J. (ed.) *The Genetic Revolution and Human Rights*, Oxford, Oxford University Press.

Putnam, R. (2000) *Bowling Alone*, New York: Simon & Schuster.

Rawls, J. (1972) *A Theory of Justice*, Oxford: Oxford University Press.

Rawls, J. (1993) *Political Liberalism*, New York: Columbia University Press.

Rawls, J. (1999) *Collected Papers*, ed. by Samuel Freeman, Cambridge, MA: Harvard University Press.

Rawls, J. (2001) *Justice as Fairness*, Cambridge, MA: Harvard University Press.

Reeves, R. (2001) *Happy Mondays*, London: Pearson Education Ltd.

Reilly, P. (1999) 'Genetic Discrimination', in Long, C. (ed.) *Genetic Testing and the Use of Information*, Washington: The AEI Press.

Reiman, J. (1998) *The Rich Get Richer and the Poor Get Prison*, 5th edition, London: Allyn and Bacon.

Ridley, M. (1996) *The Origins of Virtue*, Middlesex: Penguin.

Ridley, M. (1999) *Genome*, London: Fourth Estate.

Rifkin, J. (1998) *The Biotech Century*, London: Orion Books.

Robertson, J. (2002) 'Eco-taxation in a Green Society', in Fitzpatrick, T. and Cahill, M. (eds) *Environment and Welfare*, London: Palgrave.

Roche, M. (1992) *Rethinking Citizenship*, Cambridge: Polity.

Rodrik, D. (1998) 'Why Do More Open Economies Have Larger Governments?', *Journal of Political Economy*, 106: 932–97.

Roemer, J. (1993) *A Future for Socialism*, London: Verso.

Roemer, J. (1996) *Theories of Distributive Justice*, Cambridge, MA: Harvard University Press.

Roemer, J. (1998) *Equality of Opportunity*, Cambridge, MA: Harvard University Press.

Rogers, B. (2000) 'The Nature of Value and the Value of Nature: A Philosophical Overview', *International Affairs*, 76(2): 315–23.

Room, G. (2000) 'Commodification and Decommodification: A Developmental Critique', *Policy and Politics*, 28(3): 331–51.

Rorty, R. (1998) *Achieving Our Country*, Cambridge, MA: Harvard University Press.

Rose, N. (1996) 'The Death of the Social?', *Economy and Society*, 25(3): 327–56.

Rose, N. (1999) *Powers of Freedom*, Cambridge: Cambridge University Press.

Rose, N. (2000) 'Community, Citizenship and the Third Way', *American Behavioural Scientist*, 43(9): 1395–411.

Rose, S. (1997) *Lifelines*, Middlesex: Penguin.

Rose, S., Lewontin, R. and Kamin, L. (1984) *Not In Our Genes*, Middlesex: Penguin.

Rothstein, B. (1998) *Just Institutions Matter*, Cambridge: Cambridge University Press.

Rothstein, M. (ed.) (1997) *Genetic Secrets*, New Haven: Yale University Press.

Rowbotham, S. and Linkogle, S. (eds) (2001) *Women Resist Globalisation*, London: Zed Books.

Rubinstein, D. (2000) 'A New Look at New Labour', *Politics*, 20(3): 161–7.

Ryner, M. (1999) 'Neoliberal Globalization and the Crisis of Swedish Social Democracy', *Economic and Industrial Democracy*, 20(1): 39–79.

Sagoff, M. (1988) *The Economy of the Earth*, Cambridge: Cambridge University Press.

Sainsbury, D. (ed.) (1999) *Gender and Welfare State Regimes*, Oxford: Oxford University Press.

Sarder, Z. and Ravetz, J. (eds) (1996) *Cyberfutures*, London: Pluto Press.

Sassen, S. (1991) *The Global City*, Princeton: Princeton University Press.

Sassoon, D. (1996) *One Hundred Years of Socialism*, London: I. B. Tauris.

Sathiendrakumar, R. (1996) 'Sustainable Development: Passing Fad or Potential Reality?', *International Journal of Social Economics*, 23(4–6): 151–63.

Scharpf, F. (2000) 'Basic Income and Social Europe', in van der Veen, R. and Groot, L. (eds) *Basic Income on the Agenda*, Amsterdam: Amsterdam University Press.

Schelling, T. (1995) 'Intergenerational Discounting', *Energy Policy*, 23(4–5): 395–401.

Schiller, H. (1981) *Who Knows*, Norwood, NJ: Ablex.

Schiller, H. (1984) *Information and the Crisis Economy*, Norwood, NJ: Ablex.

Schiller, H. (1989) *Culture, Inc.*, Oxford: Oxford University Press.

Schiller, H. (1996) *Information Inequality*, London: Routledge.

Schuller, T. (2001) 'The Need for Lifelong Learning', in Crick, B. (ed.) *Citizens: Towards a Citizenship Culture*, Oxford: Blackwells.

Schwartz, H. (2001) 'Round up the Usual Suspects! Globalisation, Domestic Politics and Welfare State Change', in Pierson, P. (ed.) *The New Politics of the Welfare State*, Cambridge: Cambridge University Press.

Schwartz, J. (1997) 'The Soul of Soulless Conditions? Accounting for Genetic Fundamentalism', *Radical Philosophy*, 86: 2–5.

Searle, G. R. (1976) *Eugenics and Politics in Britain, 1900–14*, Leyden: Noordhoff International Publishing.

Selbourne, D. (1994) *The Principle of Duty*, London: Sinclair-Stevenson.

Selden, S. (1999) *Inheriting Shame*, New York: Teachers College Press.

Self, P. (2000) *Rolling Back the Market*, London: Palgrave.

Selwyn, N. (2002) ' "E-stablishing" an Inclusive Society? Technology, Social Exclusion and UK Government Policy Making', *Journal of Social Policy*, 31(1): 1–20.

Sen, A. (1992) *Inequality Re-examined*, Oxford: Clarendon.

Sevenhuijsen, S. (1998) *Citizenship and the Ethics of Care*, London: Routledge.

Sevenhuijsen, S. (2000) 'Caring in the Third Way: The Relation Between Obligation, Responsibility and Care in Third Way Discourse', *Critical Social Policy*, 20(1): 5–38.

Sewell, G. (1996) 'A Japanese "Cure" to a British "Disease"? Cultural Dimensions to the Development of Workplace Surveillance Technologies.' *Information Technology and People*, 9(3): 12–29.

Shakespeare, T. (1995) 'Back to the Future? New Genetics and Disabled People', *Critical Social Policy*, 44–45: 22–35.

Shakespeare, T. (1998) 'Choices and Rights: Eugenics, Genetics and Disability Equality', *Disability and Society*, 13(5): 665–81.

Shiva, V. (2000a) *Tomorrow's Biodiversity*, London: Thames & Hudson.

Shiva, V. (2000b) *Stolen Harvest*, London: Zed Books.

Short, J. and Kim, Y-H. (1999) *Globalisation and the City*, Essex: Addison Wesley Longman Ltd.

Silver, L. (1998) *Remaking Eden*, London: Weidenfeld and Nicolson.

Singer, P. (1998) 'The Darwin Lecture: A Darwinian Left?', The Times Higher Education Supplement Internet Service, http://rfe.wustl.edu/NewsMedia/TimHigEduSup.html.

Sklair, L. (1995) *Sociology of the Global System*, Hemel Hempstead: Harvester Wheatsheaf.

Slevin, J. (2000) *The Internet Society*, Cambridge: Polity.

Smith, G. and Wales, C. (2000) 'Citizens' Juries and Deliberative Democracy', *Political Studies*, 48: 51–65.

Smith, C. (2000) 'The Sovereign State vs. Foucault: Law and Disciplinary Power', *The Sociological Review*, 48(2): 283–306.

Smith, S. (2001) 'The Social Construction of Talent: A Defence of Justice as Reciprocity', *Journal of Political Philosophy*, 9(1): 19–37.

Solow, R. (1997) 'Georgescu-Roegen versus Solow/Stiglitz', *Ecological Economics*, 22: 267–8.

Standing, G. (1999) *Global Labour Flexibility*, London: Macmillan.

Standing, G. (2002) *Beyond the New Paternalism*, London: Verso.

Stears, M. (1999) 'Needs, Welfare and the Limits of Associationalism', *Economy and Society*, 28(4): 570–89.

Stears, M. and White, S. (2001) 'New Liberalism Revisited', in Tam, H. (ed.) *Progressive Politics in the Global Age*, Cambridge: Polity.

Stein, E. (1998) 'Choosing the Sexual Orientation of Children', *Bioethics*, 12(1): 1–24.

Steiner, H. (1994) *An Essay on Rights*, Oxford: Blackwell.

Steiner, H. (1998) 'Choice and Circumstance', in Mason, A. (ed.) *Ideals of Equality*, Oxford: Blackwell.

Steiner, H. (1999) 'Silver Spoons and Golden Genes', in Burley, J. (ed.) *The Genetic Revolution and Human Rights*, Oxford: Oxford University Press.

Stiglitz, J. (1997) 'Georgescu-Roegen versus Solow/Stiglitz', *Ecological Economics*, 22: 269–70.

Stymme, S. and Jackson, T. (2000) 'Intra-Generational Equity and Sustainable Welfare: A Time Series Analysis for the UK and Sweden', *Ecological Economics*, 33: 219–36.

Suzuki, D. and Knudtson, P. (1990) *Genethics*, Cambridge, Mass.: Harvard University Press.

Sverrisson, A. (2001) 'Translation Networks, Knowledge Brokers and Novelty Construction: Pragmatic Environmentalism in Sweden', *Acta Sociologica*, 44: 313–27.

Swift, A. (1995) 'The Sociology of Complex Equality', in Miller, D. and Walzer, M. (eds) *Pluralism, Justice and Equality*, Oxford: Oxford University Press.

Sykes, R., Palier, B. and Prior, P. (eds) (2001) *Globalisation and European Welfare States*, London: Palgrave.

Tacconi, L. and Bennett, J. (1995) 'Economic Implications of Intergenerational Equity for Biodiversity Conservation', *Ecological Economics*, 12: 209–23.

Tawney, R. H. (1931) *Equality*, London: George Allen and Unwin.

Taylor, C. (1994) *Multiculturalism*, Princeton: Princeton University Press.

Taylor, I. (1999) *Crime in Context*, Cambridge: Polity.

Taylor-Gooby, P. (1994) 'Postmodernism and Social Policy: A Great Leap Backwards?', *Journal of Social Policy*, 23(3): 387–403.

Taylor-Gooby, P. (1997) 'In Defence of Second-Best Theory: State, Class and Capital in Social Policy', *Journal of Social Policy*, 26(2): 171–92.

Taylor-Gooby, P. (2000) 'Blair's Scars', *Critical Social Policy*, 20(3): 331–48.

Taylor-Gooby, P. (ed.) (2001) *Welfare States Under Pressure*, London: Sage.

Thane, P. (1996) *The Foundations of the Welfare State*, 2nd edition, London, Longman.

Thomson, M. (1998) *The Problem of Mental Deficiency*, Oxford: Oxford University Press.

Thomson, S. and Hoggett, P. (1996) 'Universalism, Selectivism, Particularism: Towards a Postmodern Social Policy', *Critical Social Policy*, 16(1): 21–43.

Thompson, S. and Hoggett, P. (2001) 'The Emotional Dynamics of Deliberative Democracy', *Policy and Politics*, 29(3): 351–64.

Timonen, V. (2001) 'Earning Welfare Citizenship: Welfare State Reform in Finland and Sweden', in Taylor-Gooby, P. (ed.) (2001) *Welfare States Under Pressure*, London: Sage.

Titmuss, R. (1970) *The Gift Relationship*, London: Allen & Unwin.

Tocqueville, A. (1990) *Democracy in America*, New York: Vintage Books.

Travis, A. (2002) 'England Worse than China in Prison Population Rate', *Guardian*, 13 February.

Tronto, J. (1993) *Moral Boundaries*, London and New York: Routledge.

Tsagarousianou, R., Tambini, D. and Bryan, C. (eds) (1998) *Cyberdemocracy*, London: Routledge.

Turner, B. (2001) 'The Erosion of Citizenship', *British Journal of Sociology*, 52(2): 189–210.

UNDP (1996) *Human Development Report – 1996*, Oxford: Oxford University Press.

Unger, R. (1987) *False Necessity*, Cambridge: Cambridge University Press.

Unger, R. (1998) *Democracy Realised*, London: Verso.

van der Heijden, H. A. (1999) 'Environmental Movements, Ecological Modernisation and Political Opportunity Structures', in Rootes, C. (ed.) *Environmental Movements*, London: Frank Cass.

van der Veen, R. (1998) 'Real Freedom versus Reciprocity: Competing Views on the Justice of Unconditional Basic Income', *Political Studies*, 46: 140–63.

van Dijk, J. (1999) *The Network Society*, London: Sage.

van Muijen, M-L. (2000) 'The Netherlands: Ambitious in Goals – Ambivalent on Action', in Lafferty, W. and Meadowcroft, J. (eds) *Implementing Sustainable Development*, Oxford: Oxford University Press.

van Parijs, P. (ed.) (1992) *Arguing for Basic Income*, London: Verso.

van Parijs, P. (1995) *Real Freedom for All*, Oxford: Oxford University Press.

van Parijs, P. (2000) 'Basic Income at the Heart of Social Europe? Reply to Fritz Scharpf', in van der Veen, R. and Groot, L. (eds) *Basic Income on the Agenda*, Amsterdam: Amsterdam University Press.

Walby, S. (2001) 'From Community to Coalition: The Politics of Recognition as the Handmaiden of the Politics of Equality in an Era of Globalisation', *Theory, Culture and Society*, 18(2–3): 113–35.

Walker, R. (2000) *Ending Child Poverty*, Bristol: Policy Press.

Walzer, M. (1983) *Spheres of Justice*, Oxford: Blackwell.

Ward, S. (2000) 'New Labour's Pension Reforms', in Dean, H., Sykes, R. and Woods, R. (eds) *Social Policy Review 12*, London: SPA.

Warde, A. (1994) 'Consumers, Consumption and Diversity', in Burrows, R. and Loader, B. (eds) *Towards a Post-Fordist Welfare State?*, London: Routledge.

Waring, M. (1988) *If Women Counted*, London: Macmillan.

Warren, M. (2002) 'Deliberative Democracy', in Carter, A. and Stokes, G. (eds) *Democratic Theory Today*, Cambridge: Polity.

Warren, T. (2000) 'Diverse Breadwinner Models: A Couple-Based Analysis of Gendered Working Time in Britain and Denmark', *Journal of European Social Policy*, 10(4): 349–71.

Watson, J. (1998) *The Double Helix*, Scribner Book Company.

Weeks, E. (2000) 'The Practice of deliberative Democracy: Results from Four Large-Scale Trials', *Public Administration Review*, 60(4): 360–72.

Weil, S. (1987) *Gravity and Grace*, London: Routledge.

Weizsacker, E., Lovins, A. and Lovins, L. H. (1998) *Factor Four*, London: Earthscan.

Wetherly, P. (2001) 'The Reform of Welfare and the Way we Live Now: A Critique of Giddens and the Third Way', *Contemporary Politics*, 7(2): 149–70.

White, S. (1996) 'Reciprocity Arguments for Basic Income', paper presented to the Sixth International Congress of the Basic Income European Network, Vienna International Centre, Vienna, 12–14 September.

White, S. (1997) 'What Do Egalitarians Want?' in Franklin, J. (ed.) *Equality*, London: IPPR.

White, S. (1999) ' "Rights and Responsibilities": A Social Democratic Perspective', in Gamble, A. and Wright, T. (eds) *The New Social Democracy*, Oxford: Blackwell.

White, S. (2000) 'Social Rights and the Social Contract: Political Theory and the New Welfare Politics', *British Journal of Political Science*, 30: 507–32.

White, S. (2001) 'The Ambiguities of the Third Way', in White, S. (ed.) *New Labour*, London: Palgrave.

Wiesing, U. (1999) 'Social and Private Systems of Health Insurance', in McGleenan, T., Wiesing, U. and Ewald, F. (eds) *Genetics and Insurance*, Oxford: Bios Scientific Publishers Ltd.

Wilkinson, R. (1996) *Unhealthy Societies*, London: Routledge.

William, C. and Webster, R. (1999) 'Close Circuit Television and Information Age Policy Processes', in Hague, B. and Loader, B. (eds) *Digital Democracy*, London: Routledge.

Williams, C. (2002) 'The Social Economy And Local Exchange And Trading Schemes (LETS)', in Fitzpatrick, T. and Cahill, M. (eds) *Environment and Welfare*, London: Palgrave.

Williams, F. (2001) 'In and beyond New Labour: Towards a Political Ethics of Care', *Critical Social Policy*, 21(4): 467–93.

Williams, K. S. and Johnstone, C. (2000) 'The Politics of the Selective Gaze: Closed Circuit Television and the Policing of Public Space', *Crime, Law and Social Change*, 34(2): 183–210.

Wilmut, I., Campbell, K. and Tudge, C. (2000) *The Second Creation*, London, Headline Book Publishing.

Wilson, E. O. (1975) *Sociobiology*, Cambridge, MA: Harvard University Press.

Wilson, E. O. (1978) *On Human Nature*, Cambridge, MA: Harvard University Press.

Wilson, E. O. (1998) *Consilience*, London: Abacus.

Wissenburg, M. (2001) 'The "Third Way" and Social Justice', *Journal of Political Ideologies*, 6(2): 231–5.

World Bank (1994) *Averting the Old Age Crisis*, London and New York: Oxford University Press.

Wyatt, S., Henwood, F., Miller, N. and Senker, P. (eds) (2000) *Technology and In/equality*, London: Routledge.

Young, I. M. (2001) 'Activist Challenges to Deliberative Democracy', *Political Theory*, 29(5): 670–90.

Young, I. M. (1990) *Justice and the Politics of Difference*, Princeton, NJ: Princeton University Press.

Young, I. M. (2000) *Inclusion and Democracy*, Oxford: Oxford University Press.

Young, J. (1999) *The Exclusive Society*, London: Sage.

Young, M. (1958) *The Rise of the Meritocracy*, London: Thames & Hudson.

Zukin, S. (1991) *Landscapes of Power*, California: University of California Press.

Index